FINDING
THE BAD
INN

FINDING
THE BAD
INN

DISCOVERING
MY FAMILY'S
HIDDEN PAST

BY CHRISTY LESKOVAR

PICTORIAL HISTORIES PUBLISHING COMPANY, INC.
Missoula, Montana

Library of Congress
Control Number 2010930738

ISBN 978-1-57510-150-7

FIRST PRINTING August 2010

PRINTED IN CANADA
Friesens, Altona, Manitoba

TYPOGRAPHY
Arrow Graphics, Missoula, Montana

Author cover photo by Jerry Metellus Photography Inc.

www.christyleskovar.com

PUBLISHED BY
Pictorial Histories Publishing Company, Inc.
713 South Third Street West, Missoula, Montana 59801
PHONE (406) 549-8488, FAX (406) 728-9280
EMAIL phpc@montana.com

Everyone should have a chance at a breathtaking piece of folly.

—Mother to Velvet, *National Velvet*, screenplay
by Theodore Reeves and Helena Deutsch

Take nothing on its looks, take everything on evidence.

—Mr. Jaggers to Pip, *Great Expectations*
by Charles Dickens

Aila Hughes Thompson (Grandma T) with her first grandchild, Kenny West. Butte, Montana, 1946.

CHAPTER ONE

WHILE PONDERING THE MURDER mystery at the beginning of my book *One Night in a Bad Inn*, and wondering whether my great-grandmother Sarah was complicit in the fire and that dead body turning up on the ranch, I wrote that how I found out what happened was "enough to fill a volume all its own, and perhaps one day it will."

And now it has.

This is the story of how I found out who started the fire, and how the body got there, and what really happened when my grandfather saved that man in the war, and why my grandmother was sent to an orphanage when she wasn't an orphan, and so much more, and how I took those answers and wrote them into a book. It turned into quite a detective hunt, an adventure that took me across the globe, including a few misadventures I could have done without. As I discovered clues, pursued leads, followed threads, and was repeatedly dumbfounded by what I unearthed about my own relatives, I felt as if I were living in a novel. Though I had no idea what I would find when I began, I knew from the start that amid the scandals there stood at least one person of impeccable character and tremendous fortitude, an element of redemption giving me a positive reason to venture out into those uncharted waters. Otherwise, I never would have done it.

MY LAST GRANDPARENT, Grandma T, passed away on April 17, 1993. I was living in Rockville, Maryland, at the time, working for Bechtel as an engineer in the nuclear power industry. A few months later, the wheels started turning to move me back to the West: first the letter from the executive at corporate headquarters, then the interview, then I didn't get the job, then the phone call offering me a similar assignment. Soon the movers were packing my belongings, and I was on a plane to San Francisco. Though I had never lived in California, I felt I was going home, home to the West.

Two vague ideas floated through my mind: writing and family history. For some reason, I equated these with moving back to the West. I didn't connect the two, nor had I given either any thought before this. Writing? Write what? Letters I suppose. I had this idea that when I moved to San Francisco, I'd have loads of free time, and this was how I would fill it: I would write more letters, and I would fill out that family history I wrote in high school.

Living in San Francisco brought back wonderful memories of going there as a child to visit Dad's aunts and uncles. As a little girl, I loved to go to the Japanese Tea Garden in Golden Gate Park and drink tea and eat almond cookies. I still love to go there and drink tea and eat those same almond cookies. By the time I moved to San Francisco, the only one left was Uncle Ray. His wife, Dad's aunt Francie, had passed away a year earlier. Uncle Ray was in his late eighties. He lived in the Sunset District, south of Golden Gate Park, in the house he and Francie bought during the Second World War. As the story goes, Aunt Francie came home one day and announced to Uncle Ray that she had bought a house. She got it for a song because it was near the ocean and everybody was afraid the Japanese would bomb the coast. That was Aunt Francie for you—never timid, always bossy.

I saw Uncle Ray frequently. We'd go out to dinner, or I'd pick him up and bring him to my apartment and I'd cook dinner, sometimes to his exact specifications. He taught me how to make his favorite cocktail, an Old Fashioned. He mentioned a letter I wrote to him. He went on and on about how wonderful it was, how it was the most wonderful letter he ever received. I remembered the letter. I wrote it after Aunt Francie passed away. It was about what I'd been doing, a newsy letter. I was puzzled as to why it had such an effect on him.

During those two years in San Francisco, I didn't do a thing on that family history other than try to pick Uncle Ray's memory a bit about his life in San Francisco in days gone by. Did I write more letters? I don't remember. Probably not.

After my assignment in San Francisco was completed, I transferred to a job in Las Vegas. I would now be a project manager. That was how you got your ticket punched at Bechtel—by being a project manager. Though the title was big, the work was small. It wasn't nearly as challenging as what I had done working for Bechtel Power as a lowly mechanical engineering supervisor. I didn't like it. If I stayed, I feared I'd go brain dead. As I drove into the parking lot each day, an overwhelming thought swept over me: "What am I doing here?" The parable of the talents kept floating through my mind. That's the one where the master entrusts his property to his servants, each according to his abilities. To one servant he entrusts five thousand talents, to another two thousand, and to a third, one thousand. The servants with five thousand and two thousand invest their talents and double them. The master is well pleased. The servant with one thousand talents buries his. The master is displeased and orders that servant thrown out to where there is "weeping and grinding of teeth."

I didn't want to be that servant.

I began to look for a new job. Years earlier, a friend was in a terrible automobile accident, and her leg was crushed. As the orthopedic surgeon was setting her leg, he told her he liked his job so much he'd do it for free. That stayed with me. That's what I wanted—a job I'd like enough I'd do it for free. I also asked myself, am I making the most of my situation in life? I had worked for Bechtel for almost fifteen years and was a chronic saver. My parents taught us to save from a very young age. I remember as a young child walking into Metals Bank in Butte with Mom, clutching my own little passbook, there to desposit my birthday money. Because I had saved, I knew this afforded me opportunities many people don't have. Was I taking advantage of these opportunities?

Before this, every time I thought about leaving Bechtel, something happened to get me to stay. Now was the opposite.

First, my pay was cut. It was a clerical error and fixed.

Then one day I picked up the newspaper and read *Dilbert*. The boss tells one of Dilbert's female co-workers to update the company brochures. She says, but I'm a highly trained electrical engineer. The boss says he'd overlook her shortcomings.

I had just lived that.

I sent resumes to a few headhunters, thinking I would look for another corporate job. It seemed the logical thing to do, yet something told me that wasn't what I was supposed to do. But if not that, what?

In April of 1997, one year after I moved to Las Vegas, my aunt Helen Leskovar passed away. I flew to my hometown of Butte, Montana, for her funeral. As the family gathered at Uncle Joe's home (Dad's brother), the stories poured forth, all sorts of family stories.

After the funeral, we drove across the Divide to Whitehall to visit Aunt Aila, Mom's eldest sister. She wasn't feeling well so hadn't come to town for the funeral. Auntie Mary, Mom's younger sister, and Uncle Ed came too. While we were sitting there visiting, Aunt Aila got up and left the room and returned with a large box. She set the box on the coffee table and pulled out a large envelope, and from it, a piece of paper which she handed to my brother, Jeff. Only vaguely aware of what was happening on the other side of the room, I heard Jeff say, "That's quite a rap sheet," and he passed the paper to Uncle Ed who looked at it and handed it to Dad who handed it to Mom who handed it to me. Written across the top was "Descriptive List of the Prisoner." I read quickly down the page—age, born, occupation, height, convicted—murder second degree. Oh my. I looked at the pictures at the bottom of the page, one facing forward, the other to the side. Whoever he was, he was very handsome.

"Who was this?" I asked.

"Archie," Mom said, "Grandma's brother, your great-uncle."

My great-uncle?

Auntie Mary told us about the shooting, and about Uncle Archie's accomplice being hanged in Boulder, and that Grandma T wouldn't even stop there for a cup of tea because the boy who was hanged was slow and somebody else pulled the trigger, the son of a man with influence in Butte and his name was kept out of it.

Then Auntie Mary started talking about the barn burning down on the ranch near Forsyth, and how the dead body of a transient was found in it, and a neighbor started a rumor that it was Arthur, Grandma's father, and that her mother, Sarah, had murdered him, and the sheriff arrested Sarah. Later somebody saw Arthur working in another town and told him, your wife has been arrested for your murder, so he came back.

Then we passed around Uncle Bill's rap sheet, Grandma T's older brother.

Good grief.

My mind fell into abeyance. This was a lot to take in. Mom leaned over and said, "Thank God your father didn't know this. He never would have married me."

Dad joked to Uncle Ed, "Well, Ed, I guess we better start sleeping with one eye open." Everybody laughed.

Then someone mentioned the time so-and-so remarked that there were no skeletons in her family closet, and how Aunt Aila gently tapped her on

the arm and said, "That's all right, dear. We have enough for everybody."
We laughed again.

The next day I flew home. As I went back to work and resumed my
routine, these family stories kept floating around in my mind. My great-
grandmother arrested for murdering my great-grandfather—this was
incredible, not the sort of thing that readily slips from one's mind.

The following Sunday I was sitting on my back patio reading. It was
a beautiful, warm, sunny southern Nevada afternoon. The sky was brilliant blue. I put down my book and gazed off into the distance. I sat there
idly watching the fronds of the palm trees bounce gently in the breeze,
pondering these family stories, wanting a job I'd like enough I'd do it
for free, wondering if I'm making the most of my situation in life, when
POOF! The idea popped into my head—I would find out what happened
on the ranch and write a book about it. I would write a book about all four
grandparents. I would take a three month leave of absence from my job to
get started. Other things popped into my mind as further encouragement.
Somehow I knew it would work out.

I decided not to tell anyone right away and think about it. I wanted to
be sure this was real and not a passing fancy. I thought about my career
with Bechtel, how would this affect it, could it be detrimental? It seems
silly now, but at the time it seemed monumentally important. I thought, I'll
call Tom and ask him. He and his wife are long-time friends of my parents.
Though I hadn't spoken with them in quite some time, I had sought career
advice from Tom in the past. They lived in Atlanta.

The next day the phone rang, and it was Tom. I was surprised since I
hadn't called yet. He was in town for a convention. We met for dinner,
and I told him about my idea to take a three-month leave of absence to
start writing a book about my grandparents and asked what he thought
about it.

"I think it's a great idea," he said.

Also in town were Mom's Irish cousin Sam and his wife, Barbara, who
lived in England. I didn't mention the book but took advantage of my time
with them to ask questions about the family.

This was in May of 1997. The previous December, Mom's second
eldest sister, Grace, got off work, stopped at the grocery store, bought a
pie, got back in the car, and died. She was seventy-one years old. A few
weeks later, a college friend died of brain cancer. He left a wife and four

children. Two close high school friends died while I was in college. Life is short no matter how long we live. The same is true for our loved ones. We never know how long we'll have them with us. I couldn't put this off. If I was going to do it, I had to do it now.

I called Mom and Dad that Sunday, which happened to be Mother's Day, and broke the news to them. Dad sounded startled. Mom said, "I think it's a great idea." Then she said, "We got the recipes you sent." That sure brought me down to earth. Here was this momentous decision, at least I thought it was, to take a three-month leave of absence to write a book about my grandparents, and Mom's reaction was sure, great, now on to the next subject. Actually, it was the best reaction. We need those subtle, and sometimes not so subtle, reminders that we are not the center of the universe. The sun will rise, the sun will set, the earth will continue to rotate on its axis whether I write this book or don't write this book. Still, I reeled her back to my momentous life decision. I respect my parents' opinions and wanted to discuss it with them. They were very supportive.

Now I had to tell my bosses. One who had been with the company for decades warned me, "The longer you're gone, the more you'll be behind your peers." The big boss, a former admiral and fairly new to the company, said, "If this is something you really want to do, you better do it. If you don't, you'll regret it later."

We agreed that I would stay on for another few weeks to transition my work to my colleagues.

About a week after I announced my plans, Rosie called from San Francisco to tell me that Uncle Ray had broken his hip. Rosie had been a friend of Aunt Francie; Aunt Francie asked her to look after Ray if she died first. I told Rosie I would to fly to San Francisco to see him. She said, "Don't come right now, wait until he's feeling better." I said, "I'm going to come right away." My heart went out to Uncle Ray. At ninety years old, many of his friends were already gone. He and Aunt Francie didn't have children. There was no family there. Even though Rosie was as close as family, she was only one person. She couldn't be with him all the time. So I went.

He was recuperating from hip surgery in a nursing home when I arrived. I brought the newspaper so I could tell him how Cisco did that day. He bought Cisco early on and monitored it closely. I opened the paper and found the stock listings. Cisco was up. I told him I was taking a leave of absence from my job to write a book about my grandparents. He seemed distracted. He said my cousin Joey had been there buying groceries and that the sheriff was after him (Joey was in Montana). I just listened. I wondered if the pain medicine made him confuse dreams with reality. He nodded off to sleep. I sat down. There was a small book on the table next to the chair. It was the only book around. It was the only anything around. Other than the furniture, the room was bare. I picked up the book. It was a collection of essays about writing biography. I opened to a random page. It said there are two types of biography: some chronicle events in a person's life; others get at the essence of the person, the soul. That's what I wanted to do.

I sat and read until Uncle Ray woke up. We visited some more. He was still distracted. I had brought him a bunch of bananas and gave him one. He took a bite and complained it wasn't ripe enough and told me to put them on the window sill. I stayed the weekend and returned to work in Las Vegas on Monday. Uncle Ray seemed fine when I left. I figured he still had many years ahead of him, even though he was ninety. I decided I would try to get to San Francisco once a month to visit him. A few days later, Uncle Ray died. He left me a piece of his Cisco bonanza.

While going through Uncle Ray's effects, I found the letter I had written to him, the one he raved about. When I saw the will (actually a living trust), I couldn't help but notice the date—it was dated shortly after he received my letter.

CHAPTER TWO

THOUGH I DIDN'T consciously think of writing a book until after I learned about the fire and about Sarah being arrested for murdering Arthur, as I think back, it seems seeds were being sown long before.

Years earlier, I read about Edith Stein's childhood in her autobiography, *Life in a Jewish Family*. She was born in 1891 in what was then part of Germany, now Poland. Other than her father dying young and her mother taking over the family lumber business, she lived a rather ordinary childhood in a loving family. Though her life would take a dramatic and tragic turn later, I found the simple story of her childhood fascinating, a slice of life from another time, another place, another culture. I remember thinking, everybody's life could be a book.

Around the same time, I remember reading a letter St. Thomas More wrote to his daughter in which he admonished her to write every day, not necessarily to him, but to write something every day. His admonition struck me personally, as if it were meant for me. Mom would give me the same advice while I was working on *One Night in a Bad Inn*.

Many people have asked, did I study writing in college, did I always want to be a writer, was writing a book a life-long dream. The answer is no. I always enjoyed writing, I was an avid letter writer and gravitated toward assignments at work that required writing, but just as important, I read. I read books for pleasure from the time I first learned how. Except for a few years in college when my workload was terribly onerous, I always had a book going and still do.

I never thought about being a writer. I never thought about *being* anything as far as a profession. I thought about what I wanted to *do*. When I was struggling to figure out what to study in college, Dad gave me some great advice in the form of a question: "What do you like, and what are you good at?" That got me thinking. Usually the two go together. We like what we are good at. I liked math, I liked writing, I liked English, I liked foreign languages. I had already studied Spanish and French. I planned to study French in France. A few years earlier, while browsing the stacks in the library one day, I picked up *A Tale of Two Cities* by Charles Dickens. Reading the book made me fascinated with French history. Then and there, I knew I wanted to study in France.

After I did well in calculus my first quarter at Seattle University, my professors started prodding me to pursue science or engineering. My parents also encouraged me that way, pointing out that the world is becoming more and more technical all the time. An engineering background would stand me well no matter what I wanted to do. I decided to try an engineering class; I liked it and settled on mechanical engineering. Even so, as planned, my junior year I took a break from engineering to study French in Grenoble, France. After I returned to Seattle and resumed my engineering curriculum, I realized I needed only three more French literature classes to earn a French degree, so I decided to do it. Those French literature classes felt like a vacation from my engineering classes, as if I were giving one part of my brain a rest while activating another.

Shortly before graduation, the registrar summoned me to her office. She said I was five humanities credits short in my core curriculum requirements for the College of Arts and Sciences (my French degree). What about this class, what about that class, I asked. Those were all spoken for. "What else did you take?" she asked. "I took piano," I said. That worked. I had taken piano every quarter except while in France. So instead of being five credits short, I had nine more than I needed and graduated with degrees in mechanical engineering and French.

RIGHT FROM THE START I knew the kind of book I wanted to write. I wanted you to get to know the people in the book, my grandparents. I wanted them to emerge as vivid real people. I would find out what happened on the ranch, and about Uncle Archie going to prison and about Grandpa Peter saving that man's life in the First World War, and I would write about what happened, but most important, I would write about the people. To do that, I would have to get to know them. I would have to learn what influenced them. I would have to learn about their parents, the places they lived, the times during which they lived.

I resolved to keep the book nonfiction. I never considered a fictional story based on fact. That being the case, I would have to go out and find the story and the historical context. I had a lot of work to do.

The summer before I went off to study in France, while wandering through the library looking for something to read, I came across *Skid Road*, a history of Seattle. The author used the life of Doc Maynard as the vehicle for telling the story. I remember thinking, this is the most interesting way to read history, through someone's life, especially someone as colorful as Doc Maynard. Now I was setting out to do much the same but for the reverse reason.

Also right from the start, I knew the title. I think I knew the title before I knew I would write a book. A few years earlier, I heard a priest use the metaphor "one night in a bad inn," which he attributed to St. Teresa of Avila: when compared to eternal happiness in Heaven, the troubles of this life amount to just one night in a bad inn. Immediately I thought of Grandma T. She endured and overcame so much hardship, none of it of her own making, and with such dignity and grace and class. She was so good. I knew with certainty that now she rests in the good inn. It was consoling.

Actually the title started out to be *A Night in a Bad Inn*. Five years and many manuscript drafts later, I had an epiphany: I would make the bold editorial decision to change the title to *One Night in a Bad Inn*, one being more definitive, more specific, so much the better.

As for the research, I knew instinctively to take nothing on its face, to take everything on evidence. I would try to corroborate everything I was told. Though I did this simply because it seemed the responsible thing to do, I would soon discover that doing so would unlock a plethora of wonders and stories and surprises.

I began my leave of absence in mid June. My last day of work was June 13, the Feast of St. Anthony. How fitting. Not only is he the namesake of my paternal grandfather, he is also the patron saint of lost objects, and here I was setting out to find things.

And so it began, quietly, one afternoon with family, stories told, skeletons revealed, though not only skeletons, also precious family memories to be kept and not lost. And now two months later, another afternoon, I pick up the phone to begin my research, and soon I would feel like one of the children opening the door to the wardrobe and discovering Narnia.

CHAPTER THREE

I OPENED THE MAP of Montana and laid it on my kitchen table. I scanned the legend to find Forsyth. There it was in Rosebud County, in the southeastern part of the state. I picked up the phone, called information, and then called the Rosebud County Courthouse in Forsyth. I told the woman what I was looking for, and she transferred me to the Clerk of Court's Office. Liz Cole answered.

"Do you have any record of Sarah Hughes being charged with murder?" I asked. "It would be in the early 1900's."

She said she would look. After a minute or two, she came back and said, "No."

A flash of dread swept over me. I said thank you and hung up. I stood there puzzled, my hand still on the phone, thought for a moment, and called back.

"Do you have a record of Sarah Hughes being charged with anything?" I asked.

"Yes," she said, "bigamy."

"BIGAMY?!"

I started to pace the room. "Could you send me everything you have on that?" I asked. Liz said she would, and that I should send her a check for the copies and a self-addressed stamped envelope. I bought the biggest envelope I could find and put a lot of postage on it and sent it to the Clerk of Court's Office with a check for twenty-five dollars. I figured, if that didn't cover it, they could tell me and I'd send more.

A few days later I received a message to call Liz. I thought, maybe the envelope wasn't big enough. Maybe she needed a box. I called back. She wanted to know whether I had received the envelope. Not yet, I said. She told me she found depositions telling the whole story of grave robbery, fire, the murder charge, bigamy, and there were pictures, including glass plate negatives for the pictures taken in New York.

New York?

I began to pace the room again. I told her that Sarah and Arthur Hughes were my great-grandparents, and I was writing a book about them. "She *is* writing a book!" I heard her call out to the other people in the office, then to me she said, "We said somebody should write a book about this!" I told her I planned to visit Forsyth. "Oh, you should," she said. "You have to see all this."

Soon the envelope arrived. Oh my. Inside was the transcript of depositions taken in New York City of people who had seen my great-grandfather Arthur Hughes when he was supposed to be dead back in 1913. The lawyers in New York sent the transcript to the county attorney in Forsyth, and there it sat in the court file, tucked away in the Rosebud County Courthouse for the last eighty years waiting for me to request it. It was over an inch thick. Arthur told Sarah's friend Jennie in Brooklyn everything—how he went to the cemetery and dug up the body and took it to the ranch and buried it in the snow and then put it in the house and torched the place and ran off to Buenos Aires—and Jennie told all to the lawyers, and there it was in her deposition.

From the other court documents, I discovered that, when the authorities found the burned up dead man, they concluded he must be the person who lived in the house, my great-grandfather Arthur. Three weeks later, my great-grandmother Sarah ran off to Miles City and married the handyman, and the two of them were arrested for murdering her first husband, Arthur, who of course was not dead.

I read all this carefully and took notes, lots of notes. There was so much to absorb. Even Arthur was deposed in New York. I was amazed by the specificity and level of detail in his testimony. He gave his and Sarah's wedding date, he stated the year they arrived in Rosebud County, and the year Sarah's mother died, which made it easier for me to track her down. He even named the cemetery where Sarah's mother was buried in Wilkes-Barre. He described the ranch house in detail down to the fact that he bought their ACME cooking range from Sears, Roebuck. Much of this seemed innocuous and well beyond what the lawyers needed to know, but all that detail would prove extremely helpful to me, providing clues for many more leads. It was as if someone knew that I was going to write a book about this and were reaching out across time and handing me these treasures.

When one of the lawyers deposing Arthur asked where he was born, he said, "There is no positive fact where I was born, except between Australia and Pennsylvania. I was born on the high sea." That certainly piqued my curiosity.

It didn't occur to me until just now as I'm writing this—that day at Aunt Aila's when I first learned about the fire and the dead body, all my interest fixed on Sarah being arrested for murdering Arthur, who I knew wasn't dead. It didn't strike me as a bit odd that a dead guy was in the barn (I learned later it was the house). I thought, oh how sad, he was a transient, and he was dead, but that was it. Not for a split second did I stop and ask: what was a dead guy doing in the barn? I wasn't a bit curious about that, just about Sarah being arrested for murdering Arthur. I suppose that was enough to fill my wonderment, more than enough.

Some parts of the depositions were confusing—all these letters between Montana and New York City; Sarah's friend Jennie's husband, the lawyer Charles Hayes, looking for John P. Price, the sailor, who turned out to be Arthur Hughes, the farmer. How did Charles know to go looking for John P. Price?

To help keep track of all this, I prepared a time line. It was a table with three columns: Date, Family History, and World/Local History. Anything with a date, I put on the time line. I added the correspondence described in the depositions. Perhaps seeing all this laid out chronologically could help make sense of it. As with my notes, I typed the time line into the computer, which eased searches, especially when it became quite long.

Next I read the court documents for Sarah's bigamy case. So that's why there was no record of Sarah Hughes being arrested for murder. She was Sarah *Elliott* when she was arrested for murdering Arthur. I didn't know about this other husband, Tom Elliott. Since I didn't know Arthur was supposed to be dead, how would I know Sarah had married somebody else. I wonder if Grandma knew her mother married Tom.

How did the bigamy case end up? Did Sarah go to prison? It wasn't clear to me from what I had so far, or maybe it was, and I just couldn't believe it. I had convinced myself that my great-grandmother did not go to prison. I could not get my mind around the possibility that she did.

I continued to read the court documents, wading through the legalese, taking notes, entering anything with a date on my time line. I found clues in the most pedestrian places. Grandma's brothers Bill and Hector were subpoenaed to testify at Sarah's bigamy trial, and the subpoenas said where they lived. I would learn later that they were left on their own when the three younger children were sent to the orphanage, even though they were only thirteen and fifteen years old. They were living on ranches at opposite sides of Rosebud County.

Unfortunately the transcript from Sarah's bigamy trial was not in the file. Liz said trial transcripts were generally not kept.

When I read County Attorney Beeman's explanation for charging Sarah with murder, I couldn't believe it. This was the basis for a murder charge? One witness heard Sarah say she'd be better off without Arthur, another person heard Sarah say this and that, and on it went. It was gossip, pure and simple, not evidence. That song from *The Music Man* kept ringing through my head: *"Pick a little, talk a little, pick a little, talk a little, pick, pick, pick . . ."* The authorities had no tangible evidence that Sarah murdered Arthur, but they had a body, and they had a motive—Tom and the life insurance money.

While telling a friend the story, she asked, "Were some of your relatives larger than life?" I laughed and said yes. I hadn't thought of them that way, but it's true. She said, "So are mine." There was a resigned note of sadness in her voice, and I knew why. Larger than life people can be fascinating, fun to read about, but difficult to live with. I was fortunate that I didn't have to live with the notorious bunch about whom I was writing. Their shenanigans didn't wreak havoc on my life, as they did on my grandmother's.

In a letter Sarah wrote to Tom while in jail, she intimated that she was pregnant: "Let me tell you Tom if I get out on Bail I believe I will send the children home and jump in the river with the baby for by that time Tom I will be big and every body will know what is the matter with me."

I jotted on my to-do list: look for birth and death certificates, and find out what happened to the baby.

It was clear that Arthur went to prison for grave robbery, so I called the Montana State Prison in Deer Lodge and asked for his prison records. They didn't have them.

NEXT I LAID OUT PLANS for a marathon research summer. I would go to Butte, Polson, Deer Lodge, Forsyth, and Seattle. I tried to do as much up front work as possible to make optimum use of my time while on the road and get an idea of how much time I needed in each place. I prepared lists of questions to ask relatives, to-do lists of topics to investigate and documents I needed. I had an "Ask Mom and Dad" list, an "Ask Aunt Aila" list, an "Ask Auntie Mary" list, a "Rosebud County Courthouse" list, a "Butte Archives" list, and so on. These I kept in a white half-inch three-ring binder. I took the appropriate to-do lists with me on my research trips, checking off each item found, each question answered. I bought spiral notebook planners in which to take notes. They open flat making it easy to transcribe notes into the computer. These were the same spiral notebook planners I used when I worked for Bechtel. They are about seven by nine inches with lined pages and a space at the top of each page for the date and a heading. Along the left side of each page is an open vertical space. This was where I wrote what we called "action items" at Bechtel. These would be short-term things I needed to do. As I completed one, I checked it off. Anything I needed to attend to later, I noted on the appropriate to-do list in the three-ring binder. When I took notes, I wrote the name of the place I was at, for example "Butte Archives," at the top of the page and noted the date. When I took notes while interviewing people, I noted the date. When I took notes from a book I was reading, I noted the date.

I planned to record interviews, if the person I was interviewing was amenable. Even when recording interviews, I planned to take notes as well. What if something happened to the tape? Redundancy seemed prudent. I went to an electronics store and bought the best tapes I could find and a fancy tape recorder. Both would turn out to be defective. My cheap, no frills tape recorder and the cassette tapes I bought at the grocery store worked best.

Big challenges lay before me: not only to find the story, but to write the story well. A friend recommended that I speak with the husband of a friend of hers, a former *Wall Street Journal* reporter and author. He recommended the book *On Writing Well* by William Zinsser. I read it and found it be excellent. He also advised that I not feel obligated to give equal time to each relative in the book. The story would drive what to include.

Another friend recommended I speak with a shirt-tail relative of his, Rafael Alvarez, who was a reporter for the *Baltimore Sun*. Rafael advised, "If a part of the real you isn't in your book, you are cheating the reader." I pondered that a lot, and still do.

A friend of my parents suggested I contact the Montana Historical Society in Helena. It had not occurred to me that states had historical societies. I called and spoke with Brian Shovers. I rattled off the list of items I was researching, and he told me what resources they had, and if they didn't have the records, who might. For the fire on the ranch near Forsyth, they had old newspapers. For the orphanage, they had archives. For the prisoners, they had the old prison records. For the homestead, he referred me to the Bureau of Land Management.

I added Helena to my list of research destinations and started a Montana Historical Society to-do list.

Next I called the Bureau of Land Management in Billings and spoke with Ardella Berzel. I told her that I was writing a book and was looking for information about Arthur Hughes's homestead in eastern Montana. She said she would look and in no time was back with the coordinates for his homestead. She offered to send me a copy of the records and a map showing where the homestead was. She said the National Archives would have more information—another great lead.

In a few days, all this arrived in the mail. Ardella had attached a post-it to the map showing the exact spot where the homestead was. I was astounded at how easy and smooth this was.

As Ardella suggested, I wrote to the National Archives to request Arthur's homestead file. Soon it arrived, replete with copious details about the ranch—how big the house was, what it was built out of, who built it, what crops Arthur cultivated and on how many acres.

And now, to go see it.

CHAPTER FOUR

IN JULY, I FLEW to Missoula, Montana, drove north to Polson to visit Dad's cousins, and then down to Deer Lodge to see the Old Prison. In my luggage, I had a navy blue and white striped tee-shirt with horizontal stripes. I almost wore it that day but didn't when the irony struck me.

Deer Lodge is small. You don't need directions to find the Old Prison. Simply take the Deer Lodge exit, and there it is. It looks like a forbidding medieval fortress, surrounded by imposing stone ramparts, gun turrets and all. It is now a tourist attraction. I paid my admission fee and went in. The day was gray and chilly. I found it an eerie place, made more so by the gray skies. I glimpsed maybe five other people as I walked along, stopping often to jot down notes in my notebook, studying everything closely, taking pictures. I heard a muffled voice here and there, and a soft bang, bang that sounded like a door blown gently by an intermittent breeze. It was one of those somber places where I felt I shouldn't talk above a whisper but didn't know why. Looking up at the multi-level cellblock, I wondered in which cell my great-grandfather Arthur slept, a strange thing to think about. This was the "new" cell block built in 1912, the year before Arthur arrived. I didn't think much about Bill and Archie. They weren't yet as vivid to me as they would become.

I walked across the expansive yard to see the women's building. I crept tentatively inside, not venturing beyond reach of the door. I had the sense it might slam shut and lock me in there forever. I quickly retreated. Though I knew Arthur did time for grave robbery, I still wasn't certain about the outcome of the bigamy case. A mother with five children, I thought the court would have shown some leniency toward Sarah. I couldn't believe a judge would send her to prison for bigamy of all things. Even though I had heard horror stories about my notorious great-grandmother, I could not believe she went to prison. In fact, I had convinced myself that she did not. As I write this, I look at the picture of her as a pretty, young wife and mother holding my darling infant grandmother on her lap, puffy-cheeked tots Bill and Hector by her side, and I still can't believe it. Grandma used to say, "My *poor* mother, no wonder she turned out the way she did." I say, my poor grandmother; I can't believe she turned out the way *she* did.

GRANDMA T WAS the only grandparent I knew as an adult. I was nine years old when we left Butte and moved to Kennewick, Washington. After that, I saw her at least once a year and spoke often with her on the phone. During my junior year at Kennewick High School, my American Literature teacher, Laurel Piippo, gave us an assignment to write our family history. Naturally I began by asking my parents about the family. I wrote to my great-aunts in Ireland, California, and Montana. They sent back wonderful letters. During her next visit, I asked Grandma T.

"What was your maiden name, Grandma."

"Hughes," she said.

"Where were you born?"

"I was born in Wilkes-Barre, Pennsylvania."

"Where were your parents from?"

"They were from Wales. They were Welsh."

"Where did you go after you left Wilkes-Barre?"

"Oh, we moved from place to place."

I wrote my paper and turned it in. Little did I know, this was the G-rated version of my family's history—no fire, no dead bodies, nothing about her mother being arrested for murdering her father, nothing about being shipped off to the orphanage, or about her brothers going to prison. Grandma T carefully doled out stories about her life, meticulously weeding out any age-inappropriate details . When I was older, she told me much more, though she never told me about the fire or about anyone going to prison.

At my college graduation party, I overheard a friend tell Grandma that her relatives owned land in eastern Montana. Grandma replied that her family homesteaded there. That was the first I'd heard of it. Why I never thought to ask her about it later, I don't know. Too involved in my own life, I suppose. As I think back on all the time I spent with Grandma T, most of the time she listened. She wanted to know what you were doing and thinking. She was very aware of what she didn't know, and she wanted to learn more. She wanted to learn about you. By then I was old enough to hear the story of what happened on the ranch and why they left. Had I asked, she might have told me. I still wonder whether she ever knew the whole of it since she was living in the orphanage when the mystery unraveled.

Later she told me about her mother ripping up her clothes to prevent her from going to college, and how her mother tried to force her into prostitution, and about the man attacking her in the boarding house and how she scratched his face and he went tumbling down the stairs. She told that story with such intensity.

When she told me about her father leaving, I assumed that was when he left them in Butte. I got the impression that she didn't blame him because her mother was so difficult.

These conversations were usually at the kitchen table at Mom and Dad's: Grandma and Mom and I visiting over cups of tea. Mom often brought up the subject, and Grandma told me what happened. She told me about working at the post office, how some of the men were resentful, and about the married boss saying he'd give her a permanent job if "she'd go out with him." She bristled at the indignity. Of course she wouldn't, just as she wouldn't succumb to her mother trying to force her into prostitution. There was never any "poor me" in Grandma's stories. There was no "poor me" in Grandma T, period. I don't remember hearing her make a derogatory remark about anyone, about actions yes, no moral ambiguity there, and she was no Pollyanna. She simply told the facts. She told you what they did, what they said. I rarely heard her use an adjective to describe anyone. There was something perpetually gentle about Grandma T. She was a woman with no edge. Even when she was telling me about something horrible, there was gentleness. She seemed to have compassion for the flawed human condition, perhaps because she had seen so much of it.

My earliest memory of Grandma T was at her house. It was as if all of a sudden, one day, I woke up, I had memory, and there I was, at Grandma T's. Mom was there, somebody else too. Grandma T walked swiftly across the dining room. She always walked swiftly and purposefully. She was wearing a dress fitted at the waist and high-heeled pumps. She mentioned a man's name. Somehow I knew she was going on a date, and somehow I knew what a date was, and it seemed quite normal to have a grandma who went on dates.

I always loved Grandma T, but it was a warm and fuzzy teddy bear kind of love, the love of a granddaughter for a grandmother. I knew her

only as Grandma T. To write about her life, I would have to get to know
her as a three dimensional person.

What we grow up with as children, we tend to think is normal. I had
only one grandpa, Dad's father. It seemed normal that I didn't know my
other grandpa, Peter. He was killed in the mines when Mom was four. I
took for granted that I didn't know him. It wasn't until I was in my twenties that it occurred to me that I knew people who knew him, and I started
asking questions.

"Did Grandpa Peter drink?" I asked Grandma.

"No," she said. "He gambled." I understood that to mean it was a
problem. She also said, "He worked when he wanted."

When I asked Auntie Grace and Aunt Aila what their father was like,
they said almost in unison, "He would have made a wonderful uncle."

"What do you mean?" I asked.

"He'd hold you on his knee, and tell you poems such as 'Sam McGee,'
and sing to you. Then he could leave."

I knew that Grandpa Peter immigrated from Ireland, he worked in the
mines in Butte, and he fought in the American Army in the First World War
during which he saved a man's life and was awarded the *Croix de Guerre*.
I knew his family was doing chain migration where one family member
came and sent money back for the next family member until the chain
broke. His mother and several siblings stayed in Ireland. I had heard lots of
stories, but they were in swatches and remnants. I had that family history
I wrote in high school. I wanted more. There were many blanks to fill in.

FROM DEER LODGE, I drove through Butte, up the East Ridge to Home-
stake Pass, crossed the Continental Divide, and continued down the
mountain to the valley below and on to Whitehall to visit Aunt Aila, Mom's
eldest sister Aila Rose.

Day after day, we sat on her sunny porch, Aunt Aila with her stories,
me with my tape recorder and notebook. She began at the beginning and
told me about the Thomases, my great-grandmother Sarah and her parents.
I would ask a question, we'd go off on a tangent about whatever that was,
and she would pick up and resume exactly where she left off. Incredible.
She never lost her place. She was seventy-five when I started this.

She said Sarah came to this country around age sixteen. She married

Arthur Hughes in Wilkes-Barre, Pennsylvania. "Why did they leave Wilkes-Barre?" I asked. Because Arthur caught Sarah with another man and beat him to a pulp. Grandma told me that story, about how she walked in on her mother with this man. It was one of many she held off telling me until I was out of college, then a certified grown-up. I was so shocked that I didn't ask follow up questions: did the man die, did he almost die, was her father charged with anything? I asked Aunt Aila. "Mother said if they stayed, her father would be charged." She didn't know whether or not the man died.

"What was Sarah like?" I asked.

"She was very lively," she said. "She always had a man."

"What do you mean? In addition to the one she was married to?"

"Every time we saw her, she was with a man."

"How was she as a grandma?"

"She was a wonderful grandma, except when she came in the middle of the night."

"What do you mean when she came in the middle of the night?"

Aunt Aila explained that Sarah would be picked up by the police, and Grandma would have to go pay the fine to get her out. "My father didn't like that," she said. "She [Sarah] told me she thought she was an alcoholic from the time she was very small."

Grandma and Aunt Aila and Auntie Grace traveled together after all three were widowed. "This is what we talked about," Aunt Aila said, "family." Grandma talked about the homestead in Rosebud County, and about the twins being born, and when she came home from school, they were gone.

A birth certificate for the twins went on my to-do list.

When the three of them visited Forsyth, Grandma remarked, "I've traveled on a wagon and on an airplane."

I asked about the name Aila, pronounced with three syllables: A (as in say)-EYE-la. Grandma T was born Aila Mae Hughes. She married Peter Thompson. They named their first child Aila Rose; she is my aunt Aila. Two granddaughters are named Aila; one you will meet later on these pages.

As for why Sarah and Arthur named their first daughter Aila, Sarah told Aunt Aila that she had an Armenian classmate in Wales named Aila. Another time, she said she read the name in a book. I suppose both could be the case.

I've never met anyone outside my family named Aila. I decided to google it just now and see what pops up. One web site said it is a Norman name; another said it is English and Old French, which fits with Norman. Another said it is Irish. Another said it is Finnish for the Irish name Eileen. The pronunciations differed from Grandma's, two syllables rather than three. Another web site said it is Hebrew and means Oak tree. That certainly fits metaphorically. According to the web site Meaning-of-Names, it originated as a Scottish name and means "from the strong place." Indeed.

While I was still working on the book, a woman called the senior citizen's center in Whitehall and said her name was Aila. The woman who took the call was puzzled, because she wasn't the Aila she knew, my aunt Aila. She asked the woman three times what her name was and asked her to spell it. No one ever heard from her again.

After a couple days of Aunt Aila telling me about Grandma's side of the family, we switched to Grandpa Peter's side, the Thompsons and Gribbens, still sitting on that sunny porch. We ate our meals out there too. Some mornings as we ate breakfast, we watched whitetail deer lazily eat theirs in the cool shade of the trees. Aunt Aila said "Grace" before meals in Gaelic and after meals in Latin. I tried to learn the Gaelic. Her father taught it to her.

"What did your father call you?" I asked.

"Darlin'," she said, "and if we were naughty, 'You little spalpeen.'"

"Did he have a brogue?" I asked.

"No," she said, "just a soft lilt." She noticed it in the way he said Mary, it was softer, and when he said "calm" is sounded like "cam."

Aunt Aila showed me what papers she had of Grandma's. Many I already had from Mom: Grandpa Peter's naturalization papers and military records, and other documents Grandma had saved and treasured and sent copies to her children. Aunt Aila brought out an oversized magazine which Grandma had asked her to safeguard. It was her senior year *Mountaineer*, the Butte High yearbook. Inside I found newspaper clippings, clippings helpful for my research that I probably would not have found otherwise. Several were about the Vocational Congress in Bozeman and about Grandma being sponsored by the Homer Club. I asked Aunt Aila, "What's the Homer Club?" "It's a women's club," she said. I added the Homer Club and Vocational Congress to my to-do list.

As I continued to go through Grandma's papers, I found an American Legion newsletter. It was several pages long. As I turned the pages and scanned the headlines, I thought I might have to read the whole thing to figure it out why she kept it. Then on the last page, I saw the huge asterisk she had drawn next to an article called "Taps." It said Mrs. Peter Thompson, Peter's widow, would like any information about his saving that man's life in Flanders. Any members of the Post who have such information should get in touch with her.

I recognized Grandma's distinctive, huge handwriting on a paper titled "My Biggest Mistakes," and she listed them. It was heartbreaking to read. Some I included in *One Night in a Bad Inn*, some I did not. Why did she feel the need to write this down? Why did she keep it?

I also found a paper towel on which she had written: "Sometimes unless one has work to do, there is very little use to go on living."

Aunt Aila brought out a large family tree that her daughter, Mary Jane, drew for a school assignment. Peter's Aunt B provided the Irish side, the Thompsons and Gribbens. Grandma provided hers, the Welsh side, the Hugheses and Thomases. I copied it down. It's wonderful that teachers assign such things. It helps a child understand that he or she is part of a bigger world.

I remembered Grandma reading tea leaves and cards, only when prodded to do so. I asked Aunt Aila who else told fortunes and what kind.

"They were all fey," she said.

"What do you mean?"

"They knew things."

I remembered Mom and Grandma saying that Grandpa Peter did recitations at parties. Aunt Aila said he did everything—he sang, he danced, he did recitations.

"What songs did he sing?" I asked.

"'The Rose of Tralee,' 'My Wild Irish Rose,' 'I'll Take You Home Again Kathleen,' old Irish songs by Thomas Moore," and she sang one for me. She said she was astounded when she heard Bing Crosby sing "Toura Loura Loura" in a movie. She thought it was a song her father made up. She said when her father danced, he reminded her of Jimmy Cagney in *Yankee Doodle Dandy*. That gave me a wonderful visual image. Cagney was so light on his feet, as if gravity didn't bind him. What an apt metaphor for Peter—gravity didn't bind him, or he wouldn't let it.

One afternoon we drove down to Twin Bridges to see the orphanage where Grandma and her sister, Patsy, and brother Archie lived after their mother was arrested for killing their father. It closed in 1975. We saw the no trespassing sign, but no physical barrier to entry, so in we went and walked around the grounds. I took pictures. I took pictures everywhere I went in my research. It helped jog my memory and keep a visual chronology of where I had been.

After a week with Aunt Aila, I spent a week with Auntie Mary and Uncle Ed in Butte. Auntie Mary and I sat down over muffins and tea at her kitchen counter, and she told me her reminiscences and answered my many questions.

"What was Sarah like?" I asked.

"She had impeccable manners," Auntie Mary said, and, even when Sarah lived in the Cabbage Patch in a house with a dirt floor in all but the kitchen, the house was always immaculate.

What a metaphor for Sarah—an immaculate house with a dirt floor.

I asked if Sarah had a Welsh accent. She said no. When I asked Aunt Aila, she said she didn't remember, but it seemed all the adults she was around as a child had accents.

Sarah sang to them in Welsh. Recently I asked what kind of voice she had, alto or soprano. "She had a whiskey voice," Auntie Mary said. Aunt Aila said the same thing.

Auntie Mary said her friend's manicurist's second cousin's friend, or some such thing, was involved in the first reunion at the orphanage a couple years ago. I added that to my to-do list.

She pulled a book out of the cupboard and handed it to me. Grandma had given it to her. It was a nutrition book. As I opened it, a familiar fragrance wafted forth. It hadn't occurred to me that Grandma wore perfume, it was so gentle, so soft, as if it were naturally a part of her. I learned later that she wore Shalimar. To think that the little girl in the orphanage grew up to wear Shalimar.

AUNT AILA CAME TO TOWN and the three of us drove around so they could show me all the places where our relatives lived. In the 1950s, the Anaconda Company began to transition from underground mining to open pit mining. Over the years, much of the northeastern part of Butte was devoured by the Berkeley Pit. The Anaconda Company bought or moved homes in anticipation of expanding the Pit. When I was a child, two sisters refused to move, though that didn't stop mining; the Company simply dug around their house. It was a pink house and became a peninsula into the Pit. Eventually, the sisters agreed to move. In 1982, when work on the mile long pit stopped, a large swath of Butte had already been razed or the houses moved in anticipation of mining that never happened. Since many of the places where my relatives lived were on the East Side, we were often looking at an empty lot or the concrete ruins of a foundation or front steps.

Auntie Mary suggested that I talk to her friend Sylvia and arranged for us to meet for lunch. Sylvia grew up on Parrot Flat, near Sarah's boarding house at 415 Kemper Street. Sylvia told me the neighborhood children could always count on a bowl of soup from Mrs. Hughes (Sarah). I asked what the house looked like. She said Mrs. Hughes kept lots of ferns in the front room, and there was a big leather chesterfield and player piano.

After speaking with Sylvia, I made a point to ask people outside the family what they remembered about Grandma. I hadn't thought of doing that before Auntie Mary introduced me to Sylvia. It seemed all through my research, people were tugging me along, pointing me in the direction I needed to go.

Mom and Dad came to town. I listened closely and took notes while Mom and her sisters reminisced. One of them would say something and that would jog another's memory. When a memory was a song, they'd sing it. They sang that little song for me: "*Where is my father, where can he be, I'm so sad and lonesome, lonesome as can be, . . .*" Auntie Mary said she used to sing it around the house until one day Uncle Ed said, "Would you quit singing that song! It's depressing!" She laughed. She said it was something she had heard as a child and didn't think about it being depressing.

It was wonderful listening to them together, because they remembered different things, different pieces of the story. Aunt Aila, being the eldest and thirteen years older than Auntie Mary, was around when Mom and Auntie Mary weren't, and vice versa. When Aunt Aila went off to nursing school, they were still at home. With their literary ways of phrasing things, I was being gorged with delicacies, both in what they told me and how they said it. I was able to include most of what they told me in *One Night in a Bad Inn*, so I'll not repeat it here.

Several cousins joined us. I asked them about Grandma. Again, each had different reminiscences. Many stories everyone knew.

I asked about expressions people used, particularly my grandparents. When Grandma said they were going to "use Shank's mare" that meant they would walk. "Tap 'er light," meant take it easy, what miners cautioned when setting explosives. Telling the waitress, "I'll take it for the bucket," meant I'd like a doggy bag, the bucket being a miner's lunch bucket.

As I mentioned earlier, my intention was to try to corroborate everything. It wasn't that I didn't believe a person; it seemed the responsible thing to do. I wanted to be sure I had the facts in context, plus I was asking about things that happened decades ago. Information can be taken out of context, the memory of a child can be spot on, but it can also be so literal as to misconstrue things. Adults can do that too. Some people fill in the blanks with conjecture without saying that is what they are doing.

If I found a person's recollection to be suspect (which didn't happen often), I scrutinized everything all the more, and if I couldn't corroborate it, I left it out. Conversely, if I couldn't corroborate or disprove something, but the person had first-hand knowledge of what happened and had a good record for being accurate, I used it.

Also, when a person told me something that was not from first-hand knowledge, I asked from whom he or she learned it. That gave me a better idea of how reliable the information was.

NOW IT WAS TIME to take my to-do list to the Butte-Silver Bow Public Archives to see what I could find there. Mom came with me. The archives were housed in the old, historic fire station, so in effect, the archives were in an artifact. We signed in and sat down in the reading room. I pulled out my notebooks. The director, Ellen Crain, walked over and greeted us. In short order we established that Mom went to college with Ellen's uncle on her mother's side. To get there, we had to go through two layers of maiden names, but that didn't take long. In Butte, introductions often include maiden names in the form of "I'm a _____." The requisite do-I-know-any-of-your-relatives conversation goes on until we establish that somehow our families know each other. Butte people go about with the family tree of just about everyone they know in their heads. In meeting a new person, the first order of business is to establish in which slot on which tree this new person fits. That settled, we can get down to business. When Father Sarsfield O'Sullivan asked me, "Who are you?" I knew what he meant—in which slot on which tree do you belong? I'm introduced as Ted or Pat's daughter, or an aunt or uncle's niece, or a cousin's cousin. Butte is a place where you are never just you; you are you connected to a bigger world. It's nice.

Having personal connections established, Ellen explained what was available in the archives. They have the old Butte newspapers going back to the nineteenth century, naturalization cards, the *Coroner's Register*, school census logs, city directories, and much more. It is an amazing place. Though I had my laptop computer with me, I wrote notes in my spiral notebook which I would later transcribe into the computer. This worked best for me. I was actually writing the notes twice, which may sound redundant, but I found writing the notes by hand and then typing them into the computer helped sear the material into my brain. I wanted the book to be a narrative, to read like a novel, to have a familiar, natural feel to it, as if I were sitting there with you, telling you this story. I didn't want to merely pass on information. To do that, I would write from memory and then revisit my notes to be sure everything was correct and I hadn't missed anything.

Before my trip, I made tables with names across the top and a column for dates along the left side. I pulled a city directory off the shelf and started filling in the data for each person: his or her address, whether owned or rented, occupation, place of work, everything listed for that person. City directories proved to be an invaluable resource everywhere I researched. They were in essence a mini annual census of adults.

Then I bought an old map of Butte and plotted where everyone lived. It was interesting to see who lived near whom. This was the only old map of Butte I found for sale, and it happened to be for 1915, the year Grandma T arrived. How convenient.

As I was leaving the archives one evening, I told Ellen that I was also researching my great-grandparents' homestead in eastern Montana. She said the local courthouse would have the deed for the land. That sounds obvious, but I had never thought about deeds and such things or where to find them. Since I was a neophyte at historical research, every bit of advice helped. For Butte history, she recommended *Mining Cultures* by Mary Murphy. Aunt Aila and cousin Mary Jane also recommended it. I bought it and was delighted to see that the years covered in the book were the time period I was researching.

NEXT, MOM AND DAD and Uncle Joe and I drove to Helena so I could do research at the Montana Historical Society. I told Brian Shovers and Jodie Foley what information I was seeking about specific orphans and specific prisoners. I read the orphanage entry for Grandma and her siblings. (Mom signed the release as next of kin.) I made copies of the family prison records—I can't believe I just wrote that—for Sarah and Arthur and Archie and Bill, no release form needed for those. Now I knew that Sarah really did go to prison for bigamy. There was no denying it.

The prison log was kept in a huge, heavy ledger book. It gave the date the prisoner entered the prison, for what crime, and when he or she was released. I noted the data for Sarah and Arthur. Then I scanned the log to see for which crimes other prisoners were incarcerated around the same time as Sarah and Arthur. As I did, I noticed the same last name twice, an unusual name, a man and a woman, another married couple perhaps. I looked into it and found out they were married. I wonder how many times that happened—two married couples in prison at the same time and all four incarcerated for different crimes.

Later I broadened my research from specific prisoners to the prison in general and discovered the annual reports for the prison, which included a tally of how many prisoners were in prison for each crime. I'm glad I didn't know about those reports at the beginning. If I had, I wouldn't have scanned the prison logs looking at the other names and crimes, and I wouldn't have found that other married couple. The husband would pop up later in a completely different part of the story.

Jodie said she had several oral histories from people who lived in the orphanage. The historical society staff interviewed former residents at the first reunion in 1995. One of the women lived in the orphanage around the same time as Grandma T. I read the transcript from her interview. Jodie offered to inquire as to whether the woman would be willing to speak with me.

Next I sat down at the microfilm machine and began to look for articles about the fire in the Forsyth papers. I pulled out my time line to retrieve the pertinent dates: when the fire happened, when the sheriff arrested Sarah, when Sarah's trial took place. I concentrated my search around those dates and quickly found the articles. The one about Arthur being captured in New York covered the entire front page.

I FLEW HOME, ruminated over all I had collected, transcribed my notes into the computer, and started to read the books I had bought. I read slowly and took notes in my notebook which I later transcribed into the computer. I set a goal of reading one chapter of research a day every day but Sunday. I took Sunday's off. Once a week I played nine holes of golf.

While at the archives and historical society, I skimmed the old newspapers and documents to find the items on my to-do list and, once found, printed copies. I didn't take the time to read them thoroughly; I would do that later. When printing from microfilm, as with a copy machine, the machine prints what is on the screen. Most of the time, this meant I ended up with more than just the article I sought. Now I sat down to read those articles thoroughly and take notes.

The *Forsyth Times-Journal* ran lengthy, detailed articles about the fire and grave robbery and bigamy cases. The one that covered the entire front page included the letter the lawyer in New York wrote to County Attorney Beeman in Forsyth explaining how the authorities apprehended Arthur. This is gold for a researcher: the story right from the horse's mouth. The lawyer said he felt compelled to write the letter because the *World* article of that day included errors. "Find *World* article about Arthur" went on my to-do list. It would be interesting to see what it said.

A tiny headline in the November 6, 1913, *Forsyth Times-Journal* read: "Mrs. Hughes Pleads Guilty." The article summarized the trial: "The case against Mrs. Hughes-Elliott was tried . . . a large crowd was present each day . . . Hughes was brought back from the state prison . . . the two husbands of Mrs. Hughes-Elliott sat together . . . upon the release of Mr. and Mrs. Hughes from the state prison . . . other charges will be preferred against them."

"Nearly every child has worms."

What?

Oh, it's an ad for Kickapoo Worm Killer—makes children happy and healthy, says so right here. It was written as an article and seemed to be a continuation of the article about Sarah. This happened time and again, making going through those old papers even more time consuming. Articles weren't always clearly delineated, and often the headline was only slightly bigger than the text. If I didn't take the time to go slowly, it could be easy to miss something valuable.

CHAPTER FIVE

In late July of 1997, I flew to Billings. I had been to Billings once as a child when our plane was diverted there due to bad weather. That time, we landed in the dark and left in the dark, so this was my first look at the town. I liked it. The downtown has character, a well-kept western feel, just the right amount of veneer, the polish without the pretension.

I stayed the night and set off for Forsyth the next morning. I expected eastern Montana to be utterly flat and treeless and was surprised to see that it wasn't. I saw patches of flat but also plenty of hills, rim rock forming forbidding cliffs, scatterings of ponderosa pines dotting the hills, cotton-woods hugging the river bank.

As I drove along and gazed down at the Yellowstone cutting a majestic swath through the valley, my thoughts drifted to Lewis and Clark. I could picture them making their way up the river, though I didn't remember whether they were even on the Yellowstone. I looked it up when I got home. Clark was. He explored down the Yellowstone on their return trip and met Louis at the Missouri.

Up from the river, crops appeared to be flourishing. The grass along the highway was still green. I expected it to be toasted gold by now. Sprinkled among modern ranches lay relics of old abandoned homestead dwellings—our western ruins. I thought it was beautiful.

After about an hour and half's drive, I pulled into the Westwind Motor Inn on the edge of Forsyth. I walked inside and looked around. There was no one to be seen. I waited a little while and then rang the bell. A woman appeared and gave me a key. I collected my bags from the car and walked upstairs to my room. As soon as I was in my room, the phone rang. The woman at the front desk said there was a message for me. I went back down to get it. It was a note from Liz Cole welcoming me to town and saying that she and her friends were playing golf and would I like to join them. I jumped in the car and drove out to the country club. They were just finishing, so I waited at the bar. Soon Liz and her friends came in. We chatted about the story and about my writing a book about it. One of them said, "I'm trying to think of some old timers you could talk to." Liz suggested Mignon Tadsen. Somebody mentioned Whit Longley and Dorothy Spannagel. Dorothy had written a book about the area. I noted all these names.

In the morning, I drove to the Courthouse. Forsyth is a little no-stop-light town. It had a population of one thousand when my great-grandparents homesteaded in 1905. Today it is twice as big, around two thousand. If Forsyth were in Europe, I'd call it a village. Somehow the words village and Montana don't go together, unless it's an Indian village.

Liz and her co-worker Sharon Borla filled me in on what transpired the first time I called. When I asked for any record of Sarah Hughes being charged with murder, they looked her up, and of course she was in the log, but not for murder, for bigamy. They said to each other, "What should we do? Should we tell her? She asked about murder. Bigamy, murder, they're both pretty bad. Will she be upset if we tell her about the bigamy charge? Perhaps we better not tell her since she didn't ask." Liz responded to me with a direct answer to my direct question: there was no record of Sarah Hughes being charged with murder. Then of course I called back and asked the more general question: do you have any record of Sarah Hughes being charged with anything? And indeed she was: bigamy. When Liz found the bigamy case file stowed away in the bowels of the Courthouse, she discovered that the former Sarah Hughes was Sarah Elliott when she was arrested for murder, and she pulled that file for me as well, and it was all linked to Arthur's grave robbing charge. That is how my request for the bigamy file morphed into files for murder and grave robbery.

Sharon found another document related to the case, the transcript of the inquest. When there is a suspicious death, the coroner holds an inquest to determine the cause of death, and in this case since the body was burned beyond recognition, the identity. Witnesses are questioned by lawyers. Questions and answers are recorded verbatim by a stenographer. The typed transcript becomes part of the court records. I was fortunate that Liz and Sharon were tenacious in finding all this for me. Now I had my great-grandmother's actual words about what happened—she testified at the inquest.

I also had the actual words of the doctor, which filled in an important piece of the story. While conducting the autopsy, Dr. Huene discovered that the lungs were not burned, meaning the man was dead before the fire, indicating foul play; a murder investigation ensued.

I looked through those huge, old leather-bound ledger books at the Courthouse for any other Hughes records—both the criminal books and the civil books. I noted a criminal case, burglary, with a defendant named Hughes. I found several debt-related lawsuits involving Arthur, sometimes as the plaintiff, sometimes as the defendant. He usually won.

Liz suggested I talk to Judge Coate. He told her about what happened to Judge Crum, the judge who sent my great-grandparents Sarah and Arthur to prison, and gave her a magazine article about him. She made a copy of it for me.

Now why did Judge Coate save this article about Judge Crum, and why did he happen to give it to Liz? It was one of many things that would simply drop into my lap, material I didn't know I was looking for. I quickly read the article. Oh my goodness, Judge Crum was impeached.

Next I combed through the deeds and discovered that Sarah and Arthur had sold the homestead. First Arthur sold it to Sarah, then Sarah and Arthur sold it to men from Iowa, and then Sarah bought a house in Forsyth. I entered the dates of these transactions on my time line. The timing was curious. They sold the homestead only a few months before Arthur's apparent demise. It worked out perfectly since these Iowa men were absentee owners. While Sarah and the children lived in town, Arthur could live on the ranch, continue to work it, continue the milk and eggs business—or burn the place down and run off, which is what he opted to do.

What about the twins—the ones who were there one day when Grandma went to school and gone when she came home. My brother, Jeff, had reminded me to be sure to see what I could find out about them. What if something nefarious happened? I looked for a birth certificate at the Courthouse. Nothing. I thought, I'll look for a death certificate. I started at the beginning of the H's, thinking they could be out of order. I flipped through H, H, H, Hughes — I about fell off the chair — Arthur Hughes! Cause of death: murder. I couldn't believe it. I hadn't thought to look for it. It seemed bizarre that there would still be a death certificate in the file, since he didn't really die then. No twins though, just Arthur.

As for the twins, it is likely that Sarah gave birth at home. If the weather was bad, it could have been difficult, if not impossible, to go all the way to Forsyth for a doctor or even to fetch a neighbor to midwife. When the babies died, assuming that is what happened, Arthur could have buried them right there on the ranch. Absence of a birth or death record isn't conclusive. I didn't find Grandma's sister's birth certificate in the Rosebud County records. The copy I have, I found in Grandma's papers. About the twins, we know only what Grandma said: they were there when she left for school, and they were not there when she came home. The rest of the story remains a mystery.

I also looked at the birth records to see if I could find anything about the baby Sarah wrote about carrying while in jail. I found no baby Hughes or Elliott that could have been hers based on the dates.

That afternoon I went to see Mignon Tadsen. She was ninety-nine years old and lived in her own home in Forsyth. She grew up on the ranch across from my great-grandparents' homestead. Her father had been one of jurors on the inquest. I told her that I was Aila Hughes's granddaughter, and that Sarah and Arthur Hughes were my great-grandparents. We sat down on her porch. She said she knew Mr. and Mrs. Hughes, though not well. She remembered the house burning down. She thought Bill and Hector stayed on the ranch afterward. She said her cousin Whit Longley and his wife live there now. She seemed reticent. I didn't learn much. It occurred to me later that she was probably being polite. She was a teenager when the fire happened, the same age as Grandma's brother Bill. She no doubt heard plenty of gossip. She probably didn't want to speak ill of my deceased relatives. Also, I kept asking her about Sarah. I should have said Mrs. Hughes. Mignon probably didn't know that her name was Sarah.

When I visited Mignon's cousin Whit out on the old Hughes Ranch, I told him he needn't worry about hurting my feelings. I said I was writing a book, and I wanted to learn all I could. Whit said their house was in the exact spot as the house my great-grandfather Arthur built and burned down. The corral, horse barn, and large barn looked old enough to have been the ones Arthur built. Whit was only four years old when the fire happened. He didn't know anything about it other than it happened. I had a nice visit with him and his wife, Elsie, over lemonade and cookies.

Whit was eighty-eight years old when I met him. His family ran the old FUF outfit, a huge horse ranching outfit near the Hughes ranch that sold horses to the French cavalry. Seven thousand head of horses they had way back when, imagine the sight of it. Whit and Elsie had been married twelve years. It was Whit's first marriage and Elsie's second. She married as a young woman, moved away with her husband, raised her family, her husband died, and she moved back to Rosebud County. She and Whit renewed their acquaintance and married when Whit was seventy-six.

Liz and her husband took me to visit Dorothy Spannagel out on her ranch. Dorothy said, while researching her book about the families who settled on the Howard Flat, she came across something about Arthur Hughes in John Newnes's diaries, and that the diaries are in the museum in town. I bought a copy of her book *Trials and Triumphs*.

Next we drove to the Cole ranch, so I could see an old homestead house. I left my car at the main road and rode out onto the ranch with Liz and her husband in their pickup. We passed several wandering Longhorn cattle. They would have dwarfed my car. I know they're normally placid creatures, but up close, those horns look menacing. As we drove along, a mother antelope and her twins caught up with us and ran along side the truck and then, for no apparent reason, cut in front of us and ran off. Antelope are fun to watch, with those white bottoms bouncing up and down as they leap along, looking as if God pinned giant cotton balls to their behinds. (Actually they are pronghorns, only colloquially called antelope.)

As we approached the old log house, a dozen or so Herefords massed and lazily sauntered over to where they seemed to know we would stop. By the time we climbed out of the pickup, the cows were standing single file abreast, looking like an exhausted regiment awaiting inspection, staring at us with their doleful woe-is-me cow faces.

We walked over to the log house and looked around. Nobody lived in it anymore; the family used it to serve meals during branding. After I took a few pictures, we climbed back into the pickup and left. Again the antelope with the twins caught up with us and ran along side and then crossed in front of the truck, it seemed just to prove they could.

Now to see the other scene of the crime—the cemetery. Off I went to Beal's Furniture and Funeral Home to ask where John Kiernan's and Arthur Hughes's graves were. (John Kiernan was the poor fellow Arthur dug up.) It seemed unusual, furniture and funeral home together. Oh well, it's all wood. The woman unfurled the map of the cemetery and found John

Kiernan's grave. She found Arthur's grave in the log but not on the map. She said Arthur would be to the west of Kiernan. She told me where I could find them—take the road to the end and then three rows in.

I thanked her and drove out to the cemetery and found the spots she described. The graves were unmarked. I hadn't thought about their being unmarked, but it was no surprise. Johnny Kiernan had no family in the area, and I can't imagine Sarah spending one dime on Arthur. And as a practical matter, not that Sarah ever showed any evidence of being practical, she had just lost her husband, one way or another, and she had five children to support. She needed the money. I looked around the cemetery, took pictures, and thought about what happened there. It was a hot, sunny day, quite the opposite of that January night in 1913. It was eerie to stand there and think about what my great-grandfather Arthur did, digging up that body.

My next stop was the Pioneer Museum at the east end of Main Street. I found impressive little museums about local history in many small Montana towns. Forsyth's offers a slice-of-life of the old homesteading days. I asked about John Newnes's diaries. The woman directed me to a bookshelf. I pulled up a chair, sat down, and took one of the diaries off the shelf. It was a small, slim, leather-bound book, about four by six inches, something he could easily slip into his coat pocket. I started reading. I sat there and read and read and was transported back in time. It was as if I were there with him a hundred years ago, watching him go about his day. Each day was different.

I had to remind myself—I am here on a mission to find specific information. I had limited time. I focused my reading.

I took the time line out of my bag and looked up the date John Kiernan was buried—January 22, 1913. On January 18, John Newnes wrote that the weather was fine, cold and stormy, cold night, twenty-four degrees Fahrenheit. The next day, cold and stormy, got stranded, went to jury duty. The next day, cold, a chinook. The next day, weather fine, cloudy, got a load of hay. The next, weather fine, stayed over with horses and sleigh. Another chinook.

As I write, it is overcast and rainy.

On January 29, 1913, he wrote that he had been in town delivering beef and "I got back out about dark. Old Hughes was taking the wire off his fence and dragging it down the road and leaving it." The next day it was cold and snowing. Now February, very cold. February 3: "Old Hughes was snaking wire from his place over east of Emell's Creek." By mid February, everything was thawing, "water running everywhere from ditches all over fields." Then it rained, lots of mud. There was a frost. Somebody was trapping beavers on the river. He hauled hay. Somebody came by wanting to buy horses. Then it got really cold again, and stormy. A neighbor's calf died of blackleg; he vaccinated his.

I kept reading. A blizzard, another thaw, now on March 3—rain, snow, and sleet. March 4, thawing, muddy. March 5, cloudy, thawing. March 6, weather fine, cloudy.

Friday, March 7, 1913: "weather nice... Old Hughes house had burned up with some body in it. Suppose to be A.F. Hughes."

Suppose to be? Interesting choice of words.

On October 15, he wrote: "Old Hughes got 2 years for digging up grave."

On Sunday, November 2, the day after Sarah's trial ended, a blizzard blew in. How fitting.

My initial purpose in reading John Newnes's diaries was to find what he wrote about Arthur. As I read and saw that he wrote about the weather every day, I noted it, though at the time it seemed inconsequential to my story. It turned out, it wasn't. Learning there was a thaw in mid February added more drama to the story since Arthur had a dead body buried in the snow, snow that was fast disappearing. Reading about the weather also helped explain somewhat, though not completely, why Arthur kept the body those six weeks. He needed to be sure the house would burn. He needed dry weather.

Though I began my research looking for specific information, I was beginning to learn that it is best to take a broad sweep. Somewhere in the middle of that sweep, I would find the nugget of information I sought. Out around the edges, I would find gems I didn't know I needed, details that added texture and dimension to the story. When my mind gently nudged me to investigate something or keep reading something, I did, even if it did not seem to pertain to my research. In time I would discover that it did. In short, I learned to follow my intuition. Had I not kept reading John Newnes's diaries, I wouldn't have known there was a thaw in mid February, right when Arthur had a dead body buried in the snow. Of all the bad luck. Too bad Arthur didn't see it as a sign and forget the whole thing and put poor Johnny Kiernan back where he found him.

My next stop was Miles City, about forty-five miles east of Forsyth.

I took the first exit, drove into town, passed a leafy lagoon, drove down Main Street, then through a leafy neighborhood of well-kept old homes. I felt I had entered a Norman Rockwell painting.

I wound back and stopped at the library and read the old newspapers. By the time I finished, it was late afternoon. I needed to drive back to Billings, a two hour drive.

The next morning, I flew to Seattle to see my aunt and uncle and cousins on Dad's side of the family. While there, Mom called and suggested I visit her cousin Gilbert Hofling in Olympia. I thought, Gilbert Hofling, what an auspicious sounding name, it sounds like the name of somebody in a book. I had never met him and didn't know how we were related. Mom explained that Gilbert was her first cousin on her father's side, which made him my first cousin once removed.

I called Gilbert, explained who I was, told him I was writing a book about the family, and asked if I could visit him. He said yes.

When I arrived, Gilbert's wife, Maria, greeted me at the door. "Gil, your little lamb is here!" she called to her husband.

Gilbert was born in 1918, and his wife, Maria, in 1919, so they were in their late seventies when I met them in 1997. I found them to be an elegant, handsome pair, Gil with his shock of white hair, white mustache and silk scarf cum cravat, Maria with her engaging smile. Maria didn't walk through the room, she swept through it. She was absolutely delightful, wearing a long skirt and blouse—casual yet elegant, clearly Maria was always elegant. I bet as a baby she was elegant. Her name is pronounced with a hard I, as in Mariah, as in my grandmother's name, Aila, A-EYE-la. We sat down in the sunken living room of their spacious home, and I launched into my questions. Gil's mother, Mary, was Grandpa Peter's sister. I had been told that Mary used to pour forth with a verbal hand cast against her forehead about how she, a poor little waif, came to this country on the ship all by herself, all the way across the ocean, all the way across the country, all by her little lonesome.

I didn't repeat that to Gil but simply asked, "I understand your mother came here by herself."

"No, she didn't!" he declared, as if declaiming some absurdity. "She had a what-do-call . . . a chaperone!"

After we chatted awhile, Gil telling me about our common Irish kin, I asked Maria about her family.

"*My* father was born under the *last* sultan in Constantinople!" she declared with a broad sweep of her arm. Gil and Maria were definitely of a different era, and deliberately so. For them, there was no Istanbul, it was Constantinople. There was no Saudi Arabia, it was Arabia. They were inextricably tied to the nineteenth century. Maria's father was George Nazrethian, an Armenian from Turkey, then the Ottoman Empire. His family held the tobacco and silk concessions in Constantinople, granted to them by the sultan, with offices in Alexandria, Egypt. This was prior to the First World War. George Nazrethian studied at the Sorbonne in Paris. After graduation, he was celebrating with friends, and he normally did not drink, but this night he did, and he got drunk, and his friends got drunk, and they put him on the wrong ship. Instead of sailing home to Constantinople, he sailed to New York which, as history would unfold, was a fortunate accident for George Nazrethian. Walking down the streets of Manhattan, he thought, this is a curious people, these Americans, I think I'll stay awhile. He soon met Eileen Riordan, an immigrant from County Killarney. They married and stayed in New York, which no doubt saved his life. His family back home in Turkey were murdered in the Armenian genocide during the First World War.

George and Eileen Nazrathian had two daughters: Maria and — you'll never believe it — Aila. They pronounced her name I-la.

As a young woman, Maria owned Marand Antiques in New York City. She'd go off to Ireland and England on buying trips. She did retail and wholesale, though mostly wholesale. She told me about a crotchety, old Jewish man who wanted to sell a vase to a particular customer but feared he was too abrasive to make the sale. His business sense outweighing any personal pride, he asked Maria if she would negotiate the sale for him. She said she would and asked what was his final price. One hundred dollars, he said. He listened from the back room while Maria and the customer haggled over the vase. The customer threw out a number, Maria countered. They haggled back and forth, back and forth, down to $100, the customer went lower, $100, she said, he went lower, $100 is it. She wouldn't budge, he wouldn't pay, so he left.

After the customer was gone, the man burst into the room and scolded Maria, "Why didn't you sell the vase?!"

"You said $100 was your final price," she responded.

"SELL! Always SELL!" he scolded her. "Repent later but SELL!"

As for Gil, in 1940 he joined the merchant marine. He was at sea almost all the time with a week off here or there between voyages. He said he was surprised to see a lot of older men working on the ships. "It was hard on them," he said. "You get thrown around."

"How did you two meet?" I asked.

Maria said it was the summer of 1948, August, and horribly hot. She was waiting for a shipment to clear customs; otherwise, who would *dream* of staying in the city in such hot weather. She had gone out for the evening with her friends Erv and Lil. Erv was a banker and his wife Lil (or was it Lou) worked for the Red Cross. They decided to take in an ethnic street festival. "We were slumming," Maria explained, "not the sort of thing we would normally do."

As Providence would have it, that very day Gil's ship had a stopover in New York City, and while wandering the streets of Manhattan, he came upon this ethnic street festival and sat down. He happened to sit down next to Erv. The two immediately launched into a discussion of Chinese dynasties.

The four of them were sitting there, Gil and Erv discussing Chinese dynasties, when the music started for a schottische. Gil stood up and walked over to Maria, bowed, clicked his heels, and asked her name. She thought, who does he think he is asking me my name? She decided she'd really throw on airs to counter such impertinence. Tossing her head back, she declared haughtily, "*My name* is Maria --- Christina --- Beatrice --- Columba --- *Nazrethian!*"

Gil responded, "Your name will be Maria Christina Hofling!"

He said the minute he heard her name, he knew he was going to marry her. Maria Christina Hofling was his Swedish grandmother's name.

He then persisted in his impertinence by asking her to dance.

Well!

Erv leaned forward and said to Maria, "He's all right, go ahead." Anyone who could discuss Chinese dynasties so facilely was fine in Erv's book. Having received Erv's imprimatur, Maria accepted. As she stood, she glanced down and noticed that Gil had cut out the toes of his shoes. "Imagine, cutting off the toes of your shoes," she said laughing. I thought, how weird. I asked Gil, "Why did you cut off the toes of your shoes?" He shrugged. "He was a good dancer," Maria said, as if that made up for the toeless shoes.

They spent the rest of the evening together. After the festival was over, they walked through the streets of Manhattan and talked and talked and talked all night. At six o'clock in the morning, they slipped into a church for Mass, and then said goodbye.

Maria said she had a hard time remembering his name. "Gilbert Hofling?!" she said. "Who has a name like Gilbert Hofling? If his name was Myron Leibowitz, I'd remember. But Gilbert Hofling?! Who's named Gilbert Hofling?!"

Gil was supposed to leave right away, but there was a problem with the ship which kept him in New York longer. They spent much of the next two weeks together. When the repairs were finished, Gil and his ship sailed away. He and Maria spent the next four years corresponding and saw each other when Gil's ship stopped in New York. Maria said they argued and argued and argued. The end of the last argument was to get married. They were married at St. John's Church in New York City on February 23, 1952. Gil left the merchant marine, Maria sold her antiques business, and they took off for San Jose, California, where Gil owned a home in which his mother lived.

And how did they get to California? In the comfort of a train? No— they drove. And where did they stay along the way? In the comfort of hotels? No—they camped out, all the way across the country, socialite, businesswoman Maria with her designer evening dresses, camping out. I suspect this was not what she anticipated in a honeymoon. She must have really loved Gil. Along the way, they had a close encounter with bear. How does anyone spend that much time camping out and not have a close encounter with a bear. They arrived safely in San Jose where Maria was at last to meet Gil's mother.

They didn't stay long. Gil went to work in shipping-related businesses which took them all over the world, to Saipan in the Mariana Islands, to Arabia, where they lived from 1959 to 1961.

"What did you do in Arabia?" I asked.

"I worked for the Persian Gulf Arbitration Board inspecting cargo," Gil said.

"What was the Persian Gulf Arbitration Board?"

Gil explained, "It was set up by the insurance companies and others to help settle damage claims for the huge losses occurring during the build up of the big oil companies—Aramco. Insurance companies count on recovering some from the party at fault but were having no luck under Sharia law. We arbitrated claims, checked the damage, assigned the loss as required. Sometimes the ship was at fault or even Aramco. We met the ships, saw things through. Some items ran into big sums of loss. It was interesting work. I had been in the steamship business, from ordinary seaman to claims to port captain, so I was selected to sit on the board. We didn't sit much as we were out surveying the losses. It was a great time. Maria was there. Wish I had it to do over. I would have had more fun. As it was, I worked a lot."

Maria excused herself and swept off to the kitchen to finish preparing dinner, "We make haste slowly these days," she explained. I continued chatting with Gil. "What was Peter like?" I asked. It soon became clear how much Gil adored his uncle Peter, my grandfather. Sensing this, I was careful how I asked about Peter, perhaps not careful enough. I asked what he had heard about Peter quitting the job Anne McDonnell found for him (this was during the Depression when my grandfather had a wife and three children to support) and about Peter's gambling. Gil insisted that if Peter quit a job, he must have had a good reason, and he could certainly understand Peter not wanting Anne to find him a job, and if he gambled, he always won.

I see here on my list of questions for Gil, one that says, "Why didn't Peter work steady?" There is no check mark next to it. I didn't ask.

Maria announced that dinner was ready. We sat down at their round dining room table with the two of them sitting opposite each other and me in the middle. We said "Grace," I asked a question, and they were off. I became a spectator at a verbal Wimbledon. Back and forth went the volley. I could barely keep up. Gil said something, now Maria, now Gil, now Maria, now Gil, firing back and forth, back and forth, ... "Would you mind if I recorded you?" I broke in. "You wouldn't want that," Gil scowled. "Oh, yes, Gil, let her record you," said Maria. Gil scowled an acquiescing scowl, and I scampered off to fetch my tape recorder.

I returned with the tape recorder, and the volley continued. They talked about the McDonalds of the Isles and the Flight of the Earls and somehow this pertained to our family history, though I have no idea how. They said the McDonalds of Antrim (or was it McDonnells) were the only McDonalds to remain Catholic. They talked about the Easter Uprising and how Peter taught Gil to recite "Sam McGee" and "Dan McGrew," and how Gil could recite them when he was only two years old, and how the family was surprised that Peter didn't marry Nell Coughlin, and how the

Thompsons knew the Hughes family's reputation, and how Peter taught Gil to box, and how Antrim people were drier, smaller, finer, than other Irish who were big brawny people, especially in the west, in Mayo and Galway. He talked about how the Irish were clannish, how the family used to debate local politics, and how Pat was a red-hot patriot and the British were after him, and how Butte was a distant suburb of Ireland, and how kind and warm and aware Aunt Annie and Aunt B were, sincere, good people, highly moral, no guile, a joy to be around, discussed everything, interested in everything. Gil talked about the songs Peter used to sing. Maria coaxed him into singing one. They both talked at once, and jumped from subject to subject, and my head was spinning, and I thoroughly enjoyed myself.

While cleaning the dinner dishes, I asked Maria the secret to a their long marriage, then forty-five years. "We're still arguing," she said.

"Yeah," Gil said, "we wanted to get a divorce but we couldn't agree on anything, so we had to stay married."

I mentioned that a friend of mine was getting a divorce. Maria said emphatically, "You must talk to her and convince her not to get a divorce. It's the last thing she should do. You think he's easy to live with?" and she gestured at Gil.

Changing the subject back to family, I said, "Grandma T knew things, she had premonitions."

"We all do if we listen," Gil said.

"That's what Grandma T said," I replied.

I told them I was wondering how to handle this in the book. It was so much a part of Grandma, I had to write about it. I worried about it being misconstrued. I said, "Premonitions are really intuition, which Mom calls angelic knowledge."

"The word intuition is very interesting," said Maria, "*intuitus*, breathing in the spirit, the Holy Spirit. My own feeling would be, don't pull punches. Tell it straight."

Gil said, "Be objective about it. Anyone who thinks there's nothing but the material world isn't very bright."

I asked about fortune telling. Gil said Aunt Jenny read cards, Aunt B read tea leaves.

"Did they believe it?" I asked.

"They did, and they didn't," Gil said. "I remember an old lady near Randalstown [in Northern Ireland], she had a name like Butler. She told me always think positively, never think negatively. She would look into the fire, and that would focus her mind."

"Was it intuition?"

"Yes. The cards and tea leaves triggered their intuition," Gil said. "Every card had a meaning—I guess that wasn't intuition. As I saw it later on, it was kind of a hope, that something good was coming along. You always felt better after. She might give a warning but wouldn't say anything bad. They hoped the good things would come true. They weren't surprised if it didn't work out. Reading the leaves, it was in one ear and out the other. Maria reads tea leaves, she knows it by instinct."

"Keep affirming something positive," Maria said. Perhaps that was the secret to their long marriage.

She said, "When we were living on Sacramento Street in San Francisco, I was hanging clothes on the roof, and I heard my mother's voice—and she was in New York—say, 'Darling, darling, look around,' and I did, and if I had taken another step, I would have fallen off the roof."

"Do you think some people are more prone to that, to intuition and premonitions?" I asked.

"Yes," she said. "It takes belief."

I asked about Gil being in the merchant marine during the Second World War. Maria said his ship went down.

"What happened?" I asked.

"*Naaaah*," he said dismissively waving his hand. Maria tried to coax him into talking about it. "*Naaaah*."

Later when I asked again by letter and by phone, he was more forthcoming. He said he was at sea between San Francisco and Honolulu when the Japanese bombed Pearl Harbor. The army told him he could stay in the merchant marine, which he did. While aboard the *President Grant*, his ship was driven aground trying to avoid submarines near New Guinea.

He was third mate aboard the *Cape Sandy* at MacArthur's landing. The merchant supply ships came in behind the navy. A Japanese pilot fired on Gil's ship and then crashed into the bridge of the navy ship next to them. Gil got lifeboats out to rescue the sailors. He said he grabbed one of the sailors by the arm to pull him out of the water, and the man's arm came off.

He paused and started talking about something else.

Chapter Six

By now, I had been on leave of absence for two months. I had been on the road doing research almost the entire time and knew that I had barely scratched the surface. I called the office and extended my leave of absence to the end of the year.

My original idea had been to write a book about all four grandparents, and my research thus far had covered both sides of the family. By the end of the summer, I realized I had far too much story for one book, and I still didn't know the whole of it. I decided to split my work into two books and write the book about my maternal grandparents first.

A few days after I returned home, more Irish relatives came to visit, this time Mom's cousin Breda and her husband and daughter. Family stories filled our conversation, about how Rose's family didn't want her to marry Sam Thompson, and why did Sam stay in Butte and Rose in Belfast all those twenty years. (It is curious, my great-grandparents Sam and Rose had five boys and not one named Sam.) Breda said how kind her grandad Sam was to her after he returned to Belfast, though her cousins in Butte said he was very aloof. Aunt Aila said she never remembered her grandfather Sam speaking to a child.

Before that summer, it had been years since any of my Irish cousins visited, but every year the entire time I was researching and writing *One Night in a Bad Inn*, some of them came to visit. Those trips had nothing to do with my book and many were planned well before I had any thought of writing it. I could certainly write to them and ask questions, or call, which I did, but there is nothing like actually spending time with family for stories to pop up. Memories are not water faucets; we cannot turn them on and off at will. "The wind blows where it will," and so it is with memories. We must be present to capture them when they do pop up.

After Breda and her family left, I began to pore over the research materials I had collected. To learn more about homesteading, I read the actual Homestead Act. President Lincoln signed it into law in 1862, during the Civil War. As head of a family and a citizen, my great-grandfather Arthur Hughes easily qualified for his 160 acres in eastern Montana when he applied in 1905. Even if Arthur had still been a British subject, as long as he had formally declared his intention to become an American citizen, he would have qualified. He had to live on the land and cultivate it for five years, which he did, and then, after he paid the fee, was granted a patent (deed) to the land. This land could not be levied upon by creditors for debts contracted prior to the land grant.

To gain a sense of what life was like for Arthur and Sarah on the homestead, I read books by and about homesteaders. The privations were many. Dorothy Spannagel said she used to ride horseback to school; when it was really cold, she rode bareback so the horse would help keep her warm.

The descendant of an old homesteader explained why some succeeded while others did not: "The ones that did good in this country didn't spend much money. The ones that didn't do so good, the ones that had to leave, they were the ones that spent."

In addition to frugality, it seems faith was another essential arrow in the quiver of the homesteaders: faith in God, faith in themselves, faith in each other. That same rancher said, "When things get really tough, you get up . . . work hard . . . you get tired at night so you can sleep and some way the Good Lord takes care of the rest."

I tried to locate descendants of the people who owned the homestead when Arthur burned the house down. I must say, I made only a halfhearted attempt. What was I going to say, you know that ranch your ancestors owned in Montana, the one with the burned down house? Well it was my great-grandfather who burned the house down—your house. It was too weird.

The Forsyth paper said Sheriff Moses hired a Pinkerton detective in New York to help catch Arthur, so I called the Pinkertons in New York City to see if they had any information on the case. The woman said they didn't have the records there and suggested I call their world headquarters in Encino, California, which I did. The woman in Encino said they have archives, but not on every case. She looked up Arthur Hughes but didn't find anything. I can't help but wonder what does lurk in those archives about other cases from days gone by.

I reread the coroner's inquest over the dead body. Sheriff Moses said he went to the ranch to investigate the fire and "look over the premises of this desert claim on which he was fixing to build," he being Arthur. Desert claim, what is that? I asked several people in Forsyth, but none knew what it meant.

The book was always on my mind—always—a way to write something, a question to ask, something to look up. I'd quickly jot these things down, lest I forget. When I woke up each morning, the book was already on my mind, as if I'd walked in at the middle of a movie. People talk about writer's block, I had writer's overload. Thoughts about the book were bouncing around in my mind constantly, like a bunch of splitting atoms, splitting and splitting, one idea bouncing off another, creating another, and another, where to place a particular anecdote in the story, something else to research, a question to ask. And there was the puzzle aspect of it, all these clues, how did they fit together, what did they mean? Even in mentally quiet moments, when some prosaic task put my mind at rest, out would pop another book epiphany.

One day while brushing my teeth, it hit me: desert claim, claim, mining claim—land. I called Ardella at the Bureau of Land Management in Billings.

"What does 'desert claim' mean?" I asked.

"The Desert Land Act," she said.

I asked if Arthur Hughes filed for land under the Desert Land Act. She looked it up. "Yes, he did."

A few days later, I received Arthur's filing papers for the land with the location coordinates and a map and a history of land legislation. Ardella had placed yellow tabs at the Desert Land Act parts and highlighted those sections. The purpose of the Desert Land Act was to encourage settlers to irrigate the arid West and grow crops. A claimant had to irrigate the land, but unlike the Homestead Act, he didn't have to l ive on it.

I SAT DOWN at the computer to transcribe my notes and the tapes of recorded interviews. When I slipped in the tape from my visit with Gil and Maria, it was blank. I resorted to my copious notes.

What to do with all this? I had to start writing the story. Since I was sticking with nonfiction, I was limited to the facts, which wasn't much of a constraint. The facts were replete with drama and twists and surprises, mistaken identity, the wrongly accused. They needed no embellishment, yet, how to assemble them? No matter how luscious the material, every author must find an interesting way to tell an interesting story. It isn't necessarily obvious how to do that. It certainly wasn't for me. Before me lay a huge pile of jigsaw puzzle pieces, each a gem. How to piece them together, what would it look like? I had a vague idea, it was out there, in the ether. With hard work I would get there, I would see it.

Dad said, "Why don't you start with the fire and finding the body." I liked that idea. I like books that throw me into the story on the first page.

Now I had my beginning. That was a start. Even so, I became overwhelmed with the thought, I'm writing a book, an entire book, as if I had to write it all at once. It was daunting.

I mentally shoved being daunted aside and started writing about the fire. I went back through the inquest and added dialogue from it, though much abridged. Legal proceedings can be tedious. I certainly did not want my book to be so. The "show don't tell" adage has limits. My challenge as storyteller was to weed out the tedium and present these compelling facts in a compelling way.

When the lawyer asked Sarah if anyone had threatened to kill her husband, she replied, not lately. It turns out more than one man had threatened to kill Arthur. I wondered why they weren't called to testify. I wondered if Sheriff Moses investigated them as possible suspects. Perhaps he did, and they had solid alibis. But didn't Sarah have an alibi, and still she was arrested.

Since this part of the story was a murder mystery, I grappled with how to tell it, from whose perspective, which clues to drop and when and how, how to bring in foretelling. One can tell such a story from many points of view: the fugitive, the accused, a family member, the sheriff, the community. In actuality, I was telling the story from my point of view, the granddaughter/great-granddaughter researcher, but within that, I had to choose a perspective, a sub point of view, if you will. How about Arthur, the fugitive. After he torched the place, he ran off and hopped a steamer bound for Buenos Aires. This I knew because he told Jennie Hayes that's where he went, and Jennie told all in her deposition. What he did in Buenos Aires, what he did aboard ship, I knew none of that. Telling the story from his point of view would be pretty thin. What about Grandma? She was shipped off to the orphanage while her mother was in jail. To this day, I don't know whether she ever knew the whole of it. In the end, I chose the point of view of the community, that is, those orbiting around the principals, the principals being Arthur and Sarah. This gave me the most material.

Sitting here writing this, it just occurred to me, I always thought about Grandma being sent to the orphanage from Grandma's perspective. I never thought of it from Sarah's, her children being taken away to a place far, far away.

As for hints and clues to be dropped, do I announce the fugitive's true identify as soon as he resurfaces in New York? Following my point of view decision, I introduced him as John P. Price, since that's who he told the mail clerk at the Seamen's Church Institute he was. I dropped the bombshell as to his true identity when he did, when he told Sarah's friend Jennie that he was Arthur.

I decided to pull some events out of the inquest and depositions and place them where they happened in the story. I described Sheriff Moses investigating the crime scene and his conversation with the boys passing by when it happened and omitted those details from his testimony at the inquest.

While perusing old Forsyth papers at the historical society in Helena, I happened upon a description of the weather in the paper that came out the day after Arthur dug up the body. It said the temperature had been ten below the previous Friday. The next day "a warm wind grew to a Chinook," and by noon it was a balmy forty-five above, water dripping everywhere. That night "the mercury in the thermometers continued to seek seclusion" and by midnight, it was ten below.

What a poetic way to write about the weather, "continued to seek seclusion." I didn't make a note of the exact wording right then because it didn't seem essential to my research. I just noted the big swing in temperature. When storing a dead body, the weather can be significant.

In time I would learn, if anything struck me as remotely interesting, even if it didn't seem to pertain to my research, I needed to make a copy of it or write it down or take a picture. If I didn't, my subconscious would gently nudge me, relentlessly, not ill-natured guilt-ridden nagging that is to be ignored, just a quiet, persistent nudging that I had to heed or I'd never have any peace. I wanted to know those exact poetic words in that article about the weather. It wouldn't leave my mind until I found them. So off I went to the library to request the old newspapers on microfilm through interlibrary loan. When it arrived, I trotted back to the library and parked myself at the microfilm machine to look for what I had already found but had not sufficiently noted. Making a copy the first time would have been much easier. In time I learned to do that.

Since I had the microfilm, I decided to go through all the Forsyth papers from before Johnny Kiernan died in January of 1913 (he was the poor fellow Arthur dug up), until Arthur and Sarah were hauled off to prison in November.

Several times, I saw lists of delinquent taxpayers in the newspaper. How is that for shaming people into good behavior. I looked for Arthur and Sarah. They were not listed.

Here's something about bandits trying to hold up a train near Butte. Oops, they forgot the dynamite.

Here's the note to creditors for the estate of John J. Kiernan. What a chain of events his death unwittingly wrought.

Here's a story about Coroner Booth being in a serious automobile accident in May of 1913. That was only two months after he conducted the inquest over the burned up dead body found on the ranch. When Sarah wanted to take the body home, he insisted it stay put so the doctor could conduct an autopsy, which of course was how we learned that the man was dead before the fire, a murder investigation ensued, followed by Sarah's unfortunate decision to run off and marry the handyman, and she was arrested for murdering Arthur, and ultimately convicted of bigamy, and things would never be the same.

Later I would learn that his automobile accident turned out to be the beginning of quite a string of bad luck for Coroner Booth.

In those old newspapers, I came across a lively description of breakfast at the Northern Pacific Depot, which was where Sarah worked. When the waitress called out, "A wreck on the main line," that meant an order of scrambled eggs. When she said, "A mogul with two headlights" that meant ham and eggs. If she added, "And blanket those headlights," that meant eggs over. I wanted to work this into the story, thinking it would add some local color; yet, this was a serious part of the book, a little girl was grieving the death of her daddy. It wasn't the place for humor.

Ken Follett said one way to make the reader care about a character is to show that another character cares about him. Grandma adored her father. The trick was how to get that across, so you would be concerned about what happened to Arthur and, even more important, about what happened to Aila (my grandmother) because of what happened to Arthur.

With all this in mind, I continued writing the murder mystery. Now I'm at the grave digging part, describing my great-grandfather Arthur digging up poor Johnny Kiernan in the dark of night, that cold, cold night in 1913, all alone in the cemetery digging, digging, . . . or was he alone? How on earth could he get the body out of the grave by himself, a man the same size as he? Perhaps he unhitched one of the horses from the milkwagon and tied the rope under Johnny Kiernan's arms and had the horse pull him out. As I sat pondering this, I realized it was Halloween, which made it seem all the more macabre and sickly hilarious. I looked back at the newspaper reports of what Arthur said when he testified at Sarah's bigamy trial. He said she had nothing to do with it. Did anyone else? I wonder. In early drafts, I wrote, "How on earth Arthur got John Kiernan's body out of that grave by himself is a wonder." Later I deleted "by himself."

I wonder where Johnny Kiernan is now. I mean his body. After the authorities discovered the grave robbery, did they put him back in his grave, or is he still in Arthur's grave? Strange thing to think about.

When meeting with book clubs to discuss *One Night in a Bad Inn*, I often ask whether they thought Sarah was in on it. One woman said, based on Sarah and Arthur's relationship, she couldn't imagine them ever agreeing on anything. Another said she didn't think Sarah was in on digging up the body and the fire, but once she saw the body, she knew he wasn't Arthur, but she played along to get the insurance money. Another woman said she was sure Sarah put Tom up to it.

I read still more about Forsyth, about homesteading, about Montana. I took notes, transcribed those notes into the computer, read more, took more notes, more transcribing, read more, I couldn't get enough. I found the homesteading era fascinating. I had to tell myself—stop—this is only one part of the book. I have to stop. I have read enough about homesteading. It's time to move on to the next part of the book.

Why, you might ask, go to all this trouble researching the homestead era? I had a compelling murder mystery, why not just tell what happened with the dead body and forget the historical backdrop. I did it because I wanted you to get to know the people in the book. I wanted you to feel as though you were there with them. We know each other in the context of time and place. We don't think about it because we are living in the same time, and often the same place. When we want to get to know someone, we want to know where are you from, where were you born, where are your roots. To get to know my grandparents, I would have to get to know their parents. To get to know all of them, I had to learn about the times and places in which they lived, to understand the context in which they lived. The historical backdrop was necessary in order to put their lives in historical context. If I made their milieu more vivid, I hoped that would make them more vivid. Only by delving into the times and places in which they lived could I begin to comprehend what they were up against, or not up against.

I felt that everything in the book must have a purpose, bring something to the story; otherwise, it had no business being there. To determine this, I set down this rule for myself. I asked: Does it advance the story? Does it develop a character? Does it help set the stage? If I couldn't say yes to one of those questions, it didn't belong in the book. What I meant by "set the stage" was, put the story in context, show how the people bumped into history along the way, and how history bumped into them. Did this institution, this place, this event affect the people in my book? Describing what eastern Montana looked like and the unforgiving climate helped demonstrate what my great-grandparents had to contend with as homesteaders.

Even when I could answer yes to one of those questions, I still might not include it. I had to balance whether or not to include a particular anecdote against advancing the story. First and foremost I was writing a story, albeit a true one, and I wanted to tell it in an intriguing way. As such, there were many things I left out, painful though it was.

WHILE IN FORSYTH, I bought *They Came and Stayed*, a collection of family histories that provided a marvelous window into the life of the homesteaders. In addition to helping me glean a flavor of the times, the book also captured the expressions of the time. They *filed* for a homestead; they didn't apply for it. They *proved up* on it.

It also included irresistible stories about the nexus between the homesteaders and the Indians. There was the tragic story of Hugh Boyle. Hugh came to Rosebud County in 1890 to visit his aunt Ellen Gaffney and uncle Patrick Lynch. They worked his cousin Marcus Daly's cattle ranch down near Lame Deer, south of Forsyth. One evening, Hugh went out to collect the milk cows and never returned. Family and neighbors went looking for him. After several days, they found blood, moccasin prints, horse tracks, Hugh's hat, and himself dead, buried under shale. The men went to Fort Lame Deer and told the soldiers what happened. A horrible myth was going around the Northern Cheyenne that if an Indian killed a white man or short-haired Indian and died brave, he would go straight to Heaven. The two Cheyennes went home after killing poor Hugh and told their families exactly how they wanted to be laid out in their graves. The soldiers and Chief Two Moon agreed they had to be punished. The white man's punishment for murder was hanging, but the Cheyennes didn't want to go that way. It was humiliating. They wanted to die brave. So the soldiers and chief arranged an alternative. The soldiers took position, their rifles at the ready. The two Cheyennes mounted their horses and charged over the hill toward the soldiers, and the soldiers shot them.

Rancher George Beebe died in 1907 after being injured by a horse, leaving his wife Rosa a widow, living on the prairie, running their ranch near Jordan, raising and feeding her children all by herself. One day she took off on horseback in hopes of bagging a deer. She spied a deer and shot it. The deer went down, then jumped up and ran off. She spurred her horse and chased the deer. The deer ran over a hill. She followed it and galloped straight into an Indian camp. The startled Indians started shooting. She turned the horse and high tailed it back to the house. She gathered the children inside, covered the windows, quieted the children, and they waited. After a while they heard muffled footsteps outside. They waited. Silence. Rosa looked outside. There was the deer, all dressed out.

I wanted to include these stories, but I didn't. I didn't know how much Grandma and her family interacted with the Indians. And besides, I had that dead body lying there in a burned down ranch house. I needed to get back to him.

CHAPTER SEVEN

EVERY STORY TAKES PLACE somewhere. Though much of *One Night in a Bad Inn* took place in Montana, the story was not one of solely local interest, and as such, I was ever cognizant that I was writing for people outside the state as well as within. To set the stage properly, I needed to dispel myths about Montana, in particular about Butte.

From the outset, I was determined that my book would be about people. People would be at the center. I would describe institutions, places, and historic events only in so far as they affected the people in my book, to set the stage on which they lived, as a backdrop for a painting. I would not write about stuff, nor about vague people-less events, places, and institutions. I would write about real people doing real things. Wars don't happen by spontaneous combustion. Shapes on a map don't declare war. People make the decision to go to war, people cause events to occur, people make institutions what they are, and to a large extent make places what they are. That said, places can shape people in how they deal with them.

As for places, in any story in which she appears, the place that hogs the stage, steals the show, gets all the laughs and all the applause, is my hometown of Butte, Montana. I had to write about Butte. The town is irresistible. In writing the book, I found that some characters emerged by themselves. That was also true of Butte. She emerged more as a larger-than-life person than a place. As the writer of a highway marker proclaimed: "She was a bold unashamed rootin', tootin', hell roarin' camp in days gone by and still drinks her liquor straight."

On his trip around the country chronicled in *Travels with Charley*, John Steinbeck dawdled when he got to Butte. He didn't want to leave.

One could rightly say the scrubby mining town could stand to wash her face and comb her hair, and that is happening, slowly, organically, in her own Butte way. People are sprucing up the old Victorians. Driving through uptown Butte one day I noticed a beautiful old building that had obviously been there for a hundred years. I wondered why I had never noticed it before. Then I realized, it must have been scrubbed and painted, that's why I noticed it. What was once dismal and invisible now gleams and stands out.

Butte was a big city in the nineteenth century and retains much of that architecture, creating a powerful sense of time and place. Every year during my research, I went to Butte. The town is one big outdoor museum.

Just as in order to learn about my grandparents, I had to learn what came before them, about their parents, I needed to do the same with local history. Most of the story took place between 1900 and 1925, and I concentrated the lion's share of my research on those years; however, to understand the Butte of my grandparents' time, I had to learn what came before to make the town the place it was when they discovered it. Though I was born in Butte and lived there until I was nine and visited often, I knew little of the town's history. For most of my historical research, I was beginning with a blank slate. I started my research of Butte history by reading several wonderful books I found at Mom and Dad's. I learned that Butte had its own opera company way back when, and during Prohibition there were estimated to be five hundred speakeasies in the town. I read about the colorful Copper Kings—the mining entrepreneurs who created jobs, lots of jobs, good paying jobs. I took notes in my spiral notebook and then transcribed them into the computer in a file I named "notes.Butte." As I finished transcribing each page, I wrote a large check mark at the top to show that I was done.

On every research trip to my hometown, I found a reason to visit the World Museum of Mining to soak up more old Butte ambiance through pictures and artifacts, mining and otherwise. The bar from the old Rocky Mountain Café is there. *Collier's* magazine called the Rocky Mountain the finest eatery west of the Mississippi. It was quite the Meaderville supper club in its day. Though Meaderville was Butte's Italian neighborhood, the owner of the Rocky Mountain Café, Teddy Traparish, was from Dubrovnik—a Croatian ran the most famous restaurant in the Italian neighborhood—so Butte, so quintessentially American. A priest told Aunt Aila, "I grew up in Meaderville, and I thought the whole world was Italian. Then I went to the Irish Christian Brothers school, and I learned the whole world was Irish."

As I read and pondered all this, it occurred to me that Butte at the dawn of the twentieth century, when my relatives settled there, was a cross between Las Vegas and New York City. As in New York, the town was a patchwork of ethnic enclaves; as in Las Vegas, it was a 24-hour town, gambling was wide open (though illegal back then), with performances by big name entertainers and gourmet meals in fabulous restaurants. A man in Idaho told me that he and two FBI agents used to take the train all the way from Pocatello to Butte just to have dinner at the Rocky Mountain Café. "No place like it," he said.

From the late nineteenth century until well into the twentieth, Butte, Montana, was a bustling, cosmopolitan, industrial metropolis that could have been plucked from the northeast and dropped into the Rocky Mountains, a delicious melange of eastern sophistication amid a mining town's outlandishness. Rural, she was not. She was definitely cast against type.

I couldn't help but think of the Butte of days gone by as another metaphor for Sarah—lively, unabashedly confident, and naughty.

The Butte of my early childhood was a melting pot of shared recipes. Mom often made stuffed cabbage leaves for dinner. I didn't know it was called Sarma and was Serbian. We ate tamales made by Truzzolino, an Italian. It wasn't until after we moved to Kennewick that I learned tamales were Mexican (or more broadly, Latin American).

In the lead-up to our nation's bicentennial, many communities published local histories. In Butte, they wrote a cookbook. It is divided by ethnic group with a brief history followed by old family recipes and anecdotes. It is one of my favorite cookbooks on a very full shelf. Now for my research, I fetched it to read about the Welsh and the Irish.

The food I identify most with Butte is the pasty, pronounced with a soft "a," think Patsy but reverse the t and s. I will always think of pasties as endemic to Butte, though they are not. They originated in Cornwall, "a letter from 'ome" the Cousin Jacks called them. For the uninitiated, a pasty is chopped beef, potatoes, onion, shredded carrot, salt and pepper, topped with a dab of butter and wrapped in pie crust and baked in the oven. At least that's how Grandma T taught me to make them. It seems every family has its own recipe. Essential ingredients are beef and potatoes wrapped in pie crust. I wanted to write about Grandma making pasties in the boarding house, but I didn't know for certain whether she made pasties for the boarders. She told Aunt Aila about making sandwiches, so that was the vignette I included.

It wasn't until my first visit to Butte after I studied in France that I noticed—the sky really is big in Montana. Everything is big in Montana, except the people. Had I never moved away, I wonder if I would have noticed. Over time I could see the advantage of writing about the place I am from, though haven't lived in for a long time, but to which I still have strong family connections. This gave me both familiarity and distance. Distance can help see what is special about a place. When I mentioned what a spectacular setting Butte sits in (ignoring the Pit and strip mining of course), how the town is surrounded by majestic mountains, huge, close mountains, Aunt Aila said, "I've lived there so long I hardly notice." It can be easy to miss the remarkable in the familiar.

Reading more history, I was astounded to learn that my hometown was under martial law in 1914, the year Grandpa Peter arrived. That seemed incredible. I wondered how many places in the United States had been under martial law. The encyclopedia article mentioned a Colorado mining town.

As I sat in my living room in the late 1990s and read the history of mining in Butte, how mining companies were the hot stocks a hundred years ago, and eager prospectors were searching for the mother lode, be that ore in the ground or enough pay dirt to entice a behemoth to buy them out, it reminded me of the dizzy excitement over internet stocks, this idea that if you were on the internet, you'd become a millionaire, just like that.

Butte packed an immense volume of history into a very short period of time, what with the War of Copper Kings, martial law, breaking the union, the rise and fall of the Socialists, infiltration by Wobblies, infiltration by detectives, who was infiltrating whom. My time line of local history grew and grew and grew.

Learning the colorful history of my hometown further convinced me of the necessity to include the historical backdrop in the story. I already knew that Grandma T came from a notorious family. Now to realize that she lived in a wild and woolly town, through tumultuous times, and arrived there during her formative teenage years, yet she emerged an impeccable lady. From a literary point of view, the contrast was irresistible.

CHAPTER EIGHT

CLEARLY, GRANDMA T was emerging as the heroine of the story. Everything pointed to her. To know her and what she was up against, I had to get to know not only her parents, Sarah and Arthur, but also her husband, Peter, my grandfather. To know Peter, I had to know what he experienced in the war.

I needed to go to Belgium and France to see the battlefields.

Tucked away in Grandma's papers, I found the citation for the *Croix de Guerre*, the medal the French government bestowed on Grandpa Peter for saving that man's life. It was in French. I translated it and later, upon further search of family papers, discovered a copy in English. It was from General Headquarters of the French Armies of the East, signed by Petain himself, and said: "Near Steenbrugge, Belgium, on the 31st of October, 1918, he went out to the assistance of a severely wounded non-commissioned officer who had fallen in a very exposed position. Under heavy machine gun and artillery fire, gave him first aid." I obtained the rest of Grandpa Peter's military records from the National Archives, which included another English translation. This one said "violent" machine gun and artillery fire. The French version also said "violent." How vivid.

Where was Steenbrugge? I pulled out my map of Belgium but couldn't find it. I called the Belgian tourist office. I explained about my grandfather saving this man's life during World War I, and I'm trying to find Steenbrugge, the town where this happened. She started talking about Normandy. Wrong war. That's when I started saying and writing the First World War instead of World War I. It seemed whenever I said "World War," the person heard "two" even when I said "one." And besides, Grandma referred to it as the First World War, and I wanted to capture the language of the time as much as possible.

In a speech about writing, Garrison Keillor said you work and work on your manuscript, you want it to be the best it can be for the reader. Then you send it off to the publisher, the publisher sends you galleys, you make corrections. Then it is done, the manuscript goes to the printer, the book arrives in the mail, you open to a random page, and instantly your eyes fall on — a typo.

As much as one strives to eliminate typographical errors, unfortunately they slip through. The brain sees what should be there rather than what is. A typographical error that affects only spelling is embarrassing. What are most distressing and harmful are those that create factual errors, such as writing World War I instead of World War II, or vice versa, which I have seen more than once in print, yet another reason for writing out the First World War and the Second World War.

I wondered, who was this man Peter saved? What was his name, what became of him after the war? Perhaps he or his progeny went on to do something wonderful that wouldn't have happened had Peter not risked his life to save him. I wanted to know more details about what happened. In addition to the citation, all I knew was what Grandma told us: that Peter ran out into no-man's land, rescued this wounded man, brought him back to the trench, Winks Brown helped Peter pull the man into the trench, and because Winks was not decorated, Peter refused the medal. I wrote to the French ambassador and asked if the French government had more information. I enclosed a copy of the citation. The embassy staff forwarded my request to the appropriate bureau in Paris who responded that they had no additional information. I still wondered. It remained on my to-do list.

I sent the first few chapters to Mom and Dad to read. Dad asked why Sarah's family in Pennsylvania didn't take the children (Grandma and her younger siblings) rather than send them to the orphanage. Good question. He suggested I include more about Grandma, that I focus the story more on her. That meant I needed to learn more about the orphanage. They both advised, don't spill the beans so quickly, include the dialogue between Jennie and Arthur. Talk about the children, what was happening with them when their mother was arrested, include my ponderings about what happened, which we often discussed on the phone, how could the authorities arrest Sarah on such flimsy evidence, what did she know about Arthur digging up the body and torching the house. It was good advice. I set about rewriting those chapters. I would rewrite them many, many, many times.

I went back over my notes and the court documents. Some of it still didn't make sense. Who was this Thomas woman in Billings? What was Arthur's motive? Was it to get the life insurance money? Was it to leave

Sarah with the life insurance money and thereby assuage his guilt for running off and abandoning her and the children? Who told Sarah that Arthur was alive? How did Sarah's lawyer, Braz Tull, know to look for John P. Price in New York? Some of it I never did figure out. All I could do was tell you what I knew, voice my ponderings, and let you draw your own conclusions. It was after all a murder mystery, albeit a true one. Since it was true life, I couldn't tie it up neatly with a bow at the end. Some of it would remain a mystery.

Now to try to learn more about everyday life for Grandma in the orphanage. Among the papers I had collected at the Montana Historical Society was an article from the *Oregonian* about Bill Hanley, the man who organized the reunion at the orphanage. The article said he lived in Vancouver, Washington. I found listings for three William Hanleys in Vancouver and started calling. The third one was the right one. I explained who I was, and that I was writing a book, and that my grandmother lived in the orphanage, and I was looking for more background on it. Bill told me his story. His father was in prison. He and his brother were sent to the movies one day, someone picked them up at the theater, and with no explanation, took them to the orphanage.

When the press caught wind of the orphanage reunion, reporters scurried to interview former residents, which resulted in a flurry of newspaper stories. Bill had collected them into a scrapbook. I bought a copy. I read all the articles but concentrated on those about people who lived there closest to Grandma's time, from 1913 to 1915, knowing that as time passed, the world changed and, no doubt, the orphanage changed. I wanted my account to be as specific to Grandma as possible.

Former resident Mae Walsh said her stepmother made her sleep outside in a tent. Living in the orphanage was a big improvement. "Sure we had to work hard," she said, "and the discipline was tough, but it was good training that prepared us for life." She said they had plenty to eat and were taught good manners and acceptable social behavior.

Gladys Real, who like Mae lived there in the 1930s, said some of the matrons were nice but others were mean and hit the kids with hoses. She said, "There were no hugs and kisses but it was stable."

Maxine Thompson said, "It made me a survivor . . . I've always been bound and determined that what happened to me wouldn't happen to my children." That was Grandma's sentiment.

A woman, who lived there decades after Grandma, said she lived in four different foster homes after leaving the orphanage. She said she would rather have stayed put and had some stability.

I pondered all this. I thought about how traumatic it must have been for Grandma. First she is told her father is dead, then her mother is taken away for murdering him, then a stranger comes along and takes her and her little brother and sister away on the train to a strange faraway place, then she's separated from her little brother and sister, for whom she felt responsible. It's sad to think about. And yet from all I read, it seemed the orphanage staff tried to make the best of a bad situation.

A letter arrived from Jodie Foley at the Montana Historical Society saying she had heard from Rossellia Templeton, the woman who lived in the orphanage at the same time as Grandma, and that she was willing to talk to me. She did not want to talk on the phone or correspond in letters. I would have to go there. She lived in a nursing home in Stevensville, down in the Bitterroot Valley south of Missoula.

Off I went back to Montana. Rossellia didn't remember Grandma's name. Grandma was a couple years older than she, which for children can seem more like a decade. Now that I think of it, I should have said I-la instead of A-I- la in case the staff mispronounced Grandma's name. Rossellia told me about daily life in the orphanage, about their chores, how the children were segregated by age and gender. She didn't know the boys at all. She said they got lice from a German girl, but the staff took care of it right away. She said for the most part, the children were well behaved. Two girls ran away and got a spanking for that. I asked about school, did they have homework? No, she said. They had assignments to do during school. She said the staff was strict, but in a nice way. She thought Mrs. Shobe, the head matron, and her teacher were good examples. When Rossellia said, "Mrs. Shobe was a real lady," it struck me, because it sounded like something Grandma would have said.

As I discussed this with Mom, we both wondered if being sent to the orphanage could have been the best thing for Grandma, to be around positive examples at an impressionable age. She was eleven when she went to the orphanage; she entered high school the fall after she left.

Rossellia said after two years, her parents took her and her sister home. I asked about life at home on the ranch. She explained how they put up the ice, how they buried melons in oats, and stored apples and carrots in a hole lined with straw. She said everybody worked the ranch, including her and her sisters and her mother; whereas at the orphanage, the boys did the ranch chores, and the girls did household chores.

While in Missoula, I went to the University of Montana law library to see what the penal code said about the crimes in my book. In particular, I wanted to know what the punishment was for murder in 1913. I figured it was death, but I wanted to know for certain. It was death or life in prison.

IN THE EARLY DAYS of my research, acquaintances often asked, "Do you use the internet?" Considering the kind of research I was doing, I was puzzled by the question and said no. After a while I started asking, "For what?" Some people said, "Oh, I don't know." Others said, "For your research." I said I did my research the old fashioned way: reading books, finding historical documents at archives and libraries and courthouses. My neighbor Andrea said she thought those old court records and newspapers were on the internet. They were not back then. It seemed many people saw the internet as a panacea, and if it made sense for something to be there, it would be right now at no cost and with no work. It's that good ol' American optimism at work: I've heard of it, it's new, I don't know much about it, it must be wonderful. And if it's doable, it must be done, and soon.

After being asked this several times, I decided to give it a try. This was still in 1997, a year before Google was incorporated. Yahoo was only two years old. This was the Jurassic period of the internet. I searched "home-steading" and found random paragraphs floating around in cyberspace but no sources, no author, nothing I could use. I resumed doing my research the old-fashioned way.

As for searching for information using the computer, Dad gave me two encyclopedias on CD-ROM, *Encarta* and later *World Book,* which made finding a fast fact easier. Toward the end of my research, I started to use the internet quite a bit. There is so much available on line now. Today I can read the Homestead Act of 1862 at the Library of Congress website. In 1997, I had to go to the library to read it. I can find academic papers on a variety of subjects with a simple Google search, which before would have taken some digging to track down. I see the world wide web as the wild west of information, a free-wheeling electronic library and data bank, a gigantic electronic shoe box full of stuff, and anybody can put anything in it. One can find much helpful information on line, and also plenty of nonsense and mischief making. That said, the printed word is by no means immune to nonsense and mischief making. Even when no malice is involved, errors and misleading statements can creep into printed books and articles as well. When something struck me as suspect in a book, I consulted the bibliography and notes and tracked down the original source. At times, that proved to be eye opening.

An obvious use of the internet was for genealogy research. A tremendous store of genealogical data is now available on line, though that was not the case when I began my research. I already had much of what I needed as far as names, dates, and places from family records and memories. Even so, I collected copies of the actual documents from archives and courthouses: birth and death certificates, marriage licenses and certificates, naturalization papers, ship arrival records, military records. I made a table called "Data Collected" to keep track of which documents I had, which I still needed, and which I could not find. For those I could not find, I noted where I had looked. Though my reason for collecting these documents was simply to corroborate what I had been told, I was pleasantly surprised to find that doing so paid dividends. For example, Great-grandma Sarah's birth certificate, which I purchased from the British Public Records Office, showed that her mother marked her X when she registered Sarah's birth. This told me that my great-great-grandmother Ann Thomas did not know how to write, this formidable woman through whose influence her son-in-law Arthur Hughes attained the position of foreman, and she did not know how to write. I found that fascinating.

One area where the internet came in handy from the beginning was in finding people. Mom told me that Archie's wife, June, had a sister named Ellie Stathos who lived in or near Chicago. I found her phone number and called. She said she had pictures of Archie and June and asked if I would like to have them. Indeed I would. She sounded relieved to have found someone to whom she could give these things, someone to whom these pictures and records would mean something. I tried to call her again a few years later to ask about Archie and June trying to get June's brother out of the concentration camp in Germany during the Second World War. Instead of Ellie I got an auto repair place. I wrote to her again but received no response.

Mom also suggested that I speak with her cousins on Grandma's side of the family. All my life I had heard a lot about the Irish part of the family, Grandpa Peter's side, the grandfather I never knew because he died young. As close as I was to Grandma T, it was a long time before it occurred to me that she might have family besides us. In my mind, Grandma T appeared full grown one day in Butte, Montana, as my grandmother. I never thought about her being a child, a teenager, a young woman falling in love with my grandfather, or living anywhere else but Butte, even though I knew she was born in Wilkes-Barre. She was just Grandma T. When it did start to dawn on me that she had family besides us, I asked Mom, "Does Grandma T have any family?" "She has a brother in California," Mom said, and that was it.

I called two of these cousins. They were Grandma's nieces, her sister's daughters. They knew our uncles Bill and Archie (Grandma's brothers). Uncle Archie dazzled his young nieces. They thought he had the looks and presence of a movie star. One said, "It was a real treat to see Uncle Bill." I couldn't bring myself to ask if she knew they had both been in prison.

Bill told them he had been a peace officer in Rosebud County. I was skeptical. I investigated but could not confirm it. Who knows if I ever learned everything about Bill. I was fairly certain that Archie stayed out of trouble after he was paroled, but I wondered about Bill, being the mean cuss he was. These cousins said he had lived in California and Nevada, so I called the California and Nevada historical societies to find out if Archie or Bill did time in those states. Neither had. To find out if either of them was charged but not convicted, or charged with something minor, would require calling every county courthouse in those two states. I opted not to do that.

At least I thought that's what I'd have to do.

Just the other day as I sat writing this, I received an email from KC Sackman who works at the Prison Museum in Deer Lodge. We met during my book tour for *One Night in a Bad Inn*. She asked about Sarah's burglary charge in Butte. I started to say that Sarah was not convicted of burglary in Butte, then I corrected myself and said, "I'm not aware of a burglary charge in Butte." Apparently the prison staff kept track of charges against former inmates. KC sent me the note fixed to Sarah's prison record which said she was arrested for burglary in Butte on September 5, 1933.

I started hunting for the rest of the story. Tom at the Clerk of Court's Office in Butte said they had no record of Sarah Hughes or Mitchell or

Rigley being charged with burglary. He explained that if Sarah was arrested but not charged, there would be no record at the Courthouse. I remembered seeing the police blotters at the Butte Archives. I had started to look through them to find out if any of my relatives had been picked up for anything else, but the entries were by date and not name, and with no date to go on, it was like looking for a needle in a haystack. I quickly gave up.

But now I had a date. I emailed my request to the Butte-Silver Bow Public Archives, and they sent me a copy of the police blotter page. Sure enough, a woman named Hughes was arrested for burglary on September 5, 1933. It didn't say Sarah Hughes, it said Mrs. Hughes. I noticed that other women picked up around that time had the same first name: Mrs. It said the witness lived on Nevada Street. Sarah lived at 532 Nevada. As I studied the page and thought about this and again read the date, September 1933, a lightbulb went off in my head. That was when my grandparents were living outside of Helena. They lived there from 1932 to 1935. While living there, Grandma received a telegram from Mrs. Flomer, her former employer at the Family Drug, saying: Aila, please come. Aunt Aila told me about this and assumed that it must have been when Mr. Flomer died. In my effort to corroborate everything, I found out that Mr. Flomer died before they moved to Helena. Now to learn that Sarah was arrested for burglary, the dates lined up. I bet that is why Mrs. Flomer wrote to Grandma, and that is why she went to Butte. It had to be something compelling to get her to leave Peter and the children for a few days, and incur the expense of a babysitter for the little ones and for the bus trip to Butte, especially since they never had spare cash. Keeping her mother out of prison was certainly a reason to get her to go.

Now knowing that the Prison Museum had records that I did not find at the historical society, I asked KC if her records showed any further criminal activity for Arthur, Archie, and Bill. Arthur's record was clean after he left prison. Bill was charged with battery in Monterey County, California, on November 27, 1938, and found not guilty. Archie's sheet showed one additional violation: "failure to register" in Los Angeles in 1939. That was after his parole had expired. It also said he applied for a liquor license in 1939.

CHAPTER NINE

NORMALLY I WORKED on the book Monday through Friday from around nine o'clock in the morning until five or six o'clock in the evening, sometimes later if I was on a feverish writing binge. On Saturdays, I worked until around three o'clock. I took Sundays off. Writing definitely requires brain food. I always began the day with breakfast and stopped around noon for a proper lunch. I did not work after dinner. I found that if I worked after dinner, I couldn't sleep. My mind would be full of this and that about the book. In the afternoon when I got a bit drowsy, I'd go for a walk and have a cup of tea. While walking, often something that had me flummoxed would come clear. On occasion, I'd stop and chat with one of the neighbors I saw out and about. Bill was usually in his garage detailing his Corvette. He was a retired airline pilot who had flown for PSA and USAir. Bill thoroughly enjoyed a good rant, the subject of which could be politics or telling me how he had told someone off. Bill often had colorful ways of putting things, and his opinions were never in doubt. One day he told me that another neighbor asked he voted for his guy for president, and Bill exclaimed, "I WOULDN'T VOTE FOR HIM IF MY HAIR WAS ON FIRE!"

Much of Bill's flying career was in California. He regaled me with stories about riding his Harley with Boz Scaggs when he lived in San Francisco, and how Governor Reagan would always stop at the cockpit and say, "Thank you, Captain," and how Governor Reagan was always on time, and a younger governor wasn't, and one time was so late that Bill was about to lose his slot for take-off, and when the young governor and his entourage finally arrived, they took their sweet time taking their seats, and Bill told them off over the plane's loudspeaker as only Bill could, or would.

On days when I was on a feverish writing binge and took my walk late, I'd see Bill pulling out of his driveway in his Corvette. He'd roll down the window and say, "I'm on my way to work." He meant the casino, not as an employee, as a professional gambler. He played craps and video poker Monday through Friday and took weekends off.

I will never forget the time Bill told me about being forced to enter an alcoholism rehabilitation place in San Francisco—it was that or lose his pilot's license. He went on and on complaining about the place, how they wouldn't even let him smoke, "And outside my window, on and off, all night—BUD Lite, BUD Lite, BUD Lite." I said, "Bill, you mean the alcohol rehabilitation place was across the street from a bar?" I often wondered about these stories; however, there were times when he told me he had the inside scoop on something and later I'd read it in the newspaper.

While out for my walk one day, a car stopped along side me. It was Andrea. She had moved out of the neighborhood, and I hadn't seen her in quite a while. She rolled down the window and said, "You're wearing the wrong shoes," and drove on. Later I learned that she was moving back into the neighborhood. Andrea was one of the first people I met outside of work in Las Vegas. She had been a news reporter on the radio and on television and now was a private investigator. She would sometimes stop by my house to visit while out on her walk, often dressed in a white sweatshirt and white sweat pants and wearing a diamond necklace.

Andrea had two homes in the neighborhood, one she lived in and the other she rented out. One day she stopped in to tell me about the problems she was having with her tenant, an octogenarian Italian contessa with five ex-husbands in her wake. The contessa was late paying the rent again, and Andrea had just seen her playing the slot machines at a casino. Later, the contessa tried to sublet the place without telling Andrea, so Andrea put her out. The contessa was very upset with Andrea about that.

Sometimes as I set out for my walk, I'd see Alan picking up his mail. Alan was retired; he had been the chief operating officer at American Standard. He seemed to me to be in his eighties. I was surprised to learn that he was only in his early seventies. He was quite thin, which made him seem frail, even though I often saw him jogging or striding down the street with tennis racket in hand. He was from London, and the only person I ever met who attended Cambridge, Oxford, and Stanford. He started at Oxford or Cambridge, I can't remember which, his studies were interrupted by the Second World War, and he finished at the other after the war. He was supposed to parachute into Normandy in advance of the invasion but was temporarily deafened by an artillery blast during training and couldn't go. After the war, the army sent him to Germany to identify the bodies of fallen British soldiers.

I don't remember Alan ever answering the door without a jacket, even when I stopped by his house unannounced to drop off some banana muffins I had just made, or to ask if he would water my plants while I was gone. Even in the heat of the summer when it was 110 degrees, still the jacket, albeit a light-weight powder blue one.

Alan often asked how things were coming along with my book. One day I mentioned that some of my relatives were Welsh. He said he had a friend in New York who is Welsh. This friend also happened to be editor in chief at W. W. Norton. Alan offered to give this friend information about my book. He was going to New York soon and would see him.

At this point, I was still fresh from the business world, and though I didn't realize it yet, I needed a lot of reorienting. At Bechtel, I had worked on fast-paced projects, doing several things in parallel. I felt I had to hurry up and find a publisher, even though I had barely scratched the surface and didn't yet know the whole story. I looked up Norton and read that I should send a proposal consisting of an outline and sample chapter. I thought an outline was what I had learned to do in school, beginning with Roman numerals for major headings, large alphabet letters for subheadings and so on. As I learned later, that is not what publishers want in this context. It is more of a synopsis. When I look back at what I gave Alan, it was awful. Approaching any agent or publisher before I knew the whole story was a mistake. Also, I didn't yet understand the concept of selling the publisher on the story, which meant not holding back about the dramatic parts, as I do when telling prospective readers about the book, not wanting to spoil the surprises. I received a polite no from Mr. Lawrence at W. W. Norton.

With much of my work at Bechtel, I was continuing what someone else had started, and I worked with a group of people. Whenever I was stumped, I could find someone to consult. While doing book research, I found people who could point me in the right direction, refer me to an archive or book or person, but as to how to tell the story, how to write it, what to include, what to leave out, that I had to figure out for myself. I was on my own. That was a big adjustment.

Also, at Bechtel I worked on several things at once in short spurts with interruptions, on some projects incessant interruptions. That kind of work requires a short, concentrated attention span. Now I was working on one very big thing, and I needed a prolonged attention span, like a sprinter becoming a long distance runner. It took a while to adjust.

Both Auntie Mary and Aunt Aila gave me tapes they had recorded of Grandma talking about her life. I transcribed them and listened to them over and over. I'd be making dinner, I'd be listening to the tapes. I'd be doing the dishes, I'd be listening to the tapes, hearing Grandma's voice, her manner of speaking, her stories, the expressions she used. She had a such a literary way of speaking. I can't take credit for coming up with, Tom walked while she pranced, because that's how she said it.

I was reminded as I listened that Grandma's gentle voice didn't grow old sounding until the very end of her life.

As I listened to one of those tapes for probably the third time, I caught something I hadn't heard before. When Grandma talked about her father becoming a foreman in Wilkes-Barre, almost under her breath she said quickly, "That was my grandmother's doing." That simple statement told me something about her father and about her grandmother. I had the impression that Ann Thomas was a formidable woman. Now I had a concrete example.

At the beginning of one tape, Grandma said, "Did you ever see an eagle with a broken wing? A beautiful creature—fierce—but helpless." She said it with just the right amount of emphasis in just the right spots, making the meaning more profound. It pierced my soul to hear it. I thought of the wounded eagle as a metaphor for Grandma. But she recovered. She was not helpless.

Grandma was an excellent storyteller, not jumping from subject to subject, a nice smooth chronological account. As she described the train ride across the country to Montana, Auntie Mary asked if they had milk cows. Grandma said yes, "My father said that we had to have milk cows. I think we had three. They were red with white heads. That's all I can remember." Then out of the blue she said, "Well, my father was a changeable man." I wonder what she meant by that. Auntie Mary asked about her mother's matched team. "Oh, they were wonderful," she said. "One was a mare and one was a gelding . . . Everybody tried to buy them, oh how they could fly over that ground, I can still remember that."

About the homestead, she told Aunt Aila: "My father said we were going to stay until it was ours. By that time, he had a well dug, and he had fenced our section of land." Then her voice drooped sorrowfully. "He meant to stay there for the rest of his life, believe me he did, but things didn't work out very good." She paused. "My mother was a butterfly." She paused again. I was on the edge of my seat thinking she's going to talk about the fire. Then Aunt Aila asked, "Where did you go to school then?" and Grandma talked about how wonderful this particular teacher was at that little country school and how much she learned from her.

She talked about her father digging the irrigation ditch and how they put up the hay. She described life in the boarding house in Butte. She said, "In those days, after you boarded in a certain place a little time, it became family. They practically took over the house, and that suited my mother fine because she didn't want to be bothered . . . My mother always called herself the kitchen chef. She didn't like to cook, she didn't like to work. She got the other fellas to do it."

Then she said reflectively, "It was a hard life, but you learn a lot by working in a boarding house."

Did she ever.

My cousin Mary Jane asked about Grandpa Peter's experience in the war. "He saved that man's life," Grandma said. "He was bleeding to death."

"When did your mother die?"

"Was it '44 or '47?" she said. "God have mercy on me, I can't remember." (It was 1947.)

I wanted to quote Grandma T as much as possible, but I had to weigh the desire to hear her voice against smooth storytelling. I didn't want to confuse you. I had to be careful how I jumped from what was happening in Grandma's life to her recollections of it. Often I resorted to paraphrasing her because I couldn't figure out how to make an exact quote work. As with everyone else, I sought to corroborate everything. Much of what she talked about were things of which she had firsthand knowledge—her own experiences. She proved to be a very reliable source. I remember so often when I asked her a question, she would pause and think before she answered, not in trying to remember, but in forming how to answer.

RARELY DO I remember dreams, but that October I had a vivid dream that my cousin Kenny called me on the phone and said, "Hi, Christy, this is Ken West, I hear you're writing a book about Grandma . . ." He sounded very business like and matter-of-fact. All I could think was, I have to call Aunt Aila, and I didn't hear the rest of what he said. Kenny died in Vietnam. I was a small child at the time and hardly knew him.

Chapter Ten

WHILE SITTING in a waiting room idly thumbing through magazines, I stumbled across an article about a television program in which a family was going to plop itself down in the wilderness and recreate the life of the early homesteaders. No modern conveniences would be allowed. Of only the "technology" of the time could they avail themselves, such as it was. They had to raise animals, grow their own food, build a house up from the ground, just as my great-grandparents did in Rosebud County, Montana, in 1905. One of the teenage daughters said she planned to bring lots of books to read. Since they wouldn't have television or computers, she figured she'd have a lot of free time.

Clearly there were even more misconceptions to clear up. I would need to paint a vivid picture of what life was like for Arthur and Sarah homesteading in Montana in 1905. To do that I needed details, and those details had to be specific to time and place. That meant more research.

Back I went to the library. I read about Montana, I read about the railroad. I knew Grandma T and her family arrived in Forsyth by train. Which railroad took the southern route through Montana at that time? I looked that up. It was the Northern Pacific.

Though I used the library frequently throughout my research, over time I realized it was best to buy the books I needed for research. I ended up continually revisiting them, and if they were on the shelf in my house, it was much quicker and easier. Also, if I owned them, I could underline the text and write notes in the margins.

I read still more about homesteading. Those people certainly had to be optimistic even to attempt it. Simply surviving the weather was heroic. I read about a man being knocked unconscious in a hail storm.

Reflecting on ten years in northeastern Montana near Culbertson, William Alexander wrote: "The awfullest ten years of my life . . . I have worked on work-days, holidays, and Sundays. I have practiced every kind of self denial that I have been able to think of. Long hours, so long that the stars shone in heaven when I got up and went to work and they shone when I ceased work."

He wrote those words in 1921, during a drought. When Henry David Thoreau wrote, "The mass of men live lives of quiet desperation," he could have been talking about the Montana homesteaders, especially during the droughts. My great-grandparents Arthur and Sarah homesteaded from 1905 to 1913, which were good years for water. I wanted to paint a vivid picture of how hard they worked, how difficult life was; however, some of these more dire accounts from the drought years I couldn't use, because I wasn't sure whether they gave an accurate depiction of what Arthur and Sarah faced. Being specific to time and place makes research much more difficult— deciding what to use, what is appropriate, what was correct for the time and place. I found many irresistible quotes including another from William Alexander: "Folks are simply walking around to save funeral expenses." Funny and sad, yet I wasn't sure whether it applied, so I couldn't use it.

SINCE ARTHUR AND SARAH grew up in Wales, I needed to learn about their native country. The computerized card catalog at the library was in an early incarnation and was cumbersome. When I entered Wales, up popped books about Princess Diana. I was puzzled. Oh, of course, Princess of Wales. I persevered and finally found a book about Wales and the Welsh.

I had been told that Grandma's father, Arthur, was separated from his family as a small boy and ended up in the workhouse. I read almost two entire books about British workhouses for what ended up to be about a page in my book. I say almost two entire books because I skipped the parts about Irish workhouses. I wanted information specific to Wales.

The 1834 Poor Law in Britain mandated that all relief be in workhouses. In *The Workhouse System 1834–1929*, M.A. Crowther wrote that Charles Dickens valued "personal charity over impersonal public relief, he praised institutions which tried to treat each inmate individually, whereas the workhouse crushed their personality. Thus he describes the old pauper Nandy in a coat 'that was never made for him or for any living mortal.'"

At a dinner party, I was talking about what I had learned lately in my research and mentioned that Arthur lived in the workhouse. A woman asked, "Did each of them have their own room like a dorm?"

I would need to be very specific about conditions in the workhouse.

CHAPTER ELEVEN

I CONTINUED TO READ one chapter of research a day. The rest of the time I tried to weave what I was learning into a smooth narrative. Thanksgiving came and went. Now it was Christmas. My leave was about to end. I had been working on the book for a little over six months. What to do. This not having a regular paycheck bothered me, even though I had budgeted a certain amount of money to fund my writing through the end of the year and wasn't going through it nearly as fast as I thought I would. I thought, I'll quit Bechtel and spend one day a week looking for a new job and five days a week working on the book. Then I got the idea to work part time for Bechtel and part time on the book.

I prepared a plan for 1998. In January I'd prepare for my research trips and work on chapter eight. In February, I'd work on chapter seven. In March, I'd work on chapter six and go to Wilkes-Barre, Pennsylvania, to do research. In April, I'd work on chapter five. In May, I'd go to Europe for research, I'd visit relatives in Belfast, go to Wales, go to the battlefields in France and Belgium, and so on with more travel and a chapter a month for the rest of the year. In December I'd finish the last chapter and prepare a book proposal.

(As for why I was working backward, I don't remember. Perhaps I thought I had put more work into the first few chapters than the last, so working backward would even things out.)

The very day I wrote this insanely ambitious plan, I made several phone calls to people I knew at other Bechtel offices and inquired about part-time work. (I didn't want to go back to the project I had left.) The next day, a manager in San Francisco called and said he needed help on a proposal and could I fly to San Francisco tomorrow. I said yes. My idea was to work part time on the proposal, possibly from home, and the rest of the time on my book. I flew to San Francisco and immediately was swept into more than full-time work on the proposal, working long hours, six or seven days a week, and flying home every two weeks. I had committed to seeing the proposal through to the end, which was two months.

I stayed in a furnished apartment in downtown San Francisco. The place reeked of cigarette smoke. The building manager brought in an air purifier. Though it was the beginning of January, El Niño was visiting and bringing warm air with him. The apartment was quite warm. It had no air conditioning, and the window was stuck and wouldn't open. It took quite awhile to get it fixed. I didn't sleep well.

When I received my first pay stub, I discovered that a computer snafu had deleteriously affected my compensation. It took some doing but was eventually resolved many months later.

The proposal I was working on was a project for the U.S. Army to eliminate the mustard gas stockpile at Aberdeen, Maryland, there since the First World War. I told one of my new colleagues, who was a retired army officer, about my book and that part of it was about my grandfather's experience in the First World War. He said a friend of his headed the Center of Military History, and if I had any trouble finding what I needed, I should let him know. What a great tip. I didn't know there was a Center of Military History.

I continued my every two week commute back and forth between Las Vegas and San Francisco with El Niño and all his friends and relatives. The rain poured and poured and poured and poured. Looking out the window at the office one day, I couldn't see raindrops, just a wall of water. It looked as if someone had opened a fire hose on the side of the building. Water gushed down. Every flight I took was delayed and delayed and delayed, making travel all the more exhausting. There's something about waiting and wondering and wandering in an airport that I find exhausting.

After several weeks of this, I went to the ticket counter to check my bag and said I was going to Las Vegas. The ticket agent said, "You mean Los Angeles." I thought, what impertinence, I should know where I'm going. I said, "No, Las Vegas." She said, "You're in Las Vegas."

That should have been a clue I needed to take some time off.

All this time, I was thinking what should I do, what should I do, vis a vis my book. I wasn't getting any work done on it. I realized that to do it right, I needed to devote all my energy and attention to it without the distraction of an umbilical cord to another career. A life well lived, as my grandmother's was, demands a story well told. A story well told demands energy and time. I had to write the best book I could. I felt I owed it to Grandma, and in some small way, if it inspired or encouraged others, that might somehow make up for all she suffered.

But still, there was this matter of not having a steady paycheck. I had been agonizing over it for months. It was quite a distraction. I consulted family and friends.

"I'm really bothered about the thought of not having a regular paycheck," I told Cathy.

"Get over it!" she said.

As for quitting my job to work on the book full time, Cheryl said, "There's really no downside, and there's a tremendous possible upside."

Theresa said, "If you can do it, why not?"

Donna said, "When I'm not sure which path to take, I say 'Lord, I'm going this way. If that's the wrong direction, I'm counting on you to yank me back.'"

Finally, I decided. It was time to cross the Rubicon. Once the proposal was done, I'd quit my job with Bechtel, no more leave of absences. I'd quit. I'd focus all my energy on writing the book.

As soon as I made the decision, I knew it was the right thing to do. Right down to my toes, I knew it. What before seemed a tremendous, life-altering decision, now seemed so obvious, so inconsequential, a minor item on my list of things to do that day: buy groceries, stop at the bank, quit my job of fifteen years, go to the dry cleaner, do the laundry . . .

I realized my employer might not be so cavalier about it, so I addressed the subject with utmost seriousness. There were several executives and friends I wanted to tell myself and lost no time in doing so. Ed said, "As long as you're coming back, that's fine." Lee said, "Don't' quit! Take as long a leave of absence as you want. Just don't quit." John said, "I look forward to reading your *first* book." What a nice thing to say.

When I told Sandra that I was keeping the door open in case I wanted to come back, she said, "You aren't coming back. You're going to go off and write books."

The lengthy, manpower-intensive government proposal preparation process ended with delivery of the proposal to the client and an oral presentation discussing it. These presentations, called "orals" in government contracting speak, carry a lot of weight, putting much pressure on the participants. The last things they need to worry about are logistics. The project manager wanted me to go along to make sure things went smoothly behind the scenes. The presentation was to be in Aberdeen, Maryland, north of Baltimore, at the beginning of March. How convenient. My plan for the year, that I wrote in December, called for going to Pennsylvania in March.

CHAPTER TWELVE

I CHECKED OUT of my hotel in Aberdeen, Maryland, consulted the map, and headed toward Harrisburg, Pennsylvania. Just outside of Aberdeen, I stopped for gas. As I pulled out of the gas station, I turned on the radio and heard a song I'd never heard before: "I don't want to wait, for our lives to be over . . . will it be yes or will it be . . ."

Definitely yes.

Once in Harrisburg, I went directly to the state archives. I explained that I wanted to find out whether Arthur Hughes was charged with a crime, in particular assault, manslaughter, or murder, in Wilkes-Barre around 1905. That was the year my great-grandparents made their hasty retreat from Pennsylvania. The man directed me to a table and chair and brought me several old books. These were the quarter session dockets. He gave me white cotton gloves and politely told me to wear them while handling the books. As soon as I picked one up, I saw why; the leather covers had so deteriorated that the fingers of the gloves quickly turned red. I carefully thumbed through the pages. In the first quarter of 1905, a servant named Will Hughes was charged with larceny. The jury found him to be not guilty. I found no other Hughes. I looked at 1904. Nothing. No Hughes at all. The same for 1903. I found no record of Arthur beating the man. Research means looking, not always finding. Absence of a record is not conclusive. If Arthur was not charged, there would be no record, which is consistent with what Grandma said: if they had stayed, her father would have been charged. They didn't stay.

I considered looking into whether Pennsylvania law at the time included the paramour rule. This came from common law. If a husband caught his wife in the act of adultery and in the heat of passion killed his wife and/or the paramour, this could be considered voluntary manslaughter or justifiable homicide—the husband was deemed provoked. The situation as Grandma described it, with her father beating her mother's paramour to death, or near death, certainly fit the paramour rule. However, stating whether or not Pennsylvania law included the paramour rule, and explaining what it was, would have served only as an academic aside. It was a very dramatic event in the story. More detail would have diluted the drama. Anton Chekhov advised: "If you want to touch the reader's heart, be a little colder." I took this to mean pull back, leave things unsaid, best to understate, practice self-possession in prose; allow my readers to react, to draw connections, to become engaged in the story. Extra information, interesting though it may be, can suck the drama out of a passage. I didn't pursue it.

Arthur's death certificate, from when he actually did die in Oregon, said he was a veteran of the Spanish-American War. I looked at those records. No Arthur Hughes. Someone suggested I look at the Spanish-American War Veterans Compensation records. No Arthur Hughes. The man at the archives said those records would be where the veteran was living when he received the compensation in 1934. Arthur was living in Oregon then.

Later I discovered that this was compensation paid by the State of Pennsylvania under the Veterans Compensation Act of 1934. Spanish-American War veterans did not receive a bonus from the federal government, as did First World War veterans.

At lunchtime, I left to find something to eat. As I walked along, I happened upon what looked to be a quaint little café. I went in and was surprised to find it was big and modern. I enjoyed a wonderful salmon club sandwich with house-made chips of several root vegetables. The restaurant was called Stocks on Second. Should I again find myself in Harrisburg, I will definitely go back.

After I finished my research at the state archives, I set off for Wilkes-Barre. I felt a powerful sense of place as I ambled along the pine-covered rolling hills. One could almost taste the coal dust. This was surely a place where men earned their living by the sweat of their brows, where everyday life was hard work. It was March and overcast. The low, gray sky lent a sense of melancholy to the place, so fitting for what transpired there.

Not knowing which exit to take nor how many there would be, I took the first Wilkes-Barre exit. I continued down the road and turned toward the center of town, at least I hoped it was in that direction. I passed a business called Sarah's or Hughes's—something familiar. With no trouble, I found my hotel.

Before I went on any research trip, I did as much up front work as possible to determine where I needed to go, what was available, and how much time I needed at each place. While preparing for this trip, I called information and asked for the phone number for the historical society in Wilkes-Barre. The directory assistance operator said there isn't one. I thought, there has to be one. I asked for the phone number for the library. The librarian said yes, they have one, it's called the Wyoming Valley Historical Society. Never could I have guessed that one. I would soon learn that Wilkes-Barre is in the Wyoming Valley. Wyoming is an anglicized Indian word meaning large plains. The name has since been changed to the Luzerne County Historical Society.

After checking into my hotel, I walked down Franklin Street looking for the historical society. I came upon a man who was also looking for it, and together we managed to find the wrong door to the right place.

I told the woman at the desk, Ruth, what I was there to do. She directed me to the city directories, city almanacs, and microfilmed newspapers. I decided to start with the newspapers and parked myself at the microfilm machine. The machine kept falling out of focus, making this tedious work even more time consuming. I found the announcement for Sarah and Arthur's wedding. As I read, I saw many society page articles about weddings. Those seemed to be for Catholic weddings, which were in church. The Protestant weddings seemed to be smaller affairs at home, as was the case for Sarah and Arthur, with no society page article, just a notice.

My next stop was the Luzerne County Courthouse. I asked for naturalization records.

"You know this is a commonwealth," the man said.

I was puzzled as to what that had to do with my question and asked again, "Do you have naturalization records?"

He said he did and directed me to the files. They were on fiche or microfilm, I don't remember which. I sat down at the reader and easily found naturalization papers for Sarah's father, William Thomas, and for Arthur and printed copies.

For birth certificates, he sent me to another office. The woman there looked at me askance and declared that Pennsylvania is a commonwealth. I nodded. I wanted to confirm what I'd been told about Uncle Archie being a twin. I remembered that Grandma had to go through some rigamarole to get her birth certificate because records were destroyed in a fire or flood or something. Several times over the course of my research, I'd ask for a document and be told it was destroyed in a fire or flood. I wondered if it was the equivalent of the dog ate it. Maybe the person couldn't be bothered. However, much of the 1890 census did burn up in a fire, and in 1972, Tropical Storm Agnes swelled the Susquehanna such that it put downtown Wilkes-Barre under nine feet of water.

I found Grandma's birth recorded in one of those big old heavy ledger books. It seems to me the books were down in a basement somewhere, or the room seemed like a basement. Archie's birth wasn't listed. Bill's was. In among Grandma's papers I had found handwritten pages listing the date of birth for her and her siblings, including the time of day each was born and the day of the week. Grandma's sister, Patsy, wrote Archie's birth date in her birthday book, and it matched the date on those pages. Archie's prison records and marriage license have the same date. Everything I found with a date of birth for Archie had the same date, I just couldn't find a birth certificate.

While reading the old newspapers, I found William Thomas's obituary (Sarah's father). It said the funeral was in his daughter Mary Ann's home and was conducted by the pastor of the Welsh Presbyterian Church. Off I went to see the church and there met Reverend Johnson. I told him about my book and that I was having trouble tracking down my great-great-grandmother. Some people said her name was Ann, some said it was Nancy. He said he went to see one of his parishioners in the hospital and asked for Nancy ----. The nurse said they had no patient by that name. He persisted and learned that her name was actually Ann. He said, among the Welsh, if a girl was named Ann, and there was already an Ann in the family, she was called Nancy. I wondered, how do you get Nancy from Ann. Ann, Annie, Nanny, Nancy. I suppose it makes as much sense as calling Margaret Peggy.

So there we have two conflicting stories: her name was Ann, her name was Nancy. They were both right. Every once in a while I would run across what appeared to be conflicting information. I'd keep digging and find there was no conflict at all, simply two pieces of the same story. Once I found the missing link, it made sense.

The more I learned about my great-great-grandmother Ann Thomas, the more she emerged as a vivid person, and the more I confirmed what I understood from Grandma—that her grandmother was a formidable woman. For this reason I called her Ann in the book instead of Nancy, Ann being a stronger sounding name.

I asked Reverend Johnson about Welsh Presbyterians and Calvinist Methodists; Grandma said she was Methodist, yet her family attended the Welsh Presbyterian Church. Reverend Johnson explained that Welsh Nonconformists split from the Established Church of England to become Methodists. The Nonconformists learned of a new sect in Scotland called Presbyterian and were attracted to the democratic principles upon which it was run. The Welsh adopted the Presbyterian structure while retaining the Methodist theology (salvation could be lost due to sin). The resulting sect was called Calvinist Methodist or Welsh Presbyterian.

Reverend Johnson pulled out an old church directory and found William Thomas and how much he tithed. The baptism, marriage, and death records from back then were written in Welsh. He told me about the history of Wilkes-Barre and the Welsh community. "The Welsh are not influenced by fads," he said. "They are very independent in their thinking and don't like being told what to do." That certainly described Grandma T, never one to follow the crowd. I'd say she was downright suspicious of the crowd. He said the sentiment among the Welsh was, if you work with us, we'll go with you. "They were punctual and serious." That fits Grandma too.

"They were reluctant to buy on credit," he said. "If you didn't have the money, you didn't buy it. Quilting day was the sanctioned day out for wives. They made patchwork quilts." So did Grandma.

"The wife did the budgeting, and she ruled the home. She usually made the decisions about the home." That was true of Sarah. Poor Arthur.

I thanked Reverend Johnson and returned to the historical society, where I began poring through city directories. I found lots of Thomases, including eight or so William Thomases. Fortunately two of Grandma T's uncles (Sarah's brothers) had unusual names: Simeon and Isaak. I found only one Simeon Thomas and one Isaak Thomas. That's how I knew which William Thomas household was my Thomas family. The adult children were listed as boarders. One of Sarah's brothers was named Thomas. When he moved out, he floated off into the abyss of many, many, many Thomas Thomases, and I lost him.

I found only one Arthur Hughes or only one who was a stonemason.

After I finished going through the city directories, I pulled out my city map and drove around town to see all the places where my relatives lived and took pictures of each house. The houses looked old enough to be the actual houses. There didn't appear to be much new in that part of

Wilkes-Barre. I thought about how different life was for Sarah and Arthur and the children after they left Wilkes-Barre. In Wilkes-Barre the houses were so close, practically on top of one another, and then to live on a vast ranch with the closest neighbor a mile away. It must have about driven Sarah stir crazy.

As I gathered all this information, out cropped more questions. I called Aunt Aila. She and Auntie Grace and Grandma visited Wilkes-Barre on their round-the-country trip in 1987. She said Grandma was not happy when they were in Wilkes-Barre and wanted to hurry up and leave, and that it wasn't like Grandma to be impatient and restless. She was usually so easy-going.

Grandma spoke fondly of her life in Wilkes-Barre, in particular of her grandmother Ann Thomas, whom she adored; yet the circumstances of their leaving, walking in on her mother with that other man, her father beating him to death or near death, were horrible memories. I'd like to think she was impatient to get going because their next stop was my house in Maryland, but perhaps it was bad memories swamping the good.

Wilkes-Barre seemed to have an abundance of churches for a town of its size—big, beautiful, old churches made of stone or brick. Many people appeared to have come from the same stock as Grandma, Welsh stock. They had her coloring—brown hair, brown eyes, pale even complexion. They didn't look mixed. While attending Mass at the German church, I saw a man who looked like Uncle Archie, *a lot* like him. I couldn't believe it. Knowing that Sarah had several brothers, I wondered if he could be a distant cousin. I stopped him after Mass and asked if he was descended from William and Ann Thomas. He seemed startled that I approached him and said no. It occurred to me later that some people don't know the names of their great-grandparents or great-great-grandparents. I should have given him my name and number.

Someone suggested I visit Eckley, a coal patch south of Wilkes-Barre. Hollywood restored it for the movie the *Molly Maguires*. People live there, but the town, the patch, is also a tourist attraction, and there's a museum. So I went to see it. I walked slowly through the museum, studying the displays, taking notes. So depressing, the history of these coal patches—the mining company owned the homes, rent was deducted from the miner's pay, and when a man died the family was put out. Contract miners had to buy their own supplies from the company store, the "pluck me store," and hire laborers to help them. If their costs surpassed what they mined, they might actually owe the company money. It was night and day compared to the situation of Butte miners who were among the highest paid industrial workers in the country.

The museum curator saw me taking notes and asked if he could help. We had quite a long conversation about the history of the area. Another man joined us, a local historian. They recommended a couple of books and suggested that I visit the Anthracite Museum in Scranton.

Such a treasure hunt this was becoming. I went to this place and picked up a clue which directed me to the next place where I picked up a clue, and on it went.

In Scranton, as in Eckley, the museum curator saw me taking notes and offered his help. He showed me to the museum library and said I was welcome to use it. After telling him what I was researching, he pulled several volumes off the shelf and said these might be of help and left me to my research.

That evening, a high school basketball team checked into the hotel and unfortunately stayed on my floor, right across the hall. All night, they were in and out, slamming the door every time. I didn't get much sleep.

In the morning, I pored through mine inspection reports at the historical society. Grandma said her grandfather William Thomas was a mine boss. I was trying to confirm this and find out exactly what he did. I was surprised by the frankness of one mine inspector who complained about "pernicious laws"and a state certificate that in no way proved a man was a competent miner.

Next I read the city almanacs, annual histories of the town which included major crimes. I looked for something about Arthur beating the man but didn't find anything.

As I parked myself in front of the microfilm machine and resumed the tedious work of reading old newspapers, a woman came in and spoke with Ruth. I heard them mention Welsh cakes. Naturally this piqued my interest. It turned out this was an annual event—making and selling Welsh cakes. I bought some. They looked like scones.

At lunchtime, I went to a small restaurant to eat. As I sat looking out the window, all of a sudden a squall blew in, with snow blowing in every direction, like puffs of cotton being buffeted around, all of it staying in the air and not touching the ground. Then as fast as it came, it was gone. A few days later, snow fell and stuck. The patches of white on the green grass complemented the green and white St. Patrick's Day decorations. I had never seen so many St. Patrick's Day decorations.

I went to the library to look for books about the Welsh and local history. I read that the Welsh nurtured literary and musical talent, and that the Welsh were good at managing day laborers. An article written in 1870 complained about corrupt morals among the Welsh, drinking too much and fooling around, both men and women, "a disgrace even to the half civilized Irish." Oh my. And who were to blame for this calamity? Why Welshmen and Welshwomen from this place and that place and from Aberdare, where they learned "to drink beer like water." Sarah's parents lived in Aberdare.

The author of *Luzerne County: History of the People and Culture* had a different take: "The Welsh brought strong beliefs about religion and morality" and "placed great emphasis on a family centered life and abstinence from alcoholic beverages." He also wrote that "Family sacrifice combined with their somewhat better paid positions allowed the Welsh to keep their children in school longer." That was true of the Thomases. Sarah's youngest brother was a scholar, not a breaker boy relegated to long days at the colliery.

With regard to mixed marriages, meaning mixed religion, Peter Roberts wrote in *Anthracite Coal Communities*: "In a few instances the husband and wife form a compact that the female children follow the faith of the mother and the male that of the father." This was similar to what some of my Irish ancestors did way back when. Dr. Roberts cautioned that in such unions "religion which ought to be the 'bond of perfection,' becomes an occasion of strife and bitter rancor." Or as Grandma T more positively advised: "Marry someone from your own religion and culture."

I noted more titles, more threads to follow, such as comparing the day-to-day life of Slavic miners to Anglo-Saxon miners, which had absolutely nothing to do with my book. Oh, but now that I think about it, that could be helpful for my third book. I became obsessed with coal mining, the life of the coal miners, the coal mining communities. As I contemplated buying yet another book about Pennsylvania coal mining I told myself, I have to stop. I've done enough research on this. My book is not about coal mining; it is only a small part of it. I have that dead body lying there. I have got to get back to him.

In his deposition about the fire, Arthur said his mother-in-law was buried in Hollenback Cemetery. It was next to the Susquehanna, across the street from the hospital. Patients in the hospital had a view of the cemetery. How weird. I found the caretaker. He pulled out a box of index cards and thumbed through them until he found Thomas—Ann, William, and William George. He gave me the grave site numbers and told me the general area in which I could find them. I drove as close as I could and parked the car. Hunting through the cemetery was almost as tedious as searching through microfilm, but at least I was out in the fresh air. I finally found the grave markers—rusted metal stakes, round at the top, on which the grave numbers were written. There was no headstone. I was startled and saddened that there was no stone for Grandma's beloved grandmother, Ann Thomas. I asked about it and was told sometimes the stones fall down, and when the Susquehanna flooded, the stone could have floated away, if there ever was one.

Aunt Aila said she and Grandma and Auntie Grace drove all over looking for the Thomases graves when they visited Wilkes-Barre. I'm glad they didn't find the caretaker. I think Grandma would have been crushed to know there was no headstone for her beloved grandmother.

After two weeks, weary from long days of research and not getting much sleep thanks to the noisy basketball players, I packed my bag and prepared to leave. That last evening, I had a bowl of vegetable beef soup for dinner at the hotel restaurant. I got food poisoning. I was horribly sick all night. Even so, I was sad to leave Wilkes-Barre. It seemed I was leaving a part of Grandma behind.

CHAPTER THIRTEEN

STILL SICK AND miserable from the bad soup, I drove two hundred miles to Rockville, Maryland, spent a couple days visiting friends, and flew home.

I went over the papers I had collected, made notes, and transcribed my notes into the computer, read the books I bought, ordered more from the library, read those, took notes, transcribed those notes into the computer, and tried to fold all this into the story.

My computer sits on a little table in front of floor to ceiling windows. The entire wall is windows and looks out onto a golf course. I like having the natural light and the view when I'm working. As I sat typing away on the computer one day, I saw something moving out of the corner of my eye. My brain registered cat, but not cat. I looked up to see a red fox trotting along the perimeter of the house, looking quite dapper and carefree, as if he were putting on the Ritz as he cased the joint for prey. I didn't know there were foxes in the desert.

Fascinated by the contrasts between the Butte copper miners and the Pennsylvania coal miners, I wondered what the difference in pay was around the turn of the century. While at the Butte Archives I found a table listing day's pay by year for the miners in Butte. I started making phone calls to find such information for the coal miners. Lou at the Pennsylvania mine safety office gave me the name of a man who might have old payroll records for the Pennsylvania mining companies. I called him. He didn't have those records, but he had a lot to say. His family owned the Montour Iron Works in the 1850's. He said if my great-great grandfather William Thomas lived in a company house, he would have had a yard man and a horse and buggy. He said the mining companies brought the Welsh over to mine anthracite—they had jobs waiting for them, and they were family men and passed their trade on to their children, whereas "the Irish spoiled their children." (I bet those children would be surprised to hear that.) He said, "Mining wasn't a hard life, it was just a hard life when they couldn't mine." He reminded me of the stern, unyielding character in A.J. Cronin's *The Green Years*.

Reverend Johnson in Wilkes-Barre had mentioned the Lattimer Massacre. I read more about it. Back in 1897, a group of miners in Lattimer, near Hazleton, most of them Poles, Slovaks, and Lithuanians, marched in solidarity with striking union miners, carrying American flags. A sheriff's posse armed with Winchester rifles and shotguns went to the scene, tussles ensued, the posse opened fire. In the end, sixteen miners were dead and dozens wounded. (Another source said nineteen were killed.) The governor sent in the militia to restore order. The sheriff and deputies were tried and acquitted.

The whole sad event drove many more miners into the arms of the United Mine Workers Union.

The mother of a man who was killed that day said sometimes her son made only seventy-five cents a day. This was when the Butte miners were making around $3.50 per day. It's no wonder the Irish said, "Don't stop in the United States, go straight to Butte."

Child labor came up over and over while reading about Pennsylvania coal mining. At the turn of the century, hundreds of boys worked in the collieries, some as young as seven, and it was dangerous work. Child labor didn't come up at all in the books I read about the Butte mines. The Butte miners were unionized in 1878, only a few years after mining took off in Butte. By that time, coal mining had been thriving in Pennsylvania's Wyoming Valley for decades, ever since the canals were completed to get the coal to Philadelphia, and yet the workforce would not be organized for quite some time.

From all I read, the Butte copper miners had it much better that the Pennsylvania coal miners. This telling contrast was a delicious subject to tackle. And yet, that dead body was still lying there. How long was I going to flit off to nineteenth-century Pennsylvania coal mining, and union or no union, before I attended to him. Butte wouldn't be introduced for several chapters, and once I got to Butte, it didn't make sense to revisit Wilkes-Barre. Alas. There was no choice but to keep the coal mining part brief, fascinating though it was.

That said, I wasn't ready to leave Pennsylvania just yet. Aunt Aila told me that Sarah attended Bryn Mawr. Naturally we assumed it was the college in Pennsylvania. I called the alumni office to confirm this. The woman checked their records and said they had no record of Sarah Thomas attending the school in the late 1800s. I asked if there was a school in Wales by that name. She didn't think so but said there is a town with that name in Wales, and there is a high school in Baltimore called Bryn Mawr. I called the high school. Our Sarah did not attend there either.

My great-grandfather Arthur's naturalization papers, which I found at the Courthouse in Wilkes-Barre, said he was from Llandovery, Wales. Grandma said his parents were William and Mary Hughes and that Mary's maiden name was Price. I sent a request to the British Public Records Office asking for a birth certificate for Arthur Hughes born to William Hughes and Mary Price Hughes in Llandovery on March 17, 1872, the birthday he put on his naturalization papers and marriage license. I received a birth certificate for Arthur Hughes born to William Hughes and Mary Price Hughes in Llandovery on March 16, 1871.

In his deposition taken in New York City when he was supposed to be dead, Arthur said he was born on the high seas somewhere "between Australia and Pennsylvania." He also told Sarah that he was born at sea; she said so at the inquest. Obviously someone had to have told him he was born at sea. Yet I have a birth certificate for him from Llandovery. At that time, when a child was born at sea on a British-flagged ship, the captain registered the child's birth. Mary may not have been on a British-flagged ship, and even if she was, she might not have known that the captain registered her baby's birth. If she didn't know, it makes sense that she registered her child's birth once home in Llandovery. In short, the birth certificate in Llandovery is not conclusive. Arthur had two death certificates: one in Montana when he didn't die and one in Oregon when he did. Why not two birth certificates?

Now to prepare for my trip to Europe in May. I intended to go everywhere anything significant happened in the book, including the battlefields. During a visit to Mom and Dad's, while combing through their bookshelves, I found a short history of the First World War and brought it home. Now I picked it up and read it, including the bibliography. This is how I would find many research sources: by reading bibliographies. This one listed General Pershing's book. I ordered it through interlibrary loan.

Though I used primary sources for much of my research, when researching grand events, such as how the First World War began and the shenanigan-rich War of the Copper Kings, I relied on published works of history. To hedge my bets, I read more than one book on each subject. I made a point to read books written close to the events and books written long after in order to get different perspectives. I think when a person writes about the times in which he is living, to some extent, he is a pundit. Try as he may, objectivity can be difficult when one is, in essence, part of the story by living through it. Objectivity can be gained with distance. Also more archival material may be available years later. Classified papers may be declassified. Papers once private or thought lost may now be public and available to researchers. Edwin Campion Vaughan's diary, that he wrote while a British officer in the First World War, remained beyond the grasp of researchers for decades, until the family finally agreed to have it published.

Though distance from events can aid objectivity, that more personal view of someone writing about his own times and being able to interview principals is quite valuable. Opinions backed up by facts are interesting, but one must sift opinion from fact and be wary of unsubstantiated assertions presented as fact. When chronicling history, opinions not supported by facts are useless. One can run across this in books written long after the events also. What is thought to be common knowledge can be common mythology. A writer who begins his research with strong unsubstantiated preconceived notions, and cherry picks the facts to support those notions, isn't writing history.

I remember a *Dilbert* cartoon where his date says, I don't know if it's true, but that's what I think, and Dilbert replies, since when is ignorance a point of view?

One of the books I read about Butte, written long after the events, said during the 1918 wildcat strike, a Company gunman shot and killed a miner in the street. It sounded as if he just hauled off and shot the guy in cold blood. I saw it as a dramatic illustration of the times and worked it into my manuscript. Later I happened to be reading the Montana Department of Labor and Industry biennial report for 1917 to 1918 which included this incident. It said the gunman, a deputy sheriff believed to be a Company hired gun, had been "severely beaten" and was "prostrate on the ground" when he fired the fatal shot. Apparently there was more to the story.

It is not practical for every author to include every detail of every subject about which he writes. If he did, every attempt to write a book would morph into a set of encyclopedias. Editing and brevity are called for; however, in telling only a few of the facts, and not all, one can end up with something false. Leaving out one vital piece of information can give an entirely different impression of what happened.

The closest we can get to a true telling of history comes from thorough research, from knowing the facts in context. Accurate history is not told with broad brush strokes, like a modern painting with a few swatches of bold color, devoid of meaning. The more accurate telling of history is like a Seurat, a whole lot of little dots of color, little pieces of information that form the whole, and when we step back from it we see the lake, the sailboat, the tree, the shore, the sense of what the artist was trying to convey. We get more accurate history.

Pershing's book arrived. I set about reading it to help prepare for my trip. As I write this I wonder, did I actually do all this before the trip? I checked my notes. I did. It makes me tired just thinking about it. From January until I completed my European trip in May, I was on an airplane almost every week. Although some people do that effortlessly, I found it exhausting, but I kept going. I felt a tremendous sense of urgency to finish the book. I felt as if I were in a race. I would be working on it, and think ten minutes had gone by, and look at the clock, and it had been over an hour.

I was surprised by how blunt General Pershing was in his book. Clearly, political correctness had not yet been invented to choke off frank talk. He wrote that "there should be no peace until Germany is completely crushed." He bemoaned the Italian generals who seemed to be planning for a longer war rather than seizing the moment and getting it over with. Pershing recommended to Italian General Diaz that the Italians attack while the Germans were consumed with the attack from France. Diaz said, if we do that, we won't have reserves for next spring. Pershing called this "a course of reasoning which was not easy to follow."

Before embarking on my research, I knew precious little about the First World War. I knew that the archduke was shot, the *Lusitania* was sunk, we were on the side of England and France fighting the Germans, and my grandfather saved a man's life and was awarded the *Croix de Guerre*. It didn't occur to me until I was well into my research that the First World War was not fought to any extent on German soil; any incursions into Germany were quickly repelled. Where huge swaths of France and Belgium were obliterated in the First World War, this did not happen in Germany. Edith Stein wrote of her future brother-in-law Hans, who was an assistant surgeon in the German Army: "For him, the war had retained its romantic glow to the very end . . . He was unprepared for the collapse." Interesting choice of words—the collapse and not the defeat.

According to General Pershing, in the week ending October 5, 1918, the army had sixteen thousand *additional* cases of Spanish Influenza. That was almost an entire division of soldiers down with the flu, and right in the middle of the huge Meuse Argonne Offensive in France, a battle for which General Pershing needed every able-bodied man he could find and more. I needed to learn about the Spanish Influenza and how it affected my family in Butte. I added it to my to-do list.

General Pershing mentioned that Marshal Foch was a devout Catholic. Every time they passed a Catholic church, Foch went in to make a visit. The date Marshal Foch picked to end the war, November 11, is the feast of St. Martin of Tours, the patron saint of soldiers. I wonder if Foch picked the date with this in mind, or was it yet another coincidence of Providence.

Since I wanted the war narrative to be personal to Peter, and he was an American soldier, I began my research concentrating on our involvement. Some Americans were alarmed at our country's military weakness prior to the First World War. Our biggest gun was a medium machine gun. Moves toward military preparedness in 1915 were not geared toward war in Europe, even though the war had been going on for a year, a war in which the Germans could fire artillery shells a distance of seventy-five miles. Our puny machine guns wouldn't stand a chance. Other Americans held strong anti-war, anti-preparedness sentiments, the thought being, if we don't prepare, we can't get in it. One outspoken voice on the anti-war side was Henry Ford. We didn't prepare but got in it anyway.

Cousin Molly Breen had given me a copy of a letter Peter wrote while still in France after the armistice. I reread the letter and noted the places he named; those would be destinations during my visits to the battlefields. At this point, I didn't have much to go on about Peter's experience in the war, only the letter, his military records, and the *Croix de Guerre* citation. I noted all the clues I could find to bring with me on the trip.

Mom gave me a PBS documentary about the war, which I watched several times. Seeing the pictures, hearing the words of the soldiers and civilians, watching the film footage, helped sear a sense of it in my mind. I listened to it while cleaning and cooking. The haunting theme music seemed emblematic of the times and events. I never used anything from a documentary without confirming it in print. I wanted to be sure I understood the facts correctly in context. I noted the names of the historians interviewed and the soldiers quoted.

The History Channel documentary about the war said the Meuse Argonne Offensive "was the greatest concentration of defenses that Americans troops would meet in two world wars." I wondered if that was true for all wars. I watched the credits and noted the name of the writer, Norman Stahl. I took a guess that he lived in New York City and found a Norman Stahl in Manhattan. I wrote to him with my question and enclosed a self-addressed stamped envelope. He responded right away with the title of the book that was his source and the page number. It turns out, our troops faced even greater defenses in Korea.

As for personal matters, I still owned my house in Rockville, Maryland, which I had been renting out since I moved to San Francisco in 1994. I was barely breaking even on the rent income, so I decided to sell it. I called the property manager and asked him to put it on the market.

Next I turned my gaze to the Irish. I planned to visit my relatives in Belfast on this trip. In *The Irish in America*, I read that Irish immigrants were attracted to dangerous work as policemen and firemen. I would add miners to that list.

I watched the movie *Michael Collins*, about the IRA leader who was instrumental in creating an independent Ireland while agreeing to partition off the six counties in Ulster forming Northern Ireland. A fellow member of the IRA murdered him because of this compromise. The movie definitely gave a flavor for the times. Cousin Sam had recommended it.

I just found a note I wrote to myself on August 19, 1997. It said "Finish book by 5/98." Well, I didn't, not even close. I kept setting deadlines for myself and kept missing them. I kept finding more story. Instead of being done by May of 1998, I was preparing to go to Europe to do research.

The British tourist office sent me a packet of information about Wales, which included a map. I opened it and marked the places I needed to visit, town names I had culled from family records and that Grandma had mentioned. All were in south Wales. As I studied the map, I saw a town called Brynmawr. That must be the Brynmawr where Sarah went to school.

As part of my preparation for the trip, I listened to French language tapes to wake up that part of my memory. Mom and Dad planned to join me for the Belgium and France part of the trip. I would be with relatives in Belfast and on my own in Wales.

Chapter Fourteen

Shortly after Easter, 1998, I boarded the long, overnight trans-Atlantic flight to London. I had hoped to sleep on the plane, but unfortunately my seat was broken and wouldn't recline. I didn't get much sleep. My plane landed right on time at Heathrow. I raced to my flight to Belfast, which I believe took off from northern Scotland, at least it felt as if I had to run that far. I made it just in time and landed in Belfast on time. My cousin Teresa and her mother, my great-aunt Brigid, picked me up at the airport.

Though I had prepared a list of things I wanted to research while in Belfast, as soon as I arrived, I was swept up into family gatherings and forgot all about it. It was nonstop parties, luncheons, visits, dinners, and it was wonderful. Aunt Brigid was with me most of the time, allowing ample time to visit and ask questions, which was my primary reason for going. She was Grandpa Peter's youngest sibling. She would be eighty-eight years old that summer and was sharp as a tack. Only her eyes were failing her. Though they no longer served her well, they were still a brilliant, effervescent blue, and broadcast happiness. She was a delight to be around.

I had visited my relatives in Belfast once before, in 1980. My memory of it back then was no color, as if I were walking through a black and white movie. Now there was color. In 1980, we had to go through metal detectors and be frisked before walking into the shopping district. They even frisked the baby. All that was gone in 1998. We walked downtown as freely as in any other city. Policemen armed with automatic rifles still rode around standing in the top of those big, black vehicles, square and open on top. They looked like forts on wheels.

The Good Friday Accords had been much in the news, and the referendum vote was coming up soon. I asked my cousins what they thought about it.

"It will never go back to the way it was," one said.

"What do you mean?" I asked.

"You don't have to put your religion on a job application anymore."

Another cousin told me about a stamp on which he had to write the name of his school. Anyone who wrote the Irish Christian Brothers school was definitely a Catholic.

Another said, "I just want the killing to stop."

While en route to cousin Mary's house for tea (the evening meal), I saw a giant mural painted on the side of a building. It showed a man dressed all in black wearing a black ski mask. He was down on bended knee behind a barbed wire entanglement aiming his automatic rifle. The caption said, "Ready for peace, prepared for war." It was chilling. It was difficult to grasp what was going on over there without seeing it first hand.

Though the political situation hung heavily in the background and was something I was interested in, I was mostly interested in family and learning all I could from Aunt Brigid. She seemed to enjoy reminiscing; one thing would remind her of another. She hurled stories at me at a dizzying pace. Coupled with her brogue, it was all I could do to keep up. She used many expressions that were unfamiliar to me. "That's her country way of speaking," cousin Frank explained. When she said "y'ol gape," one of my cousins had to translate. It meant, you're being silly. She said, "Marrying late was as common as a wooden leg in our family, as common as a wooden leg," and she laughed and laughed. Many of them did marry later in life, so I didn't understand. I asked what she meant, but she was already on to the next story.

Aunt Brigid carried the entire family tree around with her in her head, dates and all, going back several generations, all the way back to Adam. No, not that Adam. Adam Thompson. I wrote it down as she told me. Seeing all those familiar Irish surnames on our family tree, I can only conclude that we are related to about half of Ireland. She even remembered her brother Denis's address in Brooklyn: 103 3rd Place. He lived there in the 1920s. Even better than the names and dates, she knew stories about all these people. The stories were what interested me most.

She talked about how it used to be that Catholics and Presbyterians couldn't marry. They had to be Church of Ireland.

"*Daniel* O'Connell was born when his mother was *fifty*-two years old," she exclaimed.

"Who was he?" I asked.

"He emancipated the Catholics," cousin Rosaleen explained.

"*Fifty*-two years old," Aunt Brigid repeated.

Aunt Brigid then talked about her brother Denis. "He was at a weddin' party, my mother said to him, 'How did you enjoy the party.' He said, 'If I'd 'a been the bride, I'd have got up and left.' You see, you know what he sang? 'Mother McCrea.' 'There's a spot in my heart, which no colleen may own. There's a place in my memory, . . .' Our Denis thought the song should have been for his bride, 'If I'd have been the bride, I'd have said, go you back to Mother McCrea.' 'Mother McCrea' means mother of my heart . That was no song for a groom to sing. He should have been singing a song to his wife."

It was clear that she was very fond of her brother Denis and enjoyed reminiscing about him. The way she talked about his going on French leave during the war and jumping into icy Belfast Lough right behind Peter, he reminded me of Magio in *From Here to Eternity*, a high-spirited, lovable, smart aleck looking for trouble and finding it.

About her youngest brother, she said, "Our *pur* Jimmy—that's what we always called him. He'd love you to ask him to sing."

"He had a lovely tenor voice," Teresa said. "I always felt that he would have liked to have been an entertainer, he liked telling jokes and he liked singing and he liked being praised."

"He did," said Aunt Brigid.

"I think it was his way of shining in the family," Teresa said. "Because I think it was pretty difficult. The competition was pretty strong."

When I asked Aunt Brigid about Uncle Pat, the brother who was in the IRA, she thought for a moment and said, "I never saw Pat with a book." Then she added, "He was very popular with *el*derly people."

Later I remarked to my cousin Bridgeen and her husband how amazing I thought it was, here was Uncle Pat, the red hot patriot, a leader of the Belfast IRA, and yet when his mother said go, he went, and went to Butte. He did as told. Bridgeen's husband said, "Oh, yes, that still happens today."

I pulled out the family tree I had drawn and reviewed it with Aunt Brigid to be sure it was correct. As we went through the names, out came more stories.

"All the young men of the town passed by the McCafferty home with those four maiden sisters. Only one dared enter the hornet's nest—Adam Dowdall. He went in, and he married one of those sisters and lived with those four women for the rest of his life because the other sisters never married." She laughed again. Adam Dowdall was my great-great-great-

great-grandfather on Sam Thompson's side of the family. To think we have stories going back that far is incredible.

Then she said, "*Purdy* Rosie Mooney," and laughed. "Who was Rosie Mooney," I asked. She laughed and laughed and kept on with her story.

Later after studying our family tree, I saw that Rosie Mooney was my great-great-great-great-grandmother. She married James McClenaghan. Their daughter Jane married John McDonald whose daughter Jane married Denis Gribben whose daughter Rose was my great-grandmother. Aunt Brigid explained that McDonald is the Scottish spelling which is how our family spells it. McDonnell is the Irish spelling. Why my family used the Scottish rather than Irish spelling, I didn't think to ask. By the time I scribbled that down, Aunt Brigid was on to the next story.

I am still amazed that she managed to keep all those names and dates and stories in her head. It's mental calisthenics to keep it straight. It would be a good road game to keep children occupied on long drives. Now who was purdy Rosie Mooney and whom did she marry and who entered the hornet's nest?

I asked about the house in Belfast where she and Grandpa Peter lived as children. She said the kitchen was white-washed three times a year (I didn't think to ask by whom). They used a mangle to squeeze the clothes dry after washing them in a tub. The toilet was in the back yard, no toilet inside. They kept coal in the "glory hole." When they wanted hot water, they had to boil water in a kettle on the stove; there was no hot water piped in the house. Later when they had gas, you put a penny in the slot to turn on the gas, and "when it run out, it run out."

While at cousin Frank's home for a traditional Irish fry, he brought out a box of things that belonged to my great-grandmother Rose. In it I found letters Grandpa Peter wrote while in Belgium and France after the armistice and postcards Uncle Denis wrote from the prison camp. Reading those cards, Denis sounded as if he had gone off to Boy Scout Camp rather than a prisoner-of-war camp. "Tell Nellie Jim Blake was taken prisoner along with me . . . send some socks and a shaving gear and some wool and needle . . . Have you got any idea how long this war is going to last?"

I asked if we could visit Aunt Martha, Aunt Brigid's only living sibling. "Let's go!" Aunt Brigid said, and jumped up and off we went. Martha was in her nineties and in a nursing home. She was a bit out of it, dotty as they say. "She's had so much sorrow," explained cousin Mary. All of Martha's grandchildren were orphaned almost at once. Her son Dennis and his wife were killed in an automobile accident in Paris. Martha's daughter was in her forties and already a widow and was dying of cancer. She died shortly after Dennis's funeral. After that, Martha's mind went. It was too much.

Aunt Martha kept saying, "Harry Kearney was a fine man," in her husky voice. I thought, how wonderful, here she is at the end of her life, not altogether there, but of all things, she's remembering what a fine man her husband was. I told her that I was Peter's granddaughter. She perked up at that. She and Aunt Brigid got to talking and laughing about Magheralane and working at Gallagher's tobacco factory, and they went on reminiscing and laughing and seemed to have a wonderful time.

Now a dinner, now more visiting, more cousins, now a party, now a luncheon, now another dinner, more visiting, visiting, parties, stories from Aunt Brigid, stories from cousins, I had a wonderful time, but by the end of the five days, my head was spinning. Every night I woke up in the middle of the night, my mind racing, raring to go but exhausted and couldn't get back to sleep.

The amount and level of detail Aunt Brigid provided was astounding. She had a mind like a steel trap. I don't think she forgot a thing in her life. Most of what she told me I managed to work into *One Night in a Bad Inn*. As with everyone and everything else, I sought to corroborate what she told me. She too proved to be a very reliable source. She said her father, Sam Thompson, went to America after Peter and on the return, his ship was sunk by a U-boat. After I returned home, I ordered Sam's ship arrival record from the National Archives. On it, I found the date he arrived and the name of his ship, the *Arabic*. From books about the First World War, I found out when the *Arabic* was sunk—it was during her next voyage to New York.

As I was leaving Belfast and saying my goodbyes, Aunt Brigid said, "Don't say goodbye, don't say goodbye." Those imploring blue eyes about broke my heart. I wanted to say, I'll be back, but I couldn't because I didn't know if I would. That was the last time I saw her. Over the course of my research, which turned into many years, I would write or call cousins in Belfast and they would dutifully get the information I needed from Aunt Brigid and report back to me. Shortly after the book came out, right after her ninety-sixth birthday, Aunt Brigid passed away.

CHAPTER FIFTEEN

I COULDN'T FLY nonstop from Belfast to Cardiff, but I could from Dublin to Bristol, which is near south Wales, so that was the flight I booked. I planned to take the train to Dublin, but my cousin Nell and her husband, Liam, offered to drive me. They suggested we go early, spend the day in Dublin, and then they'd drive me to the airport.

As we pulled out of their neighborhood in North Belfast, Liam yielded to one of those big black forts on wheels in which policemen were standing, holding what looked like automatic rifles. I was sitting in the middle of the back seat. As this fort on wheels pulled in front of us, my eyes met those of one of the policemen standing in the top. He trained his weapon on me. I thought, you little twit, what do you think you're doing? Not the most prudent reaction to someone aiming a gun at you, I know, but that was my reaction. It was chilling. It got me thinking about how a young man feeling such anger coupled with helplessness could act very badly on those feelings.

A man who grew up in West Belfast and whose father was in the IRA told me that when he was a young teenager, a family friend sat him down for a man-to-man talk about his future and tried to recruit him into the IRA. He declined. I asked, "Were there any repercussions to your saying no?" He said no. As a boy, he participated in a program to take children out of Northern Ireland for a few weeks at a time. He said those experiences made him the person he is today. He could have made different choices. One summer he stayed with a family in Holland. Another summer he stayed with a Catholic priest in Belgium. During the Second World War, this priest hid downed Allied pilots from the Nazis. He was found out and taken prisoner. The war ended before the Nazis could execute him.

I asked, "Why do young men join the IRA?" He said they come from a lower social class and this elevates them in the community. They can go around, chests puffed, and make threats, and back them up. "So it's like a gang," I said. "Yes, it's like a gang," he replied.

We drove out of Belfast and headed south toward the Republic. At the border, we passed an immense fort. I'd never seen anything like it. Leaving the fort and border behind, we drove through picturesque farmland, what one expects to see in Ireland. As we approached Dublin, we passed sprawling high-tech facilities. I recognized the familiar black and white logo of Gateway Computers. It has been said that Ireland leapt from the agrarian age to the information age, skipping over the industrial age.

I couldn't believe the difference in Dublin since I first visited in 1980. Back then, it was a dirty, dreary city. There were panhandlers everywhere. I had never seen so many panhandlers in my life. I remember seeing a young woman with small children sitting on the sidewalk panhandling with a brand new cigarette box. She swatted one of the children. This time I saw no panhandlers. The city was vibrant, energetic, bustling, and clean and bright. It felt like a city on the move.

As we strolled through the center of Dublin, we noticed a flyer taped to a mailbox and stopped to read it. It said Michael Collins told us these are stepping stones, now Gerry Adams says these are stepping stones, we are tired of stepping stones.

After a pleasant day strolling through Dublin, Nell and Liam dropped me off at the airport. I boarded a quick flight down to Bristol. I went to the rental car counter but found it empty. I waited. No one came. I went hunting to roust up the rental car agent. Once I found him, he was extremely courteous, couldn't have been nicer. "There you are, love," he said and gave me the keys. I walked out, pulling my suitcase behind me through the parking lot. It was dark. I had quite a time getting the trunk open. I don't know what my problem was. I was afraid I would have to go inside and ask the rental car man to help me, but I managed to figure it out and avoid the embarrassment. I put the luggage in the trunk, got in the car, started it, went to put the car in reverse, but the windshield wipers came on instead. Why are the windshield wipers on? I tried to turn them off. Oh I see, everything is reversed. Not only is the steering wheel on the right side, the gear shift is on the left side of the steering wheel. The windshield wipers control is on the right. I tried to turn off the windshield wipers, but they went faster, now slower, slower still, now again faster. Finally I managed to turn them off. I tried to put the car in reverse and again turned on the windshield wipers. I was tired. It was late. Finally, I got the wipers off and the car in reverse and headed toward Cardiff.

I had to drive through part of town to get to the M4, which gave me some time to get used to the right-hand drive. It was my first time driving on the left. For some reason, I kept wanting to go more to the left. I grazed the curb a few times. I had to concentrate more to keep the car in the lane. I flicked on what I thought was the turn signal, oops, turned on the windshield wipers again. I had noticed while in Belfast that there were dashed white lines separating all lanes, no solid lines separating on-coming traffic. On roads with more than two lanes, I wasn't sure which lane was for on-coming traffic, so I stayed in the furthest left lane to play it safe. I was afraid the roundabouts would be confusing, being the opposite direction, but they weren't. I kept concentrating—left, left, left, but not too far left, oops, hit the curb again.

I made it through Bristol and found the M4, drove across the magnificent suspension bridge over the River Severn, and entered Wales. My plan was to drive toward Cardiff until I was exhausted and then stop and find a hotel. I passed a sign that said "Services"; underneath was a long Welsh word beginning with G and almost devoid of vowels. I figured it must be the name of a town. Below it were symbols for a bed, a knife and fork, and a gas pump. A few miles later, I saw another sign that said "Services" and that same long word beginning with G and hardly any vowels, and symbols for a bed, knife and fork, and gas pump. I thought, that's odd, more than one town with the same name. After the third time I caught on that the long name beginning with G was the Welsh word for services. I didn't know I'd be seeing signs in English and Welsh.

By now, I was exhausted and famished. I pulled off at the next services sign. It was Cardiff Gate, and there was a Holiday Inn Express. That will work, not quaint, not Welsh, but comfortable. I checked in, had dinner at the restaurant next door, and collapsed in bed. I woke up in the middle of the night, my mind raring to go, but my body wanting to sleep. It took a long time to fall back to sleep.

In the morning I woke up exhausted. I wanted to sleep more, but I had so much to do, I had to keep going. I had already charted my travels to see the places where my great-grandparents Arthur and Sarah lived. I checked out of the hotel thinking I'd stay at a bed and breakfast or hotel along the way.

My first destination was Brynmawr. To get there, I headed north toward Merthyr Tydfil. The road took me through a narrow valley flanked by big grassy hills on top of which stood horses, necks gracefully bent, eating the grass.

At Merthyr Tydfil, I entered a big roundabout and took the east spur toward Brynmawr. It was lunchtime when I arrived. I parked the car, took some pictures, and looked for a place to eat. I spied a little pub and went inside.

"Do you have pasties?" I asked the woman.

"No, love, not today. We have . . .," and she went down the list.

"I'll have a meat pie, please."

When she brought it, I asked, "Do you know of a girls' finishing school that was here in Brynmawr? I'm told my great-grandmother went to school there in the 1880's."

"I've never heard of it," she said, "but I have some books about Brynmawr. Would you like to take a look?"

"Yes," I said.

"I'll go upstairs and get them."

I ate my meat pie, more of a snack really. I think it had about two tablespoons of meat in it. I then drank coffee and looked at the books she had brought me, which were mostly pictures. I noted the titles and authors. The woman working at the bar walked over and visited with the woman seated at the table next to me. Someone had died. When that woman left, she came and sat with me and related their conversation about the person who had died and asked what I was doing there and where I was from. I told her I was writing a book. She asked the other people in the pub if they knew anything about this girls' finishing school. No one knew. She said, "Ask this old guy, he's an old miner. He'll tell you all about Brynmawr."

She walked back to the bar, and he came and sat with me. He talked about mining, miner's lamps, miner's tools, and where I could get pictures of these implements. He had a raspy voice and a heavy accent. I had to concentrate really hard to understand him. I understood the woman just fine. The raspiness in his voice was no doubt due to the cigarettes that had turned his fingers yellow. After he had been talking awhile, the woman at the bar called over to me, "Give me the wink when your fed up, and I'll tell him to leave." He grumbled at her and continued telling me about miner's lamps. As I was putting on my coat to leave, they asked me to come back the next day.

Now that I think back on this, I wonder why didn't I go to the library or ask if there was a museum or historical society. My research in Brynmawr consisted of going to a pub, eating a meat pie, and listening to a chatty old coal miner. Good grief. At least I got a look at the town and took some pictures.

I didn't see any bed and breakfasts in Brynmawr nor did I look for one since I still had much of the day left and wanted to see other places. I drove west back toward Merthyr Tydfil. Teresa's husband, Gerry, had suggested I call the tourist office there to find a place to stay. I tried while in Belfast but didn't reach anyone. Since Gerry had suggested the tourist office in Merthyr Tydfil, I thought I'd look for a place to stay there. I'd been told there were B&Bs everywhere in Wales. Well, I soon learned that must mean everywhere but Merthyr Tydfil, or everywhere except the part of Merthyr Tydfil where I was driving around aimlessly. I saw taverns that offered a room for rent. They looked like places Thomas Jefferson's ancestors may have lodged. They were perhaps too quaint. Not finding any place to stay, I decided to drive on to Aberdare. That was easier said than done. I couldn't find the road out of Merthyr Tydfil. I drove around lost for probably an hour. Even if I did find a B&B or hotel, I was afraid I'd never find the place again. My luggage would be lost forever at a B&B somewhere in Merthyr Tydfil. I drove and drove, trying to leave Merthyr Tydfil but unable to find the road out of town. It was mid afternoon and since I had been driving much of the day, and only those two tablespoons of meat for lunch, I was about to faint. I didn't even see a place to eat. Those taverns I had seen earlier were long gone. I had no idea how to find them again. Places where I could pull over and ask for directions, I didn't see in time to stop, or I'd see a place, but nowhere to pull over and park.

Then at last I saw them, perched high on a hill—the Golden Arches, McDonald's, a place with parking and food and directions. I bought a hamburger and milkshake and coffee and sat down next to a window, admiring the gorgeous Welsh countryside as I ate. Who'd think there would be such an impressive view from McDonald's. I saw several horses come bounding down a hill. A man was walking with them. I didn't see any reins. They appeared unbridled. They were frisky and playful, prancing about, shaking their heads. I looked down to take the lid off my coffee. When I looked up, the man and the horses had vanished.

I had asked the young woman at the counter for directions, and she said something vague like, go down there and turn left. I wasn't convinced this was going to work. It reminded me of my visit to Dublin in 1980. My plan had been to sightsee until my cousin Dennis got off work. All I did was get lost. I'd ask for directions and the person would say, go down there a ways and turn right and then go a ways more and turn left and keep going and you can't miss it. I always did.

As I sat there gazing out the window, I saw a road with a hairpin turn going up a hill out of town—that was the road I came in on. The lane into town went straight. To leave town, I had to make a hairpin turn. Since I wasn't looking for that, I kept missing it. Now there it was. I could see it plain as day from my perch at McDonald's. At long last, I'd found the way out of Merthyr Tydfil.

My cousin Aila told me that she and her husband visited Aberdare and found a nice library there. She said Grandma had spoken of Aberdare and the Rhondda Valley. So off I went. Another beautiful drive, the road hugged the mountainside. I still didn't see any B&Bs or hotels, but I easily found Aberdare and the library. I asked the man at the desk if he had something like our city directories. I was looking for an address for Sarah's parents. "No," he said, "but we have the census. Would you like to take a look?"

"Yes, I would."

"What year?" he asked.

"Between 1875 and 1887."

"That would be the 1881 census," he said. "It's indexed. What name?"

"Try Simeon or Isaak Thomas." They were two of Sarah's brothers. I figured William Thomas would be impossible, there would be too many.

Then he disappeared. I figured something else must have come up. Then poof, he was back with the census. In no time, he found Simeon Thomas, parents William and Ann, siblings Thomas, Sarah, Isaac, Joseph. Oh, wonderful, I said, that's the right one. Then he disappeared. I didn't have a chance to thank him. The census said their address was Trebanog 22 in Llantrisant. It said Thomas was born in Cymbach Aberdare. The rest of the children were born in Llantrisant. It gave William's place of birth as Llantwit Major, and Ann's as Pencae. The librarian reappeared with a xerox copy of a map showing me how to get to Llantrisant, and whoosh, he vanished again. I looked for him to say thank you but couldn't find him. It was late, and I needed to find a place to stay for the night. I asked at the library but got no suggestions. I decided to drive all the way back to the

Holiday Inn Express at Cardiff Gate, which was quite a drive, a couple of hours. I saw some B&B's along the way but never in time to pull over, or they looked smaller than I felt comfortable staying in since I was traveling alone. I didn't see a hotel.

Back at the Holiday Inn Express, I spent another fitful night and woke up exhausted.

That morning as I set out for the day, I decided not to check out of the hotel. My destination was Llandovery, where my great-grandfather Arthur lived as a child, Grandma T's father. I drove back up the A470 past Merthyr Tydfil and into the Brecon Beacons.

The sky was gray, a scant mist fell. Again I saw horses, necks bent, forming graceful silhouettes grazing atop hill after grassy hill. I also saw lots of B&B's and charming country inns. If only I'd known. I saw much verdant pasture, a farmhouse here, a farmhouse there, the picture of pastoral peaceful silence, so I thought. I pulled over to take pictures and, to my surprise, opened the car door to a loud chorus of baaing sheep. They filled the valley with their baaing. It seemed there must have been thousands to be so loud, all baaing at once. There is something endearing about the sound of sheep baaing, such a woebegone sound. I climbed back into the car and continued on.

At the northern edge of the Brecon Beacons, I drove into Llandovery. The town looked as if it had been plucked from a picture postcard, charming, quaint, colorful, tidy, lovely. The day was still gloomy and overcast. The mist had turned into a light rain. The weather seemed to fit the ambiance of Wales, as if it were part of the decor. I saw stone ruins atop a grassy hill. The grass was thick and green and bent, matted down by wind and rain. I climbed up the hill and wandered through the ruins. I expected to round a corner and find Heathcliff and Cathy; instead, I saw a splendid view of the surrounding countryside, green and lush, hedgerows marking off tiny farms.

I remember Grandma T saying, "The Welsh are very superstitious," referring especially to her mother. A Welsh writer in the nineteenth century agreed: "there is no well or river or mountain peak or verdant copse or partly concealed cave to which no superstition or tradition has belonged." I found Wales to be an enchanting, storybook place, a land evocative of mysticism. It's no wonder superstition was in their blood. It predated the authentic mysticism born of true faith.

It was close to noon by now. I climbed down and walked over to the hotel for lunch. A hotel! If only I'd known. As I sat there, I overheard a group of elderly men at a table across the room. They appeared to be drinking but not eating and were speaking loudly. One bemoaned that his wife had gone off and left him. He had to fend for himself. Actually, his wife left him for a holiday, and he was to join her later. Their conversation drifted to the upcoming referendum in Northern Ireland. "Of course that island should be united," one of them declared. Another said they should get rid of all the Catholics. That's not exactly what he said. I'm not going to repeat exactly what he said. At the time, it seemed so ridiculous as to be funny. A few years later, it would not seem so.

As I was leaving, I stopped at the front desk to ask where the towns were that I had found on the census. Not sure of the Welsh pronunciation, I showed the woman the spellings: Llantwit Major, Llantrisant, and Pencae. She pulled out a map and said Pencae must be misspelled, it should be Pen-y-Cae. It was in the Brecon Beacons.

Next I visited Llandovery Heritage, which turned out to be a small museum. I wandered through the displays and read about the town's history. Llandovery's roots go back to Roman times. It was the site of a Roman camp. Much later, the Normans came and built a castle. Those were the ruins I had climbed on earlier in the day. The town had been a shoeing point for drovers of both cattle and sheep on their way to the London markets, though by the time Arthur was born in 1871, that was going by the wayside because of the railroad. I didn't know that people shoed cattle and sheep.

I chatted with the woman at the information desk, Mair Faulkner. She was very helpful and interested in my book. She said the Lady of the Lake legend came from Llandovery as did the herbal cures of her physician sons. She showed me books on the subject. I told her I was researching my great-grandfather Arthur Hughes, and that he was sent to the workhouse when his grandparents died. She said the workhouse is now the hospital. The facade is as it was when it was the workhouse. I told her Arthur was Catholic. She said the Catholic church in Llandovery was built in 1930. I showed her Arthur's naturalization papers. She said what was listed as the county was the parish, Llandingat. Llandovery had been divided into two parishes. These were parishes of the Established Church. The people who lived in the parish didn't necessarily belong to that church.

"Hughes, Hughes," she said thoughtfully. "I have a friend named Hughes. Give me your great-grandfather's name and I'll ask her." I wrote down my name and address and Arthur's name.

I thanked Mair for her help and walked over to the church to see if I could find any Hugheses in the cemetery. As I approached, a man walked out of the church, locked the door, and started to get on a bicycle. When he saw me, he stopped and looked at me with that I-know-you-are-a-stranger-if-you-need-help-please-ask look. Naturally, I asked. He said he didn't know much about the cemetery but told me to wait and he'd go ask so-and-so, and off he went on his bicycle. As I waited, a middle-aged man and an elderly woman walked up. "Where's the vicar?" the man asked. I said he was coming back. At least I thought he was the vicar, he had the key to the church and seemed to work there. The man asked where I was from. I said the United States. He said he was careful not to ask if I was American in case I was Canadian. "Canadians don't like that," he said. He asked why I was there and where I was from in America. I told them about my book. "Hughes," he said thoughtfully. The old woman didn't say much, and I had a difficult time understanding what she did say.

The man from the church came back. We went inside. He pulled out the old church record books and looked through the list of the deaths but found no Hughes that could have been Arthur's parents, William and Mary. Hughes did not seem to be as common a name as I expected. I asked if he was the vicar. He said he was the people's warden. He explained that *llan* means "church." I read later that the old meaning referred to the area inside the walled enclosure for the church, the church yard. He said Llandovery means church between the waters. Llandingat means Church of St. Dingat. Llantrisant means Church of Three Saints. He said he wanted to be sure I got all the help I needed since I had come so far. "Let's take a look in the cemetery anyway," he said. We wandered around looking for Hugheses but most of the grave stones were so weather worn that the letters were indiscernible.

I thanked him for his help and returned to the center of town and wandered through the little shops. Children in school uniforms were also browsing and speaking Welsh. It was the first time I heard anyone speaking Welsh on the street. I had heard it on the radio in the car. Some shops featured Welsh merchandise. I bought a few things and sat down for a cup of tea and Welsh cakes. I would have liked to have spent several days in Llandovery.

It was getting late, and I had a long drive ahead of me back through the Brecon Beacons. On my way out of Llandovery, I drove by the hospital that had been the workhouse and took pictures.

I took the route through Pen-y-Cae, which I thought was the birthplace of Sarah's mother. I stopped across the street from a farm to take pictures. An elderly man was standing on the side of the road, apparently waiting for a ride. He looked at me with that I-know-you-are-a-stranger-if-you-need-help-please-ask-me look. I said hello and told him my great-great-grandmother Ann Davies lived in Pen-y-Cae. In his thick Welsh accent, he said, "Some Davies lived here long ago," and he gestured toward the farmhouse. "Go ask them," he said, gesturing again. A long driveway led from the road down to the large white house. There were white stables, in dire need of a paint job, along the right side of the driveway and a stone fence along the left closing off an enormous pasture. I saw a man wearing high rubber boots walk into the stables. There was a gate at the top of the driveway. The man kept insisting, "Go on! Go on! Welsh people will help you!" Reluctantly, I opened the gate and started to walk down the driveway. I noticed a medium-size shaggy black and white dog sitting in the middle of the driveway near the stables. It got up as I approached and walked toward me. I didn't think anything of it. When the dog was only a few feet away, he assumed a very different posture. He didn't bark. He crouched down and ran at me. Terrified, I defensively raised my left knee, and as I did, he reached up and bit me on the side of the knee and quickly backed away. I shrieked. I turned around and limped back up the driveway to the gate.

"Did he bite you?" the man asked.

"Yes."

"I'm sorry."

So was I. Did it ever hurt. Just then the bus came, and he left. I was wearing a skirt with a slip and tights. The skirt had two little holes at the seam from the bite, but the tights weren't even snagged. I knew there is no rabies in Britain, thank God. I limped back to the car and took a closer look to be sure he hadn't broken the skin. He hadn't. Oh, it hurt.

Though it was already evening, it was spring, so the day was long. I decided to drive until dark and then stop for dinner. I made it all the way back to the hotel and got there around nine o'clock.

The next morning, I woke up exhausted after another fitful night. An ugly bruise covered the entire side of my knee. Within the black and blue, I could count the dog's teeth.

Before setting off for the day, I called the Carmarthenshire records office and asked if they had records of who lived in the workhouse in Llandovery. They didn't. Later after I returned home, I inquired again. Mr. Cooke told me there are no admission records available for the Llandovery Poor Law Union. He said they have meeting minutes; I could read them to see if Arthur Hughes was mentioned. I thought, if I return to Wales I might do that, but it sounded like looking for a needle in a haystack with dubious chance of results.

I checked out of the hotel and drove to Llantrisant. The 1881 census entry for the Thomases (Sarah and her parents and siblings) listed Llantrisant as the town and 22 Trebanog as the address. I parked the car and asked the first person I saw, could you please tell me, where is Trebanog? She didn't know and suggested I ask in the farm shop and gestured toward a place that looked to be the size of a shed. I hadn't even noticed it. I went inside. It was big, with shelves and shelves of pasties and baked goods and cases of meat. Seeing those pasties, I felt right at home. It all looked so good, I wanted to buy, buy, buy but how could I possibly eat it, and where would I put it? The wife was busy making more goodies while the husband waited on people. When it was my turn, I asked, could you please tell me where Trebanog is? He led me outside to the parking lot. Before us lay a verdant valley of farmland that swept down from Llantrisant and up another hill, atop which sat another town.

"You see that road?" he said, pointing at the town on the hill. "That's Trebanog."

"How do I get there?" I asked, and he gave me directions.

I drove down the hill, through the valley, past beautiful green meadows. This was the famed Rhondda Valley of which Grandma T had spoken. It sounds like a place in a poem, and it looks like a place in a poem. I saw more horses, their simple "fence" a large rock every two feet or so. I drove up the hill and followed the signs for Trebanog. When I had a choice but no sign, I guessed, and by some miracle, turned the right way and found it.

It turns out, Trebanog was the name of the town and the street. I learned that Llantrisant was the Established Church parish which encompassed other towns that were not contiguous.

I parked the car behind a restaurant at the top of the hill and limped along Trebanog Street looking for number 22. With each step, I could feel the sack of blood on the side of my knee slosh up and down, up and down. It hurt like the dickens. I passed row house after row house on both sides of the street. Though old, they appeared to be more modern than the mid 1800's when my great-grandmother Sarah lived there. The numbers were in order on one side of the street, not even and odd on opposite sides as in an American town. The numbers were descending, 25 Trebanog, 24 Trebanog, 23 Trebanog—then no row house. Instead, there was a high stone wall behind which stood an old stone house. Could this be it? I walked past it to where the row houses started up again—21 Trebanog. This had to be it, this big old stone house, 22 Trebanog. This was the house where Great-grandma Sarah grew up. I could see smoke rising from the chimney. Someone lived there. I wanted to knock on the door and ask, did they know the Thomases, were they Thomases, did they have a dog that bit people? I was in no mood to find out. Even if I hadn't been bitten by the dog, there was something eerie about that forbidding stone wall that made the old stone house seem mysterious and spooky. I did not venture past the gate.

Thrilled with my find, I took pictures and limped back up the hill to the restaurant. It was lunchtime. Before I sat down to eat, I went into the bar and asked the bartender about the stone house, did he know who lived there, or who used to live there. He didn't. He asked the patrons. No one knew. That seemed odd. This was a small town, the old stone house was just down the street, why wouldn't anyone in this bar know who lived there? If in Montana, someone in that bar would have known who lived there and their whole life story. Why would it be any different in a small town in Wales? Very mysterious. This piqued my curiosity even more, and still does. I thought of the mysterious Boo Radley in *To Kill a Mockingbird*, and the curious neighborhood children watching and waiting for a glimpse of him. Boo's real name was Arthur.

I enjoyed a nice lunch of breaded fish and potatoes. After paying my bill, I limped to my car in the parking lot behind the restaurant. In the morning, as I had walked along Trebanog Street looking for Sarah's house, I got a peek of the Rhondda Valley between the houses. It was magnificent. I looked every chance I had. The green hills swept down to the valley below, a valley dotted with tiny farms marked off by hedgerows. I lingered in the parking lot, soaking up every bit of that view, as if savoring the last words of a really good book I didn't want to end or the last bites of a delectable chocolate dessert. As I stood there, a voice asked, "Do you see the windmills?" I looked around. There was a young man sitting atop the wide stone pillar at the end of the fence, arms around his bent knees, gazing off into the distance.

"What windmills?" I asked.

"Over there," he said dreamily and pointed. On a hill across the valley at the end of the horizon, I could see them. These were modern metal windmills, whirling at a steady clip. "They're a national symbol," he said, and returned his dreamy gaze across the valley. A Welsh Don Quixote perhaps.

While studying the map of the area around Trebanog, I found Pencae. That was the town listed on the census as Sarah's mother's birthplace. It was spelled correctly. I didn't need to go to that town where the dog bit me. It was the wrong town. Oh, well. I drove down the hill to the area called Pencae and looked around. I glanced at my watch and realized I needed to be on my way. I still had a lot of ground to cover, and I had a flight to catch that evening.

I bid a reluctant goodbye to the charming Rhondda Valley and headed south toward the sea to Llantwit Major, the birthplace of Sarah's father, my great-great-grandfather William T. Thomas. As I drove into town, I felt as if I were entering a Charles Dickens novel—tiny white-washed houses tucked closely together, narrow streets that wound around aimlessly, as if a nearsighted drunk laid out the town. I parked the car but didn't walk far, convinced I'd get lost and never be able to find it. The sidewalks were about a foot wide or less, nothing more than a wide curb.

After wandering around and taking pictures, I asked a woman for directions to the airport, and off I went. As I drove along, the road narrowed and narrowed and narrowed to what seemed to be one lane. Now I was driving between six foot high hedgerows flush with the road. Oh, my, here comes a car. I slowed down, he slowed down, we crept past each other, a battle of nerves—for me anyway. Somehow I made it to the Cardiff airport with no scratches on the car.

My cousin Aila calls Wales a warm blanket. I agree. You want to curl up in it and never leave. I felt an attachment to places connected to Grandma. I had to remind myself that only a tiny portion of my book took place in Wales. I couldn't spend all my time there. I had to keep moving.

Now to Belgium.

CHAPTER SIXTEEN

AROUND FIVE O'CLOCK that evening, I boarded the plane in Cardiff for a quick flight to Brussels. It was a small plane, full of what appeared to be Belgian businessmen on their way home. Once the plane was in the air, as if on cue, the passengers put down their tray tables and flipped down a little ring holder affixed to the top left of the seat back. The stewardess came through and served drinks, and then came right back and served us dinner, salmon and couscous. The ring holder on the back of the seat held the small bottles of wine she passed out. I couldn't believe it, drinks and dinner on an hour flight. And it was good salmon and couscous. There was only one stewardess, and she was in motion throughout the entire flight. She looked exhausted when we landed.

We arrived in Brussels right on schedule. With the time difference it was almost seven thirty. I rented a car and set off for Ghent, about a forty-five minute drive. The hotel had sent me directions, which were sparse, but I wasn't worried. When I had driven in France, I would follow the signs for *Centre Ville* and then ask someone for directions and always found my destination pretty easily. I thought it would be the same in Belgium.

As I approached Ghent, I saw a sign for *Centrum*. I figured that was the same as *Centre Ville*. My hotel was in the old part of town which I figured was in the center of town. I took the exit and followed the signs for *Centrum*. No sign of the hotel. I kept going, now this must be *Centrum*—shops, narrow one way streets, pedestrian streets, lots of people out and about, but no sign of the hotel and not a free parking place to be seen anywhere. It was Friday night. I drove and drove aimlessly around the center of Ghent for at least half an hour, maybe longer, looking for my hotel, the Cour St. Georges. I stopped and asked a couple of pedestrians how to find the hotel. Thankfully they spoke French. Ghent is in the Flemish part of Belgium, and I don't speak Flemish (now called Dutch).

"Yes, I know the hotel," the woman said in French, "but I couldn't tell you how to drive there. I only know how to walk there." Since I couldn't find a place to park, walking wasn't an option. I thanked them and continued driving around the downtown area, thinking eventually I'd stumble onto the hotel. I saw a woman cleaning the foyer of a building and asked her, "*S'il vous plaît, madame, où est le Cour St. Georges?*" You have to walk, she said in French, you can't drive there. How can I not be able to drive to a hotel? There has to be a way. I spied a man leaving an ATM. He was getting in a car—a parking place. I waited, he pulled out, and I wedged the car into the very narrow spot. I squeezed out of the car and asked the cleaning woman how to walk to the hotel. It was straight down the pedestrian walkway through the shopping area. After about a ten minute walk, at last, I found it—the Cour St. Georges. I was exhausted. By now it was around ten o'clock at night. "I've been looking for this place for an hour," I gasped. I was about ready to drop. The cheery receptionist said, "Bring your car over, and we'll unload your bags." I said, okay, and walked out, and was almost to the corner when I remembered, I don't know how to get here in the car. I walked back to the hotel. "I don't know how to get here in the car," I told the receptionist. Even if she had given me directions, I was so exhausted I don't think I could have comprehended them. Perhaps she saw that, or she knew it was impossible. She called to one of the bell boys and said something to him in Dutch. "He'll go with you and direct you back," she said.

Once back at the hotel, he unloaded my luggage. When I made the reservation, I asked if there was parking at the hotel since I would have a car. The answer came back yes, they have parking. When I asked where to park my car, the cheery receptionist said their garage was full, I would have to find my own parking place. It was Friday night, I was in the center of town, the cafés and restaurants were full of people. If I drove around looking for a parking place, I'd never find the hotel again. There was a public parking lot about a half a block from the hotel. It was full, and several cars were waiting to get in. What else could I do? I got in line and waited, and waited, and waited. Someone came, got in their car, drove off, the next car in line pulled in and parked. The rest of us pulled forward and waited. Someone else came, got in their car, the next car parked, I pulled forward. I waited. Finally, I was next.

By now it was close to midnight. I was at once exhausted and buzzing on adrenalin. I went up to my room. The hotel was old and historic, that's why I picked it. I was pleased to see how charming the room was, lovely old world elegance. The weather was beautiful and unseasonably warm. The room was very warm. The hotel did not have air conditioning. Then I saw the bathroom. It was right in the room with no door. There was a bed, a dresser, a shower, a toilet, a sink, all there in the same room. It was bizarre. The shower was on a raised platform, as if it were on a stage, with a spotlight. Weird. To use the bathroom, I would have to close those long velvet drapes. Forget opening the window to cool things down. I thought, this will not do. I looked out the window and saw the Sofitel across the street. I called them. Do you have air conditioning? Yes. Do you have parking for my car? Yes. (Not parking for *somebody's* car, parking for *my* car.) Do you have two rooms for the next few nights? Yes. I made a reservation, starting the next day. Actually, I think I went over there to do this. I don't remember. Delirium was setting in. I went to the front desk at the Cour St. Georges and told the cheery receptionist I'd be checking out in the morning and to cancel the other room. "*D'accord*," she said cheerily.

I went back up to my room and dropped into bed. I do have to say, the Cour St. Georges had some of the nicest bed linens I have ever slept on. The room was charming and quaint, except it was hot and that bathroom right in the middle of the room, with these really modern, sleek fixtures, but no door, and the toilet wedged between the sink, shower, and wall with less room than some airplane toilets.

Other than the bizarre bathroom, it did look like a hotel where Napoleon III could have slept (according to the guidebook, he did).

I bolted out of bed the next morning, at once exhausted and raring to go. My leg still hurt like the dickens. I could still count the dog's teeth in the ugly black and blue bruise. Breakfast ended at ten o'clock. I needed to get ready and get down there to eat, plus I had a lot to do. When I looked in the mirror, I gave myself a start. My eyes were red, beyond bloodshot, blood red—horrible looking. I didn't have time to think about it. I had to eat breakfast, pack, check out, move into the Sofitel, get directions so I wouldn't get lost again, and drive back to Brussels to pick up Mom and Dad at the airport. Their flight arrived around noon.

I arrived at the Brussels airport in plenty of time. It was lunchtime, so I grabbed a sandwich and cup of water and devoured it while I waited. People poured out of the customs and immigration area. People kept coming. I kept watching. No Mom and Dad. I started to wonder. Finally, they came through. They were the last ones or close to it. "Were you worried we didn't come?" Mom asked in greeting. For some reason, it took a long time to get their luggage. Of course I was happy to see them. I told them about my adventure, or misadventure, the night before, and that I had changed hotels. We drove to Ghent and went directly to the hotel. Now that I had good directions, it was easy. We parked the car in the hotel garage and went to the front desk so Mom and Dad could check in. When I addressed the receptionist in French, she replied in English, "I don't speak French, I'm Dutch."

After settling in, we set out to see Ghent. We toured a big old church and wandered through the pedestrian shopping area. Dad wanted to go back to the hotel. I suggested that we stop at a café first. As I said that, everything started to go. I put my hand on Mom's shoulder to steady myself. She put her hand on mine.

THE NEXT THING I remember, I was lying down. Mom and Dad were sitting near my feet. Mom smiled and said, "There she is," in a reassuring tone. "You had a seizure," she said. "This is Peter," and she gestured toward the cheerful young man sitting next to me. He smiled and said a cheery hello. "Tell us about Wales," Mom said. I couldn't remember anything. Dread swept over me. I knew I was writing a book, and I couldn't remember a thing. How could I write a book if I couldn't remember anything? Then it started to come back. "I went to Llandovery where Arthur Hughes was born. He was born on March 16, 1871." I rattled off details to prove to myself, yes, I do remember. I told them about Belfast and about seeing our relatives. I was very groggy. We stopped. The back door opened, and Mom and Dad got out. As Peter wheeled me into a building, I saw a crucifix on the wall. Then I knew I was in a hospital, and I knew I would be all right.

Peter wheeled me to a bed. He and a nurse started to help me onto it, but I said I could do it myself. I climbed off the Gurney and onto the bed. Sheets hung as curtains on either side. It was very quiet. Mom and Dad were there with me. Soon a cheery woman with long red hair and wearing a white lab coat bounded in. She checked this and that, tapped my foot with a mallet and such things. She said she was the emergency room doctor and that another doctor would be in to see me. Soon he arrived, Dr. De Potter. He said he was a neurosurgeon. He tapped my foot with a mallet and checked this and that. He left and somebody else came and wheeled me to a big machine that did something or other. Later I discovered that I had had a CT scan. Then I was moved to a room. Either there or in the emergency room, I don't remember where, somebody drew blood. The nurse connected me to an IV. I barely felt the needle poke my wrist. I was hungry for dry Melba toast and a hard boiled egg, things I normally don't eat, but that's what sounded good. I was nauseous and sore. My muscles ached.

This was the first time I'd been a patient in a hospital since I was born. Everything was white and clean and pristine. If you have to be hospitalized overseas, and I hope you never do, have it be at Sint-Lucas in Ghent. They were wonderful.

In the morning, the priest swept into my room and gave me communion. "*Bonne Fete, madame*," he said and turned and swept out of the room.

Bonne Fete? Oh, yes, Mother's Day. I remembered I had a card for Mom somewhere.

I wanted to move around, so I got up and pushed my IV tree up and down and hall, slowly. I was still groggy.

Mom and Dad arrived with clean clothes for me. I wished Mom a happy Mother's Day. She was very chipper. "I'll go see about springing you," she said and dashed off.

She came back and said the nurse called Dr. De Potter, and he said I could go. I was to see him in his office Monday morning. We tried to pay, but the nurse said they would send a bill.

We spent the rest of the day sightseeing. We had lunch in the main square near the hotel and then visited *Het Gravensteen*, the Castle of the Counts.

The next morning, I saw Dr. De Potter at his office. He said the CT scan and blood work came back normal. He said I should see my doctor when I get home for a full work up. I showed him the bruise where the dog bit me in case he thought I should do something about it. "Yuk!" he said, or the Dutch equivalent.

As we got up to leave, he gave me the CT scan. He said I might as well take it since he wouldn't be needing it. That was definitely the most unusual souvenir I ever brought back from a trip—a picture of my brain.

That done, we set off to do my research.

Dad drove, and I navigated. Despite being groggy and dull and frequently lightheaded, I managed to read the map and give directions.

We easily found the Flanders Field American Cemetery south of Ghent near Waregem. The cemetery is located where Grandpa Peter's division, the 91st, jumped off on their first day of battle in Flanders. We pulled into the small parking lot and walked into the building at the entrance to the cemetery. A man came out into the reception area and greeted us warmly. He was Christopher Sims, the cemetery associate. Each American cemetery is supervised by a superintendent who is a member of the American Battle Monuments Commission. They are transferred frequently, staying at a particular cemetery for only a few years. Christopher is a permanent local employee who runs the day-to-day operation. Christopher was very interested in why we were visiting. I told him about my grandfather, and that I was writing a book about his experience in the war. He gave me a copy of the portion of the 91st division history that described the battle in Flanders. He asked if I had any information about my grandfather. I said yes and showed him Grandpa Peter's military records. He asked if he could make a copy. I said, certainly. I told him Peter saved a man's life near Steenbrugge. Did he know where Steenbrugge was? No, he said. He asked for my address in case he found something else. He said he would be on the lookout for anything that might be helpful. We thanked him and wandered through the cemetery. It was impeccably kept.

Next we drove to Audenarde (Oudenaarde in Dutch), the largest town Grandpa Peter's division took during the war, and the second largest taken by American forces. The Church of St. Walburga in the center of town was damaged during the final bombardment of the war but has since been restored back to her medieval glory. We drove through the area around Audenarde so I could survey the countryside over which Peter and his fellow soldiers fought. It was farmland with trees and farmhouses sprinkled throughout. The land was flat as could be. I thought about our troops attacking through German bullets and bombs and snipers; it was so flat, there was no cover. Plus our troops were heading for the river, which meant the land was sloping down, leaving them even more exposed. The River Scheldt which cuts through Audenarde certainly looked forbidding as far as attempting to cross under fire carrying a heavy pack and rifle.

As always, I took pictures, and thank God, I did. When I got home and had the film developed, some of the pictures were completely unfamiliar to me, even though I took them. I had to ask Mom and Dad what they were. Mom said, remember we went here for lunch and did this and that.

I still don't remember. I remember the day before and the days after, but part of our day in Audenarde is a complete blank.

We looked for Steenbrugge, the place near where Peter saved that man's life, but didn't find it. We drove around to see if we could find the convent where Peter was billeted after the Armistice, the one he mentioned in his letter to Aunt B.

I'm looking at my itinerary for the trip as I write this. I had planned to visit the Flanders Field American Cemetery on Sunday and go to Bruges on Monday. Being in the hospital put a crimp in that plan. We went to Flanders Field on Monday instead. Had we gone to the cemetery on Sunday as planned, I wonder whether Christopher would have been there since it was Mother's Day. He proved to be so much help.

The next morning, we checked out of the hotel in Ghent and headed toward Bastogne. The drive along the Meuse was beautiful, lush green vegetation swelling over the river banks. We stopped at Dinant for lunch. After struggling to figure out how the parking fee machine worked, we went into the first restaurant we saw. It was a bright, sunny day. The weather was unseasonably warm and sunny during our entire stay in Belgium and France, not one drop of rain, hardly a cloud in the sky, and it was early May. We sat outside on the veranda overlooking the river. Though my brain was decidedly operating in low gear, I could still speak and understand French. I don't know the French words for all foods and often order something without knowing what it is, just to be adventurous. Usually I'm pleasantly surprised, but not this time. I never did figure out what I ordered.

Across the street stood a huge medieval church and, high on a cliff, a stone fort. Later while reading *The Guns of August* by Barbara Tuchman, I learned about the civilian massacre in Dinant during the First World War. German soldiers lined up men on one side, and women and children on the other, and with a firing squad down the middle, shot them all dead. The Germans killed 664 civilians in Dinant. In an essay, Tuchman wrote of seeing gravestone after gravestone in the cemetery that said in French, shot by the Germans, shot by the Germans. Had I known, I would have visited the cemetery.

As I did more reading about the First World War, I was struck by how dismissive some authors were of atrocities. They seemed to have the attitude, if some atrocities were exaggerated, none happened. The reasons they provided were hollow or nonexistent. I heard one such historian mention a famous American lawyer who went to France and Belgium looking for civilian victims of a particularly horrible atrocity allegedly inflicted by German soldiers. Since no victim came forward, the historian assumed this was proof it didn't happen. He calls that proof? The people could have died, or it could be they didn't know this lawyer was looking for them, and even if they did, perhaps they couldn't reach the lawyer.

Barbara Tuchman found accounts written by the German soldiers themselves who claimed to have inflicted atrocities on French and Belgian civilians. I found such references in other sources as well.

Another author seemed to dismiss atrocities in the First World War because they were not as extreme as in the Second World War. I'd say, another way to look at it is, the First World War was the warmup act for the Second World War.

Barbara Tuchman thought this dismissive attitude toward atrocities in the First World War contributed to disbelief in Nazi atrocities.

After lunch, we drove to the Ardennes American Cemetery and Memorial, which was actually near Liège. A friend of Dad's fought in the Battle of the Bulge, so he wanted to pay a visit. The monument, as you might expect, was quite impressive. Again, the cemetery was impeccable.

Back in the car, we continued on our way to Verdun. We had no problem finding Verdun, but once there, we couldn't find the road to the hotel. Ah, there they are again, the Golden Arches, a place to pull over and park and ask for directions. We went inside, and I asked one of the employees at the counter. She summoned the manager who came over and sat down with us. Hearing that I had a foreign accent, she carefully and slowly enunciated each word and gave me clear directions, *"Descendez cette rue, tournez à gauche, ..."* French spoken so carefully is a delight to hear. After clearly and precisely giving me directions, she whipped out a place mat, turned it over, and drew us a map. We found our hotel *sans problème*.

Over the years on several trips to France, I have found getting around to be quite easy, and when I did need to ask for directions, I found French people to be great at giving directions—very precise, no extraneous detail to confuse me. It's no surprise Descartes was French, that lovely x-y Cartesian graph, such delightful order. When in Wales and Ireland, receiving directions in my mother tongue, it was hopeless. It's only by some miracle that I am not to this day still driving around aimlessly in Merthyr Tydfil.

I had wanted to stay at a particular hotel in Verdun, but it was full. The guidebook listed a chateau nearby, Le Chateau des Monthairons, so I reserved rooms there. It was no more expensive than the hotel. Since the guide book didn't rave about it, I wasn't expecting much. Was I in for a surprise. We pulled up to a magnificent stone chateau. It was like something out of a movie. And it only got better the more we saw. A cheery young woman greeted us and showed us to our rooms. They looked like the kind of apartments Napoleon and Josephine would have inhabited, with long elegant tied-back drapes all the way to the floor, and large bathrooms with *doors*, bathrooms the size of a New York City apartment.

After settling into our rooms, we walked around the expansive grounds. We looked for herons but found none. They must have been hiding. We went back inside for dinner. Right after we ordered, a group of French business-men sat down. Since we were out in the country, it had to be a destination restaurant for them, a good sign. After the wonderful main course, we awaited dessert. Unbeknownst to us, the simple act of ordering desert set in motion a three-course pageant. First, the waiter brought a small portion of chocolate mousse, *le entremet sucre*. I suppose this is to wake up one's pallet to the prospect of dessert, as if such an awakening were necessary. After we finished the mousse, followed by an appropriate pause, out came the dessert we had ordered. After we finished that, another pause, and out came a plate of petits fours, the dessert of the dessert. Oh my. It was delicious. Any one of those courses would have sufficed as dessert for me, but I was happy to have it all.

In the morning, we went down to breakfast and found a table set for three. We sat down, and you'd think a sensor on the chairs announced our arrival because immediately out came a cheery waitress to take our orders for tea and coffee. There was a basket of delicious croissants and rolls already on the table, and of course butter and jam. Wonderful.

After breakfast, we set out for St. Mihiel, south of the chateau. It was another bright, sunny day. The road took us through farmland blanketed by brilliant yellow mustard. We drove into the center of town, parked the car, and wandered around. Grandpa Peter's division waited in reserve near St. Mihiel in early September of 1918, during the battle in which the American First Army smashed the salient and took the town back from the Germans. The Germans saw a huge fresh army coming at them and bolted. It ended so quickly that Peter and the rest of the 91st Division just got to sit and watch. They were not called in.

After taking pictures and surveying the landscape, we drove north past the chateau to Verdun, the site of one of the most horrific battles of the First World War, or any war for that matter. The Germans began bombarding Verdun mercilessly in February of 1916. The idea was to kill as many French soldiers as possible, to bleed the French white, the thinking being that the French would never give up Verdun and would defend it to the death. The German officers were right. The French did defend it to the death. During the prolonged siege that dragged on for months, the people moved underground and lived in tunnels. When the battle was finally called off in December, the Germans had about as many dead soldiers as the French. They bled each other white in a fight to the death that ended in a draw.

We took the underground tour of the tunnels, riding around on a little programmed car and listening to narration. Talking holograms appeared and disappeared depicting life underground during the siege.

After lunch, we drove farther north through the Meuse Argonne battle-field, where the American Army fought in the fall of 1918 between the Meuse River and the Argonne Forest. We passed more swaths of yellow mustard, now recently plowed land, now something green in cultivation, now thick forests, now cattle grazing, enormous black and white Holsteins. The land undulated softly and continuously, not at all flat as in Flanders. Though the war histories I had read thus far included little about my grandfather's division, the books did mention some place names. We set out to find them.

Our first stop was Epinonville. I knew Grandpa Peter's division had taken the town, but since I had not yet read the division and regimental histories, I did not know they had to take it several times. We found a First World War monument next to the church. Unfortunately I did not yet know about Gesnes, so I didn't know to look for the monument to the Montana men.

At the American cemetery at Montfauçon, we wandered through the ruins of the old church high atop the hill, the high ground held by the Germans, quite a view those German lookouts had, a great help to their gunners. Looking down from the high ground, I imagined our troops advancing down below where I saw a wide lawn flanked by rows of tall trees and behind those trees, row upon row upon row of white crosses, our soldiers buried where they fell. As in the Ardennes, as in Flanders, as in Arlington, as in Gettysburg, the cemetery was beautiful and impeccably kept.

The superintendent gave me a copy of the portion of the 91st Division history about the Meuse Argonne Offensive. He was kind and polite but not nearly as enthusiastic as Christopher.

The next day, we drove to Fort Vaux, which looked as though it had been burrowed into the hillside, a fort with a daylight basement. I walked inside and peered out through the barred windows.

We drove on to the museum. As we were walking across the parking lot to the entrance, I heard a man yell, "*Mademoiselle! Mademoiselle!*" and something more in French. I stopped and turned around. He ran up and handed me a small flyer. I said *merci*, and he ran off. I looked down at the flyer. It was for a restaurant. I stuffed it in my purse, and we went inside. We spent the rest of the morning touring the museum. A film was about to start. We went into the theater and sat down. It was about the Battle of Verdun and was in French, of course; we wore headphones to hear it in English. The Battle of Verdun blared on the screen, artillery blasts and all, with loud narration in French, and loud narration in English in our ears, and Dad managed to sleep through the whole thing.

By now it was lunchtime. Since we were out in the country and didn't know where to go close by, I pulled the flyer out of my purse and said, "Why don't we try this place?" Off we went, following the excellent little map on the flyer the man had given me, and soon arrived at *L'Auberge au Feu de Bois*. It looked, well, rustic. Beyond rustic. And it looked more like somebody's house than a restaurant. A very, very old house. We ventured inside. Is this the barn or the house? I looked around. Yes, it was the house. Against the back wall I saw a very large, very blackened, obviously well-used fireplace. I suppose it would be called a hearth. It was big enough to cook in. An impressive old clock sat atop the mantle flanked by pottery. Baskets hung from the rafters. A woman came out, thrust her fists to her hips, and glared at us. "*Est-ce que c'est trop tard?*" I asked meekly, is it too late? I was careful that we left for lunch in plenty of time, knowing that many French restaurants, especially small ones, adhere to strict meal hours, and if the stated hours say open from noon to one o'clock, that does not mean it is acceptable to arrive at a quarter to one, and if you do have the temerity to commit such an affront, well, God help you. The way I see it, I am a guest in their country. It is my job to adapt.

"*Ça va,*" she said, or something to that effect. It wasn't too late for lunch. But she still didn't look happy.

Her husband came in, smiling, looking quite cheerful, and said something to her. She said something back and glared at him. He seemed unfazed and cheerily left. She motioned for us to sit down. No one else was there. She rattled off what she was serving for lunch, a set meal, *le menu.* The main course would be *dindon*, turkey. She brought out the first course, which we enjoyed, then the turkey. I had a leg. It had been braised in a tomato-based sauce, no doubt with beer or wine in the braising liquid. It was simple and delicious.

When she brought dessert, she stayed and visited. She seemed to have warmed up to us. She was easy to understand. I translated as she spoke and as Mom and Dad spoke, and we had a nice chat. Dad asked how long the place had been here. (My guess was five hundred years.) She said everything was destroyed in the First World War. (Apparently they rebuilt it to look as though it had been there five hundred years.) In the Second World War, the Germans came through so fast they didn't do much damage.

In retrospect, I still can't believe, groggy as I was, that I could speak and understand French as well as I did. Even though I was the one translating, and I was translating quite effortlessly, Mom and Dad remember the conversation better than I do. It was as if the French language resided in the autopilot part of my brain, and that part worked fine. It was the today part that was operating in slow motion.

Next we toured Fort Doaumont, which also appeared to be burrowed into the hillside. What a view we had from the top, gazing over thick forests and meadows as far as the eye could see to the east, forbidding terrain for German soldiers to fight through, which most of them didn't. The bulk of the German army came in through Belgium and swept down from the north. We wandered through the battlefield and stood in the old trenches. We saw the French monument listing the names of 150,000 missing French soldiers. That is mind boggling. The equivalent of a large town—missing. I cannot imagine how it must have been for all those wives and mothers and fathers and children, hearing someone approach the house and thinking, could it be he, but it wasn't. I wonder how long that lasted. Possibly forever.

In the morning, we checked out of the chateau. The cheery receptionist presented us with a beautiful poster of the place. Outside on the front steps while waiting for the car, I met an elegant Dutch couple. They looked to be in their sixties or thereabouts. The woman wore blue patent leather loafers. I had never seen blue patent leather loafers before. She held up a red book and said firmly, "This is what you have to use." It was a Michelin guide for booking hotels. I had seen only the slim green Michelin sightseeing guides, never these hardcover red books. On my next trip to Europe, I would wish I had heeded her advice.

En route to Paris, we stopped at Chateau Thierry and Belleau Wood. American troops fought there in the spring and summer of 1918, before the American First Army went into battle at St. Mihiel and in the Meuse Argonne. General Pershing had been waiting until he had sufficient troops to comprise an American army before sending them into battle, but by the spring of 1918, the situation was growing desperate. The Germans were advancing rapidly on Paris. The Allies urgently needed any help he could give, so he threw three divisions and the marines into the fight. He sent the marines to Belleau Wood. It was a ferocious battle. After three long, grueling, deadly weeks, they won the day. The Germans were impressed. They called the marines *teufel hunden*, devil dogs.

While reading *The Last Magnificent War*, I stumbled upon the memoir of one of those brash young leathernecks who fought at Belleau Wood. Right after we declared war on Germany in 1917, J.E. Rendinell quit his job in the steel mill and enlisted in the marines. One of his buddies wanted to enlist with him, but he was five pounds underweight. The recruiting sergeant told him to eat as many bananas and drink as much milk and water as he could, so he would meet the weight requirement.

"There were fourteen Marine recruits leaving Cleveland that day," Rendinell wrote. "We got a dollar traveling expenses for the day . . . One of the boys got a quart of whiskey with his dollar. We nicknamed him Pork Chop. He sure was funny.

"The conductor gave us a coach to ourselves. Pork Chop took a colored boy along with him who could play the banjo. The kid knew that below the Mason-Dixon line all colored and white folks separated, but not Pork Chop. 'He is riding with us, see, or we Marines will wreck the coach!'

"What fun we had that night. Nobody could sleep. Conductor locked us in our coach, but he forgot the windows could be broken and they were too."

He said his first meal at their quarantine camp at Parris Island, South Carolina, "looked as though it was made of beef stew, boiled potatoes, hash, dish rags, and a few old shoes mixed together."

Once in France, on their way to the front, he said the road was full of French refugees, and as the marines passed by in their trucks, they knelt down along the side of the road and prayed.

About his first day in the battle at Belleau Wood, he wrote: "My gun got so hot I could not touch it, so I crawled over & took one of my buddies rifles for he was done for and I used both guns, alternating as they got too hot."

During the night, he and another marine crawled out to see if the Germans were getting ready to attack. It looked as though they were. As the marines scurried back, they came across a German patrol. In hand to hand combat, the two marines killed the German soldiers. "No attack came from the Germans that night," Rendinell wrote.

He said the woods were full of German soldiers: on the ground, behind woodpiles, in the trees, everywhere. "We had to advance from tree to tree, looking all around to see where those shots were coming from. It was like playing Hide & Seek, only if you lost you were out for keeps."

The Germans were relentless in firing poison gas shells. Apparently Corporal Rendinell had trouble keeping his gas mask on. The next thing he knew, he was in a field hospital. As he was being transferred to a base hospital in Paris, French people ran along side his ambulance and gave him cookies.

When a nurse asked when he was scared the most, he replied, "All the time."

IN THE MORNING, we flew from Paris to Lourdes, which sits in the heart of the Pyrenees. I had been there before and so had Mom. I had reserved rooms at the hotel where I stayed before. I remembered the proprietress being uppity and snippy, but the location was convenient, the food was good, and it had been recently renovated and was very clean. We unloaded our luggage from the taxi and went inside to check in. On the wall behind the front desk was an enormous poster of the proprietress shaking hands with Pope John Paul II. When I attempted to check in, she curtly informed us that she had cancelled our reservation. There she was, throwing us out, standing before that huge picture of herself with the Holy Father. Yes, our reservation secured with a credit card—cancelled. She said she booked us at another hotel. We hailed yet another taxi, loaded our luggage into it, and had him take us to the other hotel. It turned out to be fine. The rooms had little balconies with beautiful views of the Pyrenees which the hotel with the snippy proprietress didn't have.

After settling into our rooms, we went down to the hotel restaurant for lunch. When I attempted to order in French, the waitress replied timidly in English, "I don't speak French, I'm Polish." We cracked up laughing, at which she became flustered almost to the point of tears. "It's all right, it's all right," I said, trying to reassure her. Her boss hurried over, looking as if he were about to scold her. "*Ça va, ça va,*" I assured him, everything was fine, she hadn't done anything wrong.

After lunch, we walked through town down to the Grotto. I was surprised to see Lourdes full of soldiers, military men of every stripe, and it seemed from every country. At any moment, a group of soldiers would appear marching in formation down the middle of the street. I asked what was up and was told it was the International Military Pilgrimage. We saw French soldiers, Brazilian soldiers, American soldiers, Swiss Guard from the Vatican, the town was an array of uniforms. I remarked that they seemed so young. Dad said, "The same age as the men in those cemeteries."

That evening we participated in the candlelight procession. I was still having severe bouts of lightheadedness.

The next morning, we were fortunate to find seats in the Basilica of the Rosary for Sunday Mass. The church was packed. When it came time for the sign of peace, usually a handshake or polite nod, the young French soldier next to Mom leaned down and gave her a more familiar French greeting: a kiss on each cheek. Was she ever surprised.

We then went out for a nice lunch at what I understood to be the best hotel in town. I had tried to reserve rooms there but no luck. I figured it would have a nice restaurant, and I wanted to see the place. The maitre'd led us to a table in a little cubby by itself with a curtain to close it off from the rest of the dining room. Soon, the waiter burst in, rattled off the menu in French, and disappeared behind the curtain. I heard fish and lamb but couldn't make out the rest. We expected him to come back and ask whether we wanted the fish or the lamb. We had no menus. We waited. After a little while, he burst through the curtain with the first course and again disappeared. After we finished that, he cleared the plates and brought plates of sole. I guess we're having the fish. After we finished that, he returned with lamb chops. Now I got it. We were getting *le menu*, as at the little place out in the country near Verdun, except this was a formal dinner with a fish course, a meat course, and so on. After dessert and coffee, the waiter came back and with a perfect John Wayne swagger and accent, asked in English, "Would ya like anything else?" and then cracked up laughing. So did we. Again, lunch was an adventure, and delicious, and delightful.

Chapter Seventeen

Throughout the trip, I experienced periods of severe lightheadedness, so much that I felt I needed to hold on to something or someone, or I'd fall down. It was similar to the sensation of being on a ship as it suddenly lists. My brain was still operating on a decidedly low speed. When someone spoke to me, it would take a moment or two to register. Background noise made it worse.

After, I returned home, still feeling loopy and knowing I needed to see a doctor to be sure there was nothing horribly wrong, I decided to spend a couple months at Mom and Dad's and see their doctor. He sent me for a battery of tests. Everything was fine. Sleep deprivation was the only answer. Before this, when I would hear about someone being hospitalized for exhaustion, I thought, how can a person be hospitalized for exhaustion? Now I know.

When I told Aunt Aila, who is a nurse, what happened, she said, "You need to sit and twiddle your thumbs." I should have heeded her advice, but I didn't. I kept working.

One thing being knocked off my horse in Belgium did was make me completely forget about looking for another job. From then on, I put my hand to the plow, just worked on the book, and quit glancing back at my former career. At least I didn't turn into a pillar of salt.

It was now the spring of 1998. I had been working on the book for a year. I laid out another schedule. My goal was to spend two weeks on each chapter. I thought I had fifteen chapters, that's thirty weeks, I'd be done in seven months.

I received a letter from Doris Black in Llandovery. She was Mair Faulkner's friend, the woman I met at Llandovery Heritage. Doris said her mother was Regina Hughes, the daughter of William and Mary Hughes. Those were my great-grandfather Arthur's parents' names. With nothing more to go on, no dates, I thought it could be a coincidence. I wrote back with questions but didn't hear from her again.

The trip to Wales made me want to learn more about Welsh traditions and culture. I went to the bookstore and asked for books about Wales. "Over here in natural history," the clerk said and began to lead me there. I was puzzled, but I followed, then I realized the confusion. "Not whales the animal," I said, "Wales the country." "Oh," he said and led me to the right place.

I learned why coal miners were paid monthly. Way back when, the Welsh mine operators paid the miners once a week. After being paid, the miners would descend on the pubs and get so drunk and be so hung-over they couldn't make it to work the next day. The mining companies were losing significant production because of this and resolved the problem by paying the miners once a month. That way they would lose only one day a month instead of four.

Bonfires, or bone-fires, were a popular Welsh ritual. Long ago, they believed they could read the future by the way the bones burned. One author speculated that the tradition of fireworks to celebrate the Fourth of July could have stemmed from Midsummer's Eve bonfires.

It was customary in some parts of Wales to set an extra place for "Morris from over the mountain," the unexpected guest. Grandma T used to do that.

People would walk into a house and call out, "Are there people here?" I wondered if that was what Sarah used to call out when she climbed out of the buggy at the Anderson/Tadsen ranch after galloping the horses there.

On a wedding day, the groom's friends would go to the bride's house to fetch her and take her to the church, but first they had to overcome an obstacle course thrown up to block their way. Once they'd overcome the obstacles and were at the door, they would find it bolted shut. In order to gain entrance, they had to sing out a verse, which was answered by a verse from someone inside the house. The groom's friends would be sure to bring along an adept versifier for this. The volley of poetic verse would go back and forth across the closed threshold until someone inside decided, that was enough, and opened the door to let the groom's friends take the bride to the church.

Speaking of poetic verse, Grandma collected poems. She kept them in a large envelope; one of my aunts had it. As I read them, I wondered why she kept each one. I thought of those poems and how to work some of the poignant ones into the narrative.

I read more Irish history. I went back pretty far, several centuries, in order to understand how things got to where they are now. I focused on the north, where Grandpa Peter was from, County Antrim, and specifically Belfast. Ireland is a tiny country with an enormous history. I decided not to tackle it in a big way in my book, because much of it is generally known; however, to put my forebears, the Gribbens, the McDonalds, and the Thompsons, in historic context, I had to learn about what came before them. To understand the now, we must know the past. G.K. Chesterton said, "History is a hill or high point of vantage from which alone men see the town in which they live or the age in which they are living." Without a sense of history, only vaguely can we understand the present, including a present long ago.

I wanted to read a book about Irish history by a Catholic author and one by a Protestant author. As I mentioned before, I think it is difficult to write history objectively when one is living through it, especially such emotionally charged events as the troubles in Northern Ireland. The story is unfinished. Thackeray said, "To have 'an opinion about Ireland,' one must begin by getting at the truth; and where is it to be had?" One needs distance in time or space to be objective, and yet I do like to read the perspective of those living through the events.

Jumping to the early twentieth century, as I read, I watched the trouble brew and build in Belfast. The coal heavers were locked out in July of 1907. Grandpa Peter's father, Sam, was a coal heaver. I noted the lockout on my time line and saw that it was the same year Peter started going to the half time, meaning he went to school half time and worked in the linen mill half time.

In 1910, the Ulster Unionists began stockpiling guns to stop home rule in Ireland. Sir Roger Casement said he was "appalled by the threat of fellow Protestant Ulsterman to resist Home Rule by force." He became a militant separatist. He sailed to America to raise money for the Irish Volunteers and, while here, met with the German ambassador to request military aid for the Irish rebellion.

Hibernians attacked a Sunday school outing in Derry. Protestant shipwrights attacked Catholics. Knives and guns were drawn at a soccer game. Now the Irish Republican Brotherhood re-surges, now gun running, now Ireland totters toward civil war, assassination and counter assassination in Belfast. I could see why my great-grandmother Rose wanted her son Pat, the one who was in the IRA, to leave the country before he got himself and the rest of the family killed. I wonder if Rose asked Sam to send money for all of them to emigrate. That was in 1922, and Butte was just catching its breath from the 1921 shutdown. Perhaps it was all the family could do to scrape together enough money for Peter's siblings Pat and Jenny to come here.

I took copious notes and later transcribed them into my "notes.wales" and "notes.irish" files on the computer. Then I started writing the Irish part of the story, wanting to capture the voices of my Irish kin while still fresh in my memory. From Aunt Brigid's stories, I took it that Great-grandma Rose's favorite retort to her husband was: "How dare you, sir!" I wanted to work that in but never did figure out how.

As I thought of more questions, I called Mom and Auntie Mary and Aunt Aila. It seemed every answer spawned six more questions. Answering my questions would prompt more memories which would prompt more questions, and on it went, never ending, like the loaves and fishes. I'd write letters to cousins Molly in Palo Alto and Gilbert in Olympia and Rosaleen in Belfast. They were wonderful about writing back. These were old-fashioned letters sent by mail, giving me a wonderful record of what they told me. I keep all letters. I always have. "Keep asking questions," Molly would say. She seemed to enjoy reminiscing.

Gilbert wrote that his uncle Peter, my grandfather, "reflected courage, not one to trifle with . . . he feared nothing and no one." Every letter from Gil included glowing remarks about his uncle Peter.

When I sent questions by letter, I typed the questions, leaving ample space in between so the person could simply jot down the answers and send the letter back to me. With domestic letters, I included a self-addressed stamped envelope. I wanted to make it easy for people to help me.

A letter arrived from Christopher Sims in Belgium. He found Steenbrugge and took several pictures for me. The land was flat as could be. Peter really did put himself in danger when he crawled out of the trench to save that man. Snipers and machine gunners had a clear view of him.

Mom's cousin Sam in England sent me information about getting British war records. My great uncles Denis and John served in the British Army during the war. Most of the British First World War records were destroyed by fire during the Nazi Blitz. Those that were salvaged are in a collection called Burnt Documents.

Cousin Mary said in one of her father's first battles (Peter's brother John), the line broke, and the sergeant yelled, "Every man for himself!" and John ran. Another soldier stopped him and said, "You want to be running *that* way. You're running *toward* the Germans." We laughed. He was only a teenager. If he hadn't survived in one piece, it wouldn't have been funny, but he did. It says a lot about the chaos of battle. It must be like being in a blinding blizzard only much worse, becoming disoriented by the smoke, the fog, the noise, bullets whizzing at you, exploding bombs throwing dirt sky high, that dirt raining down on you, all the while terrified that any moment could be your last.

As I read *The Story of the 91st Division*, written by members of Grandpa Peter's division, I was astounded by all the drama—how they advanced far ahead of the adjacent troops and could have been pinched off by the enemy, the ghastly losses they suffered. For all I knew, Grandpa Peter could have served in a division that saw little action, and his saving that man's life in Flanders the only bit of high drama. That was not the case.

I read slowly and carefully. There was so much detail. I prepared a separate time line for the battles which made it easier to keep everything straight. In my loopiness, I could concentrate on only one thing at a time, and yet, that was all I needed to do, that's what one does when writing a book. All I could bear was the present moment, and yet that was all I needed to bear.

Later I would realize the cause of my loopiness—I was still utterly exhausted. Had I taken time off from my book and just rested, I probably would have bounced back more quickly.

And thanks to Doctor Mom, I discovered the cause of my waking up in the middle of the night and not being able to fall back to sleep—I needed more magnesium. I started taking a supplement.

I read more general histories of the war, as always, entering dates on my time line. Czar Nicholas abdicated on March 15, the Ides of March. How telling. No soothsayer to warn him. Evidently he did not have the Celtic sensibility for luck or he never would have picked that date.

Several authors wrote of the First World War bringing an end to innocence, that an age of innocence prevailed in the years leading up to the war, an innocence shattered by the cataclysm of a war far worse than any before it, a war in which the marvels of the industrial age were brought to bear to kill and maim at heretofore unfathomable levels.

There seemed to be two contrary sentiments prior to the First World War: that war in Europe was inevitable, and that it was impossible. Barbara Tuchman wrote about this in *The Guns of August*. She said in *Germany and the Next War*, Count von Bernhardi proffered the notion that Germany needed war to progress, that war was a "biological necessity" and "a carrying out of the natural law." In *The Great Illusion*, Norman Angell propagated the more comforting notion that war between developed nations would never happen again. Because of trade, war didn't make sense, and if it didn't make sense, it wouldn't happen.

John Dos Passos wrote that Americans of his generation "were confident that industrial progress meant an improved civilization . . . the European war of 1914–1918 seemed a horrible monstrosity, something outside of the normal order of things."

When Kosovo was exploding in the 1990s, one of my neighbors remarked derisively, "And in this day and age," as if to say, "What's wrong with those people? Don't they know better?" From her tone, you'd think they were committing the faux pas of using the wrong cutlery, or that war was as much an anachronism as an out-of-style dress, something relegated to old movies, not real life, not today. I remembered something a Romanian colleague at Bechtel, a recent immigrant, said to me in 1992: "Americans are very innocent." News of the Balkans unhinging was a faraway unpleasant perturbation "outside of the normal order of things," in 1914 and in the 1990s. My contemporaries and I, far away from the trouble, all the way across the Atlantic Ocean in America, could ignore it if we chose by turning off the television and ignoring the newspapers. Another age of innocence. It gave me a sense of foreboding. The words of St. Paul kept ringing in my head: "Just when people are saying 'peace and security' ruin will fall on them . . . and there will be no escape." I had to find a way to work that into the war narrative, as well as the part about the end coming "like a thief in the night."

As I continued to write and do more research, the news was full of warnings of "irrational exuberance" over internet stocks. I thought of the exuberance over mining stocks in the late nineteenth century, except I'd say that exuberance was rational. The mining companies were extracting and selling a physical commodity that the modern industrial world needed. The story of how Butte's biggest mining company, the Anaconda, went public is a fascinating story. Imagine if Microsoft had grown into a behemoth as a private company and, while high on the upward slope of its rise, joined with several other big high tech companies to form a mega-behemoth technology company, and then went public. This is essentially what happened with the Anaconda Copper Mining Company. In 1895, it was a private company; only eleven stockholders owned it, and they reaped tremendous profits. In 1899, several industrial titans, including Henry Rogers of Standard Oil, set about consolidating, or you might say amalgamating, much of Butte mining into a holding company called the Amalgamated Copper Company. It included the Anaconda, the Butte and Boston, and several other mining companies. If I understood this correctly—I found it a bit confusing—they bought the Anaconda and immediately went public and, with this avalanche of cash, paid for the company. So in essence, they bought it with no pre-public-offering cash. According to Isaac Marcosson, author of the company biography, *Anaconda*, "The flotation of the Amalgamated stock developed a sensational chapter in American finance."

Chapter Eighteen

In the books I had read thus far about the war, other than General Pershing's, the American experience in general and my grandfather's division in particular were in the first case only touched upon and in the second case ignored. I had few specifics, and specifics were what I wanted. The 91st Division history was a big help, but it wasn't enough. I wanted more. I wanted to tell you the story of this particular foot soldier, my grandfather Peter Thompson. I wanted you to feel as though you were right there with him, right on his heels, slogging through the mud in the Argonne, trying to avoid shot and shell, dashing out of the trench to save that man's life in Flanders. I wanted the war narrative to be as personal to Peter as possible, which would be difficult since he didn't talk about it. I needed ground-level details. I would have to go hunting for them.

Again I read bibliographies looking for soldiers' memoirs, collections of letters, diaries, anything personal. I wanted to know what it was like for the soldiers on the ground, what were they thinking, feeling, doing. I wanted to dig deeper than a broad overview of the battles, I wanted to peek behind the curtain of history. The titles that looked most promising were old and obscure and long out of print. Still in the olden days of the internet, the on-line vehicles we have today for finding out-of-print books weren't nearly as prevalent, so I depended on the library. The trouble with doing research in Las Vegas is everything is new, including the books in the library; however, the able interlibrary loan staff managed to track down everything I requested. We were soon on a first-name basis. It could take quite a while to get the books. As a result, I was continually putting down and picking up a subject of research as I waited for those old, obscure books to arrive.

They were worth the wait. I found letters written by French soldiers, by American soldiers, by German soldiers, by Canadian soldiers. I read diaries and memoirs. I read about the elite of the French officer corps going into battle wearing white gloves and sporting red and white plumes on their caps, so emblematic of the clash of history, these nineteenth-century warriors with their nineteenth-century traditions facing the horrors of twentieth-century warfare.

In a letter home, a German prisoner implored his mother to aid the French wounded because of how kindly he was treated in a French hospital.

French writer and soldier Gaston Riou was captured early in the war and held in a Bavarian prison. He wrote of incessant hunger. "It seems strange to a man who believed himself to live on ideas to be reduced to become nothing but a stomach."

Pierre-Maurice Masson said he abandoned the "trenches of the Sorbonne" for Verdun and called this bit of bad luck a mere "bagatelle" when compared with the future of the world.

The French soldiers sounded gung-ho about going to war in 1914 and 1915, and at the same time fully realized and accepted that they may be killed. They wrote frank letters to their loved ones; quite a contrast from my Irish grandfather and great-uncles who never wrote or spoke of the horrors of the war or of being afraid.

While reading a biography of Winston Churchill by an English author, I noticed a marked change in tone when the First World War entered the narrative. Opinions were coming through, though not couched as such, strong opinions. I quit reading. I find opinions interesting, and I like to read them, but I was seeking facts for my research. I needed to shield myself from opinion as best I could so as not to confuse the two. The facts alone were confusing enough. The war seemed personal to British historians, even for those born after it ended. American historians seemed more dispassionate, as if they had more emotional distance from the events. I made a point to read books about the war by British authors and American authors.

A man from Australia told me he was reared on the First World War. In school, he studied the history, the heroism, the tragedy, the poetry. "It's in our marrow," he said, "probably always will be." Perhaps the proliferation of English poetry that came out of the First World War made it all the more poignant. A poet can strike at the marrow. I read much of that poetry.

I discovered British officer poet Siegfried Sassoon in the PBS documentary Mom gave me about the war. His poems helped give me a sense of the horror. In "A Mystic as Soldier," he wrote: "Now God is in the strife, and I must seek him there." In another called "Editorial Impressions," he wrote: "I am writing a little book called *Europe on the Rack*." Wasn't that the truth.

I wondered why the assassination of the Austrian heir to the throne by a Serbian nationalist could lead to a fight to the death between Germany and France and Britain and Russia and us. I wanted to know more about why the war started and why we got involved. I read and read. What a story it was: diplomats bungle or make mischief, leaders wield unflinching ultimatums drawn in anger, the first domino tips, entangling alliances line up the rest, the guns follow, and *they all fall down*.

It took only sixteen days to put the entire country of France on a war footing. That is astounding. Six million French soldiers would become casualties in the First World War, more people than live in the entire country of Costa Rica today.

I decided to include a brief description of how the war began, because I didn't think it was part of the collective memory in our country, and also because right from the start, even before we were in it, the war had a direct bearing on the people of Butte, where my family lived, a city of immigrants whose kin in the Old Country were now at war with each other. Though far away, this war was very real, very personal to the people of Butte, Montana, right from the start. I needed to demonstrate that.

Following up on my Bechtel colleague's recommendation, I called the U.S. Army Center of Military History. The woman I spoke with found a regimental history for the 362nd, Peter's regiment. She said they did not normally have such things in their collection. She remarked what a literary war the First World War was, a reflection of the culture. She suggested I contact the Military History Institute at the War College in Carlisle, Pennsylvania.

Soon the regimental history arrived in the mail. It was written by Captain Joseph M. Scammel and was a poor copy of a copy of a copy, difficult to decipher though worth the trouble. Captain Scammel included the personal details I was looking for, down to what they ate and how they felt, and he went down to the company level, which was a tremendous help in getting closer to details specific to Peter. As with Pershing, I was surprised by Captain Scammel's frankness, such as in this passage where he quotes Colonel J.B. Woolnough: "'The Regiment was inadequately equipped, about 75% trained' but the morale of the men 'promised to offset these other deficiencies.'"

About being ordered to withdraw from Epinonville after they had taken the town, he wrote:

> The ostensible reason for this order was to allow Epinoville to be shelled, but not only was it safely in our hands, but no shelling ever came.
>
> As the fathers of the illegitimate are ever backward about proclaiming their parenthood, the origin of this unfortunate order will doubtless remain in obscurity. Such incidents are common to the confusion of battle.

A PACKAGE ARRIVED from Christopher. It was the regimental history for the 361st. Since they were in the same brigade as Peter's regiment, he thought it might be helpful. It was.

Historical research is akin to getting copper out of raw ore. As it takes tons of ore to yield pounds of copper, it takes volumes of research to yield pages of text. For the war narrative, which turned out to be about one hundred pages, I read all or part of fifty books, plus newspaper articles, letters, operations reports, memos, memoirs, division histories, regimental histories. I'm fortunate I had the time to do it.

One of my aunts, or perhaps it was Uncle Ed, suggested I talk to some of the old timers at the American Legion. I tracked down the head of the Butte post, Neil Neary, and called him. He said there were no surviving First World War veterans and most of their First World War records burned up in a fire. One thing that did survive was the bottle of cognac for the Last Man's Club.

CHAPTER NINETEEN

IN JULY, I returned to Montana to do more research. Mom and Dad took me. I still couldn't do the driving.

Our first stop was the historical society in Helena. My to-do list had grown considerably. The more I learned, the more I knew I didn't know. Always with me, I kept my lists of questions, things to look up, and documents to find. As I found something on the list, I wrote a check mark at the left margin. When I completed an entire page, I wrote "done" at the top right corner. Completed pages I placed in a folder called "Completed Questions."

Throughout my traipsing around the world doing research, I met many archivists and historians. I came to learn that archivists know where the bodies are buried; historians know who they are.

At the top of my to-do list was to find out what daily life was like for the prisoners in 1913, when Arthur and Sarah were incarcerated. I set out to plumb all I could from the prison records. As in other parts of the book, I would write a bit about the institution, but my primary interest was the inhabitants—what was everyday life like for the prisoners in the prison, for the children in the orphanage, for the miners, for the soldiers. I found this ground-level history very difficult to find.

Back in 1913, when my great-grandfather Arthur was sentenced to hard labor at the Montana State Prison in Deer Lodge, I thought hard labor meant hard labor, images of chain gangs. I was surprised to discover that only half of the inmates had work. The documents showed that the warden was trying to find work for the rest of them. Those who worked did so on road crews and ranches, they butchered cattle, made bridles. Their work did not appear to be much different from a man on the outside. Mining was hard labor. Ranching was hard labor. Hard labor was what many a man did for a living in 1913.

While plowing through the archives for the orphan's home, I found reports prepared by the executive board for the time when Grandma lived there. They were a pleasure to read, so well written, so clear headed. I looked for ways to quote from them, not only because of the eloquence, but also to capture the language and way of thinking of the time.

I found a list with the names of the staff and each person's salary. The head matron, Mrs. Shobe, made $50 per month. (Days pay for a miner in Butte was $3.50 at that time.) As I read down the list I saw a familiar name: Miss Myrtle Dragstedt. Grandma spoke fondly of her teacher Miss Dragstedt on one of those tapes, when she told the story about dancing in the parade. Now I knew that happened when she lived in the orphanage.

Only once did I hear Grandma mention living in the orphanage. It was that Thanksgiving I described in *One Night in a Bad Inn*. She told me a lot about her life, but that whole episode with her father believed to be dead and her mother in jail, and she and Archie and Patsy sent off to the orphanage—that she didn't talk about. Considering the horrible things her mother did later, it still amazes me that Grandma grew into the impeccable woman she was. She certainly had everything stacked against her. I think a person in Grandma's situation either makes a firm decision not to follow the bad examples she grew up around or else slothfully falls into those familiar destructive patterns. Grandma said, "I was not going to live like that. I was going to be a lady." She lived life deliberately. She knew she was captain of her own ship with regard to character. She set her own course, the direction on her compass was clear. She did not aimlessly drift.

After I completed the items on my to-do list for the historical society, we left for Butte. My first stop was the Silver Bow County Courthouse where I pored through the deeds, looking for records for all family members. I went through everything very slowly. It took probably twice as long as it would have if I had been feeling fine. My brain was still running on slow speed. I noted addresses and dates. Using this information and the addresses I had collected from city directories, I prepared another table, this one by address. It had three columns: year, address, and the names of the people who lived there. I wanted to see who lived with whom and when and for how long, who moved frequently, who stayed put. As I did this, it became quite clear that my great-grandfather Sam Thompson was living with his children and in-laws, not the other way around. He lived with his daughter Mary and her family, he lived with his daughter Jennie and her family, he lived with his sister-in-law and her family. For twenty years, Peter's father, my great-grandfather Sam, lived in Butte while his wife, Rose, stayed in Ireland. A twenty year separation—why? It didn't dawn on me until Mom pointed it out—what was Rose to come to? Sam didn't have a home. Even though I had all this data in front of me, often it takes someone else to point out the obvious. Being steeped in the story is good, but others can help provide the distance needed to see things more clearly. While counting the petals on a daisy, I could miss the garden.

I sat down to more chats with Mom and my aunts. One of them would say something and it would remind another of something, and the stories kept coming. Mom and her sisters are good at distinguishing the important, entertaining, and interesting from the unimportant, dull, and trivial, and they stuck to the important, entertaining, and interesting. The same was true of my cousins and their spouses and Dad and my brother and uncles. Thinking back on it, I am very fortunate, blessed really. The challenge for me would be how to knit this mother lode of wonderful stories into a smooth, readable narrative. Not easy. Not one bit.

One morning we drove out to Twin Bridges to visit Uncle Sam, Mom's brother. The last time I saw Uncle Sam was when he made a cameo appearance at the grave site after Grandma's funeral. He pulled up in an old beater of a pick-up truck. It took me a minute to realize who he was. He looked older than Grandma. He had been a career enlisted man in the navy and later in the air force, and was now retired. His ship was bombed and decorated during the Korean War. That day we visited him in Twin Bridges, he looked and sounded like a crusty old salt, with his gray straggly beard, ruddy cheeks, and red suspenders. Clearly those suspenders served a utilitarian purpose—he was rail thin. He spoke with a perpetual note of derision in his voice. He smoked heavily and had the worst smoker's hack I had ever heard, no doubt exacerbated by his lungs being injured in a boiler accident at the shipyard in Bremerton years ago.

I would visit Uncle Sam several times while working on my book, and he always told me bits of family lore that I didn't hear from anyone else. Over time I figured out that when he was absolutely certain about something, he was wrong. On those rare occasions he voiced uncertainty, he was right. When he was matter-of-fact, not strongly certain or uncertain, I'd say he was pretty reliable. Back in 1981 when Mom and Dad threw an eightieth birthday party for Grandma, Uncle Sam called to tell Mom it was the wrong year. He insisted that his father, Peter, immigrated in 1912. It was 1914. I asked everyone about that college scholarship Grandma won. No one knew how she won it, except Uncle Sam. He said, "I *think* she won it in a sewing contest." While reading the old newspapers at the Twin Bridges library, I found an article about it and sure enough, Uncle Sam was right.

He said only thirty-nine of the original members of Grandpa Peter's company survived the war. (Company E left Camp Lewis with 150 men.) I don't remember whether Uncle Sam was absolutely certain when he said that or not. I wasn't able to verify the number and so left it out. Based on everything I learned about Peter's experience in the war, in particular the massacre at Gesnes where his company was at the vanguard of the attack, the number may be accurate. The specificity tends to lend credence to it. To use it, I would have had to include a caveat, and that didn't work with the tone and pace I wanted for the war narrative. I had solid casualty numbers at the battalion and division level, so I used those to demonstrate how horrific the fighting was and how great the loss of life.

Uncle Sam said the man whom Grandpa saved in the war wrote to Grandma. I wish we had the letter. He said Winks Brown, the man who helped Peter pull the man into the trench, was from Philipsburg.

During his travels with the navy, Uncle Sam visited Grandma's siblings, Archie and Bill and Patsy, in California. He said Archie told him what happened in Forsyth, that Arthur was on his way back to Wales, that Sarah couldn't get any more money from her family in Pennsylvania, and she was in on the whole thing. I silently wondered, how would Archie know this? He was in the orphanage when the story unfolded. Who told him? Did he know ahead of time that his parents planned to dig up the body and burn the house down, assuming Sarah was in on it as he supposedly claimed? Was this simply Archie's take on things or was it Uncle Sam's take on Archie's take on things? It may be true, but the sources were too far removed from the events, and I had no idea how reliable Archie was. I also thought, if Arthur's intention was to return to Wales after he left Forsyth, why didn't he? There had to be lots of ships heading to Britain out of New York in 1913. Instead, he hopped one bound for Buenos Aires. And why would Sarah need money from her family in Pennsylvania? She and Arthur had just sold the ranch for $4800. There were too many holes in the story to consider any of it reliable.

Uncle Sam said Archie and his accomplice, Roy Walsh, robbed stores for two years, meaning the car theft in Butte and the attempted robbery turned murder in Renova were not the beginning of their crime spree.

(Later in my research, I was able to confirm that Roy had been arrested several times before he met Archie. As for their crime spree ensemble, I wasn't able to confirm what Uncle Sam said.)

He said Archie talked about all the money he was going to make, and that he would pay for Sam to attend Stanford, and he was sure he could get him in.

Then out of the blue in his cranky, raspy, chain-smoking voice, Uncle Sam said, "There was nothing ghoulish about him digging up that body."

Nothing ghoulish? It struck me as a bizarre non-sequitur. Somehow nothing Uncle Sam said seemed funny at the time, now it seems hilarious. Nothing ghoulish indeed.

He insisted there was nothing wrong with the way his grandmother Sarah lived. "She just liked to party," he said apologetically.

As for Sarah being pregnant while in jail, which she intimated in one of her letters, he declared, "There was no baby!"

How would he know? I listened politely and took notes, knowing I planned to corroborate everything, or try to.

Uncle Sam's travels also took him to Portland where he met his grandfather Hughes. "What was Arthur like?" I asked. He said Arthur was talkative and well informed and that he was slowly losing his leg to diabetes—first the toes, then the leg up to the knee. He said Arthur did not like farming.

I asked what he remembered about his father. He was five when Peter died, and being the only boy, I wanted his perspective. He said nothing that was based on first-hand knowledge.

A woman who knew Uncle Sam as a child, though not well as an adult, to this day swoons over him. From his pictures, he certainly was a cute little boy and grew up to be a strikingly handsome young man. But to see him in 1998, that chain-smoking curmudgeon of an uncle of mine, with constant derision in his voice and that straggly gray beard, I had to shake my head. I couldn't see cause for swooning. It seemed, to her he would always be that cute, funny, little boy in Butte.

As we said our goodbyes, I mentioned that we were going to Virginia City. Uncle Sam recommended that we stop at the Sump in Sheridan for lunch. "They have good pasties," he said. That's a great thing about these small Montana towns—you don't need directions. All you need to know is: the Sump in Sheridan. You drive into Sheridan, and there's the Sump. As per the name, it was in the basement. It was a bar with tables, a saloon really, but with tables. Very smoky. The cheerful waitress had quite a cough. She explained laughing, "I'm allergic to cigarette smoke, and I work in a bar." The pasties were delicious.

Chapter Twenty

BACK HOME AGAIN, I transcribed my notes, tried to corroborate what I had been told, and began to weave all this into the narrative. I'd write part, and as I did, gaps in the story would emerge, and my to-do list grew, I'd go off and follow new threads. I read more books, called relatives, asked questions, listened to their stories, asked more questions, and in the process learned many things I didn't know to ask about. Then I tried to weave that into the narrative. The process repeated itself over and over. Something would pop into my head, and I'd chase after it, be it about Butte history, homesteading, Forsyth, elements of the murder mystery. I'd be in the middle of one thing and get an idea about another part. I'd order research materials, I never knew when they'd arrive, I'd go on to something else, and then get back to work on that part when the research materials arrived. I researched, wrote, researched some more, wrote some more, building the story in layers. As I read what I had written, even more questions would pop up.

Though I continually unearthed gems, at times my search ended in nothing, or something of no apparent use. Probably five percent of my research ended up in the book, though I never knew until I looked whether what I was looking for would end up in the ninety-five or the five. I needed the ninety-five percent to understand the five percent in context, to get a better sense of the people, the place, the events. From time to time, after I thought I had finished part of the manuscript, something would emerge from the recesses of my memory, something I found interesting but didn't think had anything to do with the story, and now, suddenly I saw that it did and added it, and I was glad I had followed that particular thread.

From the outset, I was concerned about pacing. I knew the story was replete with drama and sadness. Grandma was beset by untold trial and tragedy, yet she rose above it and overcame it, and with such dignity. I remember when reading *Oliver Twist*, right at the point where I thought, if one more bad thing happens to this little boy, I won't be able to stand it, the story turned and something good happened. Even though I was writing nonfiction, which meant the facts drove the story, the manner in which I presented those facts was up to me. I didn't want to depress you so completely that you would give up and put the book down and say enough already.

Another thing always on my mind was the purpose of my book—which was to tell the story of my maternal grandparents and great-grandparents so you could get to know them—not to hurt people. As such, I left some things out or included the event but used no name or a pseudonym, which I identified as such. The descendants of these people aren't responsible for what their ancestors did, and they don't need to hear about it from me, especially not in a public setting, and a book is a public setting.

I was able to corroborate much of what Uncle Sam told me, despite his curmudgeonly way of saying it. Everything he told me about Sarah's accident, where she had been, where she was going, where she was living at the time, agreed with her friend's testimony at the inquest over her death. It seemed he, Mom, my aunts, my cousins, each had different pieces of the story, not conflicting pieces, just different.

Not only with Uncle Sam but with everyone, if I couldn't corroborate something and it seemed questionable and the person telling me the story did not have first-hand knowledge of it, I didn't include it in the book. I was able to find documented evidence for the most dramatic parts, or Grandma told me what happened herself. When I sought to corroborate what Grandma told me, I would find it be exactly as she said or more dramatic.

Though I didn't intend it for this purpose, an accidental benefit of keeping a time line was in fact checking. Cousin Molly said certain relatives' actions were because they were on hard times on account of the Great Depression. I had no reason to think otherwise. It made sense. She said this happened right after her father died, before school started in the fall. With so many dates and so much information swirling around in my head, it wasn't until I entered his date of death on my time line that it dawned on me—the Depression hadn't started yet. Her father died in July of 1929, the stock market crashed in October.

The story about Ves Hall caught my interest because of the connection to Judge Crum's downfall. Ves Hall was the Rosebud County rancher who was arrested during the First World War for saying it was okay to sink the

Lusitania if she was carrying munitions and other such things. Crum was the judge who threw the book at Sarah. He testified as a character witness for Ves Hall, which led to his altercation with County Attorney Felkner Haynes, and Crum pulling his revolver on Haynes (not a good idea), and Haynes filing affidavits which led to Crum's impeachment. The first book I read that mentioned Hall said he was charged with sedition. I had already noted the dates of the sedition acts on my time line. As I entered the dates pertaining to Hall's case, I realized that the sedition acts had not passed yet. Ves Hall's trial was in January of 1918. The Montana Sedition Law passed in February, and the federal act passed in May. What was he charged with? A new mystery. The question went on my to-do list. Yet another hunt and another example of how that time line proved quite handy.

It turned out, Hall was charged under the Espionage Act—a rancher out in the boonies of Rosebud County, Montana, complaining about President Wilson. Knowing the facts makes his arrest all the more ridiculous, not to mention the first amendment implications.

Where initially I thought I would rely on published books of history for the broad historical backdrop, now I began to seek out more primary sources even for those parts. Aunt Aila told me that a priest told Uncle Hugh that he could not receive communion because he was a Socialist. I had a vague understanding that the Catholic Church condemned socialism but no specifics. Some authors had mentioned it, but rather than take their word for what the Church taught, I decided to go right to the source: *Rerum Novarum*, the encyclical letter written by Pope Leo XIII in the nineteenth century. My pastor printed it for me from the Vatican web site.

Getting back to the time line, in addition to being a convenient way to organize a mountain of information, seeing family events juxtaposed against historic events often helped explain a person's actions or give me a possible time frame for when a particular event occurred. Grandma told me prostitutes lived in their boarding house. That was something of which she obviously had first-hand knowledge, not something I questioned. As I read Butte history, I discovered that the Montana attorney general closed the Line (the red light district) during the First World War, and when he did prostitutes did not leave town, they simply moved into hotels and boarding houses. It fit with what Grandma said.

Speaking of the boarding house, I was well into my research and writing before it dawned on me that the bad inn was not only a metaphor, it was literal. Grandma lived in a bad inn. Not only did prostitutes live in their boarding house, Great-grandma Sarah told the men they could have their way with her daughter. Grandma refused, of course, even if it did result in a whack across the head. It truly was a bad inn.

NOW TO DELVE INTO the Anaconda part of the story. (Here I mean the town in Montana near Butte. I had already researched the company of the same name.) I wanted to know how long my great-granduncle John Gribben lived there before moving to Butte and I wanted to confirm what he did for a living. This may sound inconsequential—why did it matter exactly how long he lived in Anaconda—but I often found, in looking for a rather pedestrian piece of information, additional gems would pop up. I'd been told there was a museum in Anaconda, so I called there. "John Gribben," the man said, "I have information on him." Then he hurriedly said he was busy, I should call back later, and hung up. I didn't have a chance to ask his name. A couple weeks later I called back. A gruff, older sounding man answered the phone. I explained that I had talked to this man and what I was looking for. He said gruffly, "The man you talked to is buried." His voice dropped off as if in sorrow. Oh, my goodness, I thought, how awful. "I'm so sorry," I said. Silence. After a moment or two, he said, "No, he's not dead! He's busy! Call back in November!" and he hung up.

Some days I felt completely overwhelmed—I'm writing a book, an entire book, all at once. I had to tell myself, I'm not writing a book all at once, I am writing this sentence, I am writing this paragraph. I don't eat everything on the plate in one bite. I eat the meal one bite at a time. The same applied to writing a book. I'd take bite-size pieces. I would take one chapter at a time, beginning with chapter one, read over my notes and fill in any blanks. Before, as I read or wrote the manuscript, I'd be taken up with story and didn't want to stop and go look something up, so I'd insert a bracketed question mark and keep writing or reading, which was fine, since I wanted to keep the flow of my writing. But now was later, no more procrastinating. I needed to fill in all missing information. It took real discipline to force myself to do this. I'd rather just read and be caught up in the story.

I could see distinct stories emerge as I wrote and decided to split the book into four parts, each with a title. Part one would be about the fire. I'd call it "The Forsyth Episode" or perhaps "Trouble in Rosebud." Part two would be about Grandpa Peter's life in Ireland and about the family arriving in Butte, part three would be the war, and part four would be the rest, about which I still had much to learn. Grandma T was the thread who tied it all together.

Dividing the story into parts immediately made it seem easier to tackle.

As I reread the newspaper articles about the fire, I wondered why Arthur put a railroad tie in the coffin. Why go to all that trouble? Why not just take the body and leave the coffin empty? I wondered why County Attorney Beeman suspected that Arthur was alive, even though the inquest said he was dead. Perhaps some missing piece of the story not reported in the newspapers, not in the court files, beyond my reach, something floating around in the local scuttlebutt made him believe Arthur was alive. I went back through the sequence of events leading to Arthur's capture to see if I had missed anything.

CHAPTER TWENTY-ONE

FROM THE BEGINNING, I tried to steep myself in the times and places in which my grandparents and great-grandparents lived—in all things Welsh, in all things Irish, all things about Montana, all things about the First World War. To put you there, I had to be there. I wanted to get the language of those times and places into my head. I watched those documentaries about the war again; I watched documentaries about the Irish, about the West, over and over. I noted the historians interviewed and looked for their books. I read novelists who were contemporaries of my grandparents and great-grandparents, or close to it, and who wrote about the times and places in which they lived. I did this to help gain a flavor of the times, always taken with the caveat that these novelists wrote fiction and never claimed otherwise. Also, since I wanted my book to read like a novel, I wanted to get the lyric prose of good novelists into my head, to sate my mind with it. I read more Dickens, I read the Brontë sisters, and George Eliot, and Hemingway, and John Steinbeck, and F. Scott Fitzgerald, and Somerset Maugham. As I did, I stumbled across parallels to the lives of my ancestors. Jane Eyre attended a pauper school. Oliver Twist lived in the workhouse. Somebody in *Ashenden* turned the money over in his pocket for luck, just as my great-grandfather Sam did. I was careful to avoid fiction that was too close to my research, so as not to confuse fiction with the facts, which were difficult enough to ascertain from the historical record. A few novels I started and put down because they were too close to my subject and without authority. Even when writing historical fiction, it is the novelist's prerogative to take liberties to fill in the blanks, fiction is fiction; though I prefer that if a novelist uses real names and writes about real events and places, he use the knowable facts.

I did not consider novels to be source material. Even if the novelist wrote about his own time and lived in the setting, even if he did extensive research, unless I am already completely versed in the historical setting,

I don't know where the facts end and his imagination begins. The fiction writer has complete license. He is not bound by facts. When I read *David Copperfield*, I wondered if Charles Dickens placed his own thoughts in the mind of David when he visited the prison and happened upon the villainous Uriah Heep. Upon seeing the dinner served to the prisoners, David observed "a striking contrast between these plentiful repasts of choice quality, and the dinners, not to say of paupers, but of soldiers, sailors, laborers, the great bulk of the honest, working community; of whom not one man in five hundred ever dined half so well." Perhaps Dickens did put his own observation in the mind of his character, but I don't know that. I would not take the word of a fictional character in a fictional story. To have used such an observation, I would have had to corroborate it with nonfiction sources. That done and found to be accurate, a gifted novelist can have a much more elegant or profound way of presenting those facts, of cutting quickly to the essence of things. Though Charles Dickens was a journalist, he did not claim to be writing journalism when he wrote *David Copperfield*. He was writing a novel.

As for the Welsh, I listened to the recording of Dylan Thomas reading his poem "A Child's Christmas in Wales." I read *How Green is My Valley* and watched the movie, a wonderful story about a Welsh coal mining family. In it, young Huw says, "My father was night shift." That's how Aunt Aila says it, not my father was on night shift, or he was working night shift, "My father was night shift." When Huw falls into the river, his mother wraps his legs in goose grease. Auntie Mary said her grandmother Sarah's house always smelled of goose grease.

I watched *The Corn is Green*, about an Englishwoman who starts a school in Wales to teach young coal miners. In the movie, the students sing: "Sleep my child and peace attend thee, all through the night. Guardian angels God will send thee, all through the night." It sparked a latent memory.

Remembering those Welsh cakes in Wilkes-Barre and Llandovery, I looked for a recipe. I figured there must be one in the Butte cookbook, and sure enough, there was. I made them. They are similar to a scone but with more butter and are cooked on the griddle. They were delicious, especially with tea.

I listened to the audio book of *Dubliners* by James Joyce, read by Donal Donnelly. Hearing Donnelly's lyrical voice render Joyce's lyrical prose was a delight. About boarding house matron Mrs. Mooney, he wrote: "She dealt with moral problems as a cleaver deals with meat," a delectable simile if there ever was one. I could almost hear the cleaver falling as Mrs. Mooney prepared to deal with the moral problem under her roof.

I read the Robert Service poems that Grandpa Peter used to recite at parties and to Aunt Aila and Auntie Grace when they were children. The beginning of the "The Cremation of Sam McGee" awakened another memory from my childhood: "There are strange things done in the midnight sun by the men who moil for gold . . ." Somebody must have read it to me as a child; perhaps Mom recited it for me and my brother when we were little to keep us entertained on road trips.

I read books written by soldiers in the war. Erich Maria Remarque, who wrote *All Quiet on the Western Front*, was a German soldier in the war. His book is not about particular battles, it is about what it was like to be a German soldier in the war. Something about that book brought untold inspiration. I'd be reading it and get an idea about something for my book, put it down, and dash over to the computer and go on a writing binge. Usually it had nothing to do with the war. This went on the whole time I was reading it.

Siegried Sassoon's book *Memoirs of an Infantry Officer* I understood to be a novel based on his experience in the war. I read it for his observations, such as the one about poison gas being in its infancy and they'd probably all be dead before it had time to grow up.

I started but did not finish *Three Soldiers* by John dos Passos. It didn't mesh with the letters and memoirs I had read by American soldiers. Even though Dos Passos was an ambulance driver in the war, the story did not seem to be from his personal experience.

I watched every First World War era movie I could find: *Legends of the Fall*, *All Quiet on the Western Front*, *The Lost Battalion*, and many others. As with novels, I didn't consider movies to be source material, but by now I had done enough research to discern what was depicted realistically and what was not. Modern movie makers with large budgets often give great attention to visual historical detail, though not always. The visual images that were consistent with the historical record were helpful in searing what I already knew into my brain. One of my favorite movies was *La Grande Illusion*, about French prisoners of war. The cordial civility between enemy officers charged with killing each other was surreal. The senior German officer almost apologizes to the French officers for having to capture them. I thought about Uncle Denis getting care packages from home while in the prison camp. I wondered if the director and screenwriter, Jean Renoir (son of the painter), chose the title as a scoff at the book *The Great Illusion* by Norman Angell. That was the book I mentioned earlier, published in 1910, which proffered the notion that due to "financial and economic interdependence of nations," in any war both victor and vanquished would suffer. Since war was unprofitable, it wouldn't happen, no one would start it. Don't we wish. Four years after Angell's book was published, the Great War began—the war to end all wars that didn't. The great illusion indeed.

Normally I had three books going: a novel, a nonfiction book for research, and an audio book that could be either of those two. I found both reading and listening to good books to be great ways to get good writing into my head. Reading is to the writer what exercise is to the athlete. To be a good writer, I needed to absorb good writing, visually and audibly. I didn't want to contaminate my subconscious with bad writing. And to write something meaningful, I'd better not contaminate my subconscious with nonsense. Our minds can be a safe where we keep treasures or a trash bin where we collect garbage. We choose.

Also, to write well I needed to expand my vocabulary. Reading those nineteenth-century English novels turned out to be a great way to do that. Every time I came across a word I didn't know, or knew but didn't use, I looked it up and wrote down the definition in a little notebook. This was especially important for me, coming from the engineering and business world. To some extent, each profession has its own vocabulary, and there has been an unfortunate trend in business, due to the onslaught of management consultants, to make the simple sound complicated, which does not make for good writing. It doesn't make for good anything. Clarity makes for good writing. An expansive vocabulary aids clarity.

William Zinsser advised in his book *On Writing Well*: don't write something you wouldn't say. I understood this to mean, don't use words or expressions that I wouldn't use while speaking. Using words or expressions that do not sound natural can sound stilted. The purpose of an expanded vocabulary is not to show off, it is to make sense.

I would include an attendant admonishment: I wouldn't write about things I wouldn't discuss in polite company. My readers are, after all, polite company.

Great authors of days gone by didn't resort to tossing in gratuitously salacious or vulgar tidbits to shock us. I dare say everybody knew what was going on between Anna Karenina and Count Vronsky. Tolstoy didn't have to spell it out for us. I knew Bill Sikes was a vile creature because Charles Dickens effectively drew his character. I didn't need a string of profanities to make that clear. As film critic Kenneth Turan noted about a grisly movie scene, "it's not realism—it's making us squirm for squirming's sake." There's no need for that.

As for words, it is curious that we are attracted to some more than others, just like people. There are words I simply like the sound of, such as flummoxed and pixilated and trollop and prairie, such a poetic sound to prairie. Dipping further back in time, I was captivated by Daniel Defoe's use of language in *Moll Flanders*. I wanted to write that Sarah sallied forth, and whither she went, but I couldn't make it work.

I wanted to use "daft" somewhere. I like the sound of that one too. Grandma was the only person I ever heard use that word, usually about something she had done. I never did find a spot for it.

CHAPTER TWENTY-TWO

ON MY NEXT VISIT to Butte, I headed back up the hill to the archives, this time in search of newspaper articles about the war. I had been told that Marshal Foch tried to give Grandpa Peter the *Croix de Guerre* for saving that man's life, but Peter refused to accept it because Winks Brown, the man who helped pull the wounded man into the trench, had not been decorated. As with everything else, I wanted to corroborate this and figured Marshal Foch's visit would be in the newspapers. The trouble was, I didn't know the date. I sat down at the table in front of the big picture window and began the tedious process of going through old newspapers. Thankfully, the actual newspapers are at the archives. At least I didn't have to resort to microfilm. I sat there skimming the headlines, reading, turning the page, skimming, reading, lifting my eyes now and then to gaze at the mountains off in the distance, then more reading, turning, skimming, mind going into a fog after hours of this when my eyes fell on a tiny headline in the *Butte Miner*:

BRIDE'S FATHER STARTS ACTION
Son-in-Law Is Charged With Perjury in Allegation That He Declared 15-Year-Old Girl to be 18 Years of Age

I don't know why, but I read it. The son-in-law was William Hughes.
Oh my. Could he be our Bill, Grandma T's brother? I had to find out. Off I went to the Courthouse and found the marriage license and certificate. Yep. There was enough corroborating information. No doubt, he was our Bill. He was all of twenty, though he claimed to be twenty-one.
The girl's father had the marriage annulled. When I entered all this onto my time line, I realized that Bill was in jail awaiting trial for robbery when the annulment papers were filed. The perjury complaint was dropped.

While at the Courthouse, I looked for marriage licenses for my great-grandaunts and uncle. I had been told that Peter's uncle John Gribben waited until all his sisters were married before he got married. It sounds noble. Yet, as I collected wedding dates, I quickly saw that John married after his sisters Mary and Maggie, but before Bridget and Annie. I was disappointed.

I returned to the archives and resumed my forced march through the old newspapers, hunting for stories about Marshal Foch's visit to Butte after the war. I stumbled across several articles about men returning from the war, detailed accounts by Butte soldiers. The accounts of the battles tracked well with the division history, which gave me more confidence in the reporter's accuracy. I'd be reading along about a soldier's account of the war, and then—thin, nervous women need phosphate. What? Oh, it's an ad. I kept reading. These articles included many quotes by soldiers, making it all the more personal, exactly what I wanted.

At long last, I found the articles about Marshal Foch's visit to Butte. The papers included detailed articles about what was planned but next to nothing about what actually happened.

Oh, and that's another thing. Grandma always referred to him as Marshal Foch which was correct, but before he was named a marshal of France, he was a general. In writing the war narrative, I had to find out exactly when he was named a marshal of France, so I could identify him by the correct title at the time. That is why I introduced him in the narrative as General Foch and later called him Marshal Foch.

Next on my to-do list was the Homer Club, the literary club that sponsored Grandma for the vocational congress in Bozeman when she was a teenager. I read their meeting minutes over several years. It was interesting to see the books they read and discussed: *The Great Hunger* by Johan Boyer, *War in the Garden of Eden* by Kermit Roosevelt, *Letters from France*. None of this sounds light or trivial. Being trivial is a luxury. I doubt even the well set in Butte could afford it back then.

In the fall of 1917, the ladies hemmed hospital slings while discussing H.G. Wells. What an image.

I looked up the address of the woman who hosted the Homer Club meeting at which the members voted to send Grandma to the vocational congress in Bozeman. Then I drove over to see the house. It was way, way into the West Side, as far from an East Side boarding house as one could get and still be in Butte. It struck me how far apart these worlds were, literally and figuratively: Sarah's bawdy boarding house and the far reaches of the sophisticated West Side. Had I not looked up the address and driven over to see it, I might not have observed the vivid contrast between Grandma's world and the world of these well-to-do women.

In search of any record which might contain a familiar name, I looked up Grandma and her siblings in the school census records. More surprises. Great-grandma Sarah kept changing her name. Some years she was Anna, some years she was Sarah. Since there was only one Aila Hughes, there was no question it was our Sarah changing her name. I'd been told she used aliases. Quite by accident, now I had proof.

Next stop was the Butte library to look up census records. Again, I wasn't looking for anything in particular, just casting a wide net, never knowing what I might drag in. I slipped the microfilm roll for the 1920 census into the reader and found 415 Kemper, Sarah's boarding house on Parrot Flat. I proceeded to write down all the information for the family and all the boarders. Oh my—Roy Walsh was one of Sarah's boarders. I didn't know he lived with them. He was Archie's accomplice in the shooting at Renova. He was the boy who was hanged. So when Grandma said Roy was slow, she had first-hand knowledge of this. He lived with them. But then, Grandma wouldn't have said such a thing if she didn't have first-hand knowledge.

I noted the exact date the census was taken. It was in January 9, 1920. Archie was only fifteen years old.

Later, I would find these simple bits of information from the 1920 census significant for several parts of the story of which I was as yet unaware.

The census said Archie was born in Texas. Texas? Where did that come from? Oh, of course, Dallas, he was born in Dallas. Dallas, Pennsylvania.

That year Sarah called herself Anna in the census and in the city directory. At least she was consistent. I prepared a separate chart to keep track of Sarah's name changes.

I needed to find out when "the dry" was built. I wanted to know whether it was in place when Grandpa Peter started working in the mines in 1914. The dry was where the miners cleaned up and put on dry clothes after their shift, so they wouldn't catch their death walking home in sweat-drenched clothes in forty below weather. I needed to read the other Butte papers for stories about the war. Butte had three dailies back then: the *Butte Daily Post*, the *Butte Miner*, and the *Anaconda Standard*. I needed to look for stories about Butte High's graduation when Grandma graduated. I needed to find a description of Butte circa 1915, when Grandma arrived.

It was time to go home. I was exhausted. Two weeks was all the research I could do at one time. There came a point when I could not absorb another thing without a break. I would have to come back.

As I was readying to leave, Uncle Ed handed me a box of papers and said, "Here's something you might want." He pulled out the biggest bundle. "It's the abstract for your grandmother's house," he said. I thanked him and stuffed it in my luggage.

Chapter Twenty-three

HOME AGAIN. Transcribe notes into the computer, ruminate, read, ponder, write. As I sat at my computer one day gazing out the window at the long sweep of hole number six on the golf course behind my house, thinking about the war narrative and how to describe the terrain of the Argonne that Grandpa Peter and the Wild West Division fought through, wondering whether I should take another trip to France to look it over again, it occurred to me—the undulation of the fairway, with those swells and knolls throughout, was much the same. I had the Argonne battlefield in miniature behind my house.

Another afternoon as I sat there typing away, out of the corner of my eye I saw something hurtling toward me and BAM, crashed into the window. It gave me quite a start. The smaller bird flew off. The other righted himself, shook and straightened his feathers, and stood there next to the sliding glass door. He was a golden brown bird of prey, a magnificent looking creature, but those talons, oh my, did they look fierce. Thank God I wasn't sitting outside when they crashed into the window. I sat very still and watched him. After a few minutes, he flew off. I looked in the encyclopedia and found out he was a falcon.

MOM AND DAD and Uncle Joe came to town for my birthday. We spent the afternoon exploring Valley of Fire, north of Las Vegas, seeing petroglyphs drawn on the red rock, the same red rock from which burst tenacious sage green leaves adorned with white blossoms. When we returned to my house, I had a message from my realtor in Maryland. My house in Rockville had been on the market for three months with not one bite. The message said he had an offer. I called back. It was a good offer. I said, take it. The house had appreciated considerably, giving me more of a financial cushion for writing the book, which was clearly not going to be finished by the end of 1998 as I had planned.

Turning now to Grandma's house, I unfurled the abstract Uncle Ed had given me. I had never seen one of these before. It's a history of who owned the house and what loans were taken against it. I flipped ahead to my grandparents' purchase of the house. Oh my goodness! Grandma's name is the only name on it, meaning the house was never in Peter's name. There must be a story behind that. I started making phone calls. Mom was surprised. She didn't know the reason. Auntie Mary and Aunt Aila were astounded to learn that the house was never in their father's name, only in their mother's. I wondered if Judge Lynch or Uncle John Gribben had anything to do with it, or maybe Grandma was putting her foot down with Peter. He couldn't sell it out from under her or lose it in a card game if he didn't own it.

Mom said her father had life insurance from the war and named his mother as beneficiary. He refused to name his wife and children. Even so, Grandma paid the premium until they could no longer afford it. He said he didn't want to name Grandma as beneficiary because, if he died first, he didn't want another man to get the money if she remarried, and yet always insisted he would outlive her. Perhaps this had some bearing on her insisting the house be her name, assuming she insisted on it.

Over and over again I learned: don't overlook anything. The abstract for a house—how pedestrian, and yet look where it led. Until I followed a thread, I didn't know how ornate a tapestry I would find.

I requested a copy of Grandma's high school transcript to confirm that she started high school in Butte in 1915. On it was a handwritten note saying a copy had been sent to Radcliffe. Radcliffe? I had never heard mention of Radcliffe. It didn't say anything about her transcript being sent to Bozeman, which was where I always assumed Grandma was planning to go to college when her mother ripped up her clothes to keep her from going. Knowing her scholarship was to Bozeman, I never thought to ask, Grandma, where were you going to go to college? I called Radcliffe. The woman said they keep records only for those who attended, not for those who applied and were accepted but did not attend.

These days I am listening to *House of Mirth* by Edith Wharton. At the part about Lily allowing that odious man to invest money for her, so she thought, and his expecting something in return, I thought about Grandma declining the offer of financial help to attend law school. "You never know if there are strings attached," she said. Wharton's Lily would have done well to be so wise. I wonder if Grandma read the book.

Grandma told me about her married boss at the post office saying he didn't hire women (in permanent positions, she had a temporary appointment), but he'd make at exception for her if she'd "go out with him." Of course, she wouldn't. After this pestering went on for quite some time, Grandma confided to her friend Rhea, Rhea told her boss, who was Senator Murray, and Grandma's boss was replaced. I had Grandma's employment records. Her employment card listed the date, her job title, and her pay, and whenever any of those things changed. While at the archives, I found out when the reprobate boss was sacked and the new man took the job. I entered these dates on my time line. Oh my gosh. The day after he was named to the job, the new boss gave Grandma her regular appointment. Though I knew what happened, I had no idea it was one of the first things he did.

CHAPTER TWENTY-FOUR

STILL IN SEARCH of more about Grandpa Peter's experience in the war, in October of 1998, I flew back east to do research at the U.S. Army Military History Institute at the War College in Carlisle, Pennsylvania. To write a personal story, I needed personal details. I hoped to find them in Carlisle.

"Which brigade?" the woman asked.

"The 181st," I said.

While I waited, a man printed something from the computer and handed it to me. It was a bibliography. "The biggest file is from Farley Granger," he said. We both wondered if he was related to the actor.

The woman returned with a box. I sat down at a table and opened it. By far the fattest files were marked Farley Granger. He was an officer in Peter's regiment. Thank God he had the foresight to save all this and donate it to the archives, or his family did. The thought of someone throwing such things away makes me want to weep. Methodically I started going through the contents of the box, reading every piece of paper pertaining to the 362nd Regiment. I was reading the actual field messages and field orders written by the officers right on the battlefield, also memoirs, letters, operations reports. It was raw data, that's the best, not someone's interpretation. It's like using fresh ingredients in cooking, so much the better; though as in cooking, it's also much more work. I tried to make sense of all these fragments of information, all these pieces to a giant jigsaw puzzle, what would it look like?

Sergeant Major George P. Dykes had collected field orders and messages, and he just happened to be with the Second Battalion, Peter's battalion. What luck. They were addressed to Regard, Racoon, Regard 2, Regard 3. Such urgency came through. I must find a way to use them verbatim, but first I'd have to figure out who was Racoon, who was Regard . . .

One message was from "Queen." I figured that had to be a code name too. Later I would discover that Captain Clyde Queen was the first commander of Peter's company.

I was starting to see discrepancies, or I should say, apparent discrepancies. Was there an artillery barrage before the attack on Gesnes or not? I would have to investigate further.

In "Who Won the War, by William Johnston in collaboration with John Pershing," General Johnston (Peter's division commander) complained that Pershing did not credit the 91st for their bravery and accomplishments in his book *My Experiences in the World War*. General Pershing wrote: "The 91st Division overcame strong initial resistance and advanced rapidly to Epinonville, which it entered but did not hold." They didn't hold it because they were ordered to withdraw because the flanking divisions had not advanced as far. Pershing neglected that detail. Johnston also said Pershing seemed more interested in criticizing the Allies than in writing about the accomplishments of his own troops. I had the same reaction when I read Pershing's book.

Pershing's response to Johnston, dated June 13, 1931, was curt: thank you for your letter, I'm sure my book is accurate.

But Johnston wasn't done. "Every man of the 91st knows the 35th ran away, 9/29, under artillery fire alone," meaning they weren't up close fighting the German infantry, as was the 91st. It sounded akin to having McClellan and Grant side by side in the same battle; McCellan falling back, while Grant blazed ahead. Then the powers that be booted out the divisions led by McClellan types and left the Grant style commander, Johnston, in place.

What little I know about them, I admire both these men, Pershing and Johnston. It is easy to criticize historical figures, to judge them with the benefit of hindsight, something the criticized soul did not have. He was on the ground, having to make difficult decisions on the spot with limited information, flawed though it might have been, but he didn't know how it was flawed. Military officers in battle make such decisions in such circumstances every day. Granted, some are better at it than others.

About the order to attack and subsequent order to withdraw from Gesnes, Johnston speculated that the corps command sacrificed the 91st in their reports to cover their blunder. I read elsewhere that Pershing replaced the corps commander shortly after the disaster at Gesnes. Even before the attack on Gesnes, there had been much confusion coming from the corps command. The 91st was in and out of Epinonville at least twice because they were ordered to advance and then withdraw. It was confusing—the chaos of war, the fog of war research.

The table of killed and wounded showed that Grandpa Peter's regiment, the 362nd, suffered the most casualties in the division, no doubt because of the massacre at Gesnes. I read about the moments leading up to the attack. A soldier said he fell over a dead Yank, dead in a hedge. I read the day-by-day description of the battles. Sitting in the mud, sleeping in the mud. Miserable. No hot food. Traffic jams, rain, more rain, bullets and bombs, no sleep. Miserable. Dead men, dead horses. Confusion on the battlefield, who was where, who had advanced, who had not advanced. Into Epinonville, out of Epinonville, into Epinonville. Such confusion. Little or no support from flanking troops, little or no artillery support. Grim. Taking land, ordered to give up that land. Depressing. Gas, lots of poison gas. Grisly. Gas masks on, gas masks off. How did any of them survive this with their wits intact? It sounds superhuman.

I found questionnaires completed by members of Grandpa Peter's regiment. Unfortunately these were sent to the veterans in the 1970s. By then, many had already passed away. Farley Granger wrote copiously on his, and yes, he was the father of the actor. He complained that the officers were lawyers and bankers with no horse sense, no guts. He praised the Salvation Army for being right up there with them at the front, under heavy artillery, serving them hot coffee. "God bless them and remember them," he wrote.

Stanley Kerr of Big Timber, Montana, wrote: "A man cannot be trained for combat, it's too varied, too demanding. A man has that in him or he does not, cannot be trained . . . The Nation had no right to draft a German citizen to fight Germans."

He also wrote: "Our nation's existence depends on patriotism." He was eighty-eight years old and sounded disillusioned about the state of affairs in the country.

Amos Hatch of Utah remembered Colonel Parker's pearl-handled sidearm. He was Parker's runner. As for what the soldiers spent their money on, he wrote: "Wine and women, and gambling—cards and dice." As for the battles, he said he was scared and soaked to the skin. "We were sure we had made the world safe for democracy. How naive we were."

Kendloss Jacobsen, a Utah farmer and cook in Company I, remembered taking cold baths in a lake. He said their uniforms weren't adequate for the cold. He said he was more patriotic after the war.

Eugene Knoke, a rancher from Livingston, Montana, said their rifles jammed when the least bit dirty, rations were poor, their leaders were good. He said, "Our unit was almost all Westerners used to living an open life where a man's personal property is respected." He said there was very little theft in the unit and morale was good. He said they didn't get along well with the English soldiers but did get along with the Belgian and French soldiers.

Harold Meyer, a businessman from San Francisco in Company L, said the rations were fine if you could get them. Did he have any unusual assignments? Yes, all of them. He thought the Aussies and Zealanders were very good troops.

Earl Morrison of Minnesota explained some of the slang. Canned Willie was corned beef. Slum gullion was stew. Somewhere else I read that canned goldfish was canned salmon.

Chaplain Ralph Davis of Hollywood noted the disparity between the officers' quarters and the living conditions of the men on the troop ship. He said rations were insufficient until they reached France. Once at the French rest camp, they ate well. He said most divisions were at the front no more than five days at a time. The 91st fought and held the line much longer, under constant shelling. He said it rained most of the time and was cold and miserable. "What a blessing to be dry and clean," he said.

Quite a treasure trove these questionnaires turned out to be. I wish one of the questions had asked about acts of bravery they witnessed.

After spending several days going through that box, taking notes, making copies, I went to the library at the Military History Institute. I told librarian John Slonaker what I was researching and showed him the bibliography I'd been given. It listed a regimental history. I asked where I could find it. I didn't find it in the archives. He said, "James Controvich has it." I asked how I could find him. "He lives in Springfield, Massachusetts," he said. He recommended the Harries book, *The Last Days of Innocence*, about American involvement in the war. I noted the title. He gave me a tour of the library—quite a collection, a bit overwhelming. I said I'd like to know what was happening with the German troops who opposed the 91st. I thought it would be helpful to read German accounts of the battles and find out what they were anticipating. John showed me those books. Unfortunately they were in German, and I don't read German. I told him

I was looking for information about the Prussian Guard. He disappeared and soon reappeared with a book, in English, open to the right page.

I mentioned that I was looking for information about Irish soldiers in the British army. He said a book had been recently published about the Irish Catholic Division, *Ireland's Unknown Soldiers: The 16th Irish Division in the Great War, 1914–1918.* That was the division in which my great-uncles fought.

He had so much knowledge in his head that was of great benefit to me. The internet is a great convenience; more and more research materials are becoming available through it all the time, but it can never replace actually going to these archives and libraries. So often, things came up in the course of conversation, and the librarian or archivist mentioned something I didn't know I was looking for. I was fortunate I went to Carlisle when I did. Later I called and asked for Mr. Slonaker and was told he had retired.

Since I was staying in Carlisle awhile, I thought it would be fun to stay at a bed and breakfast rather than a hotel and booked a room at Jacob's Resting Place. What a find it turned out to be. A husband and wife owned it. She ran the bed and breakfast. He was a retired military officer who collected Civil War artifacts, which were all over the house. It looked like a place you would visit on a historic tour but would be relegated to the walkway behind the velvet ropes. To top it off, she was a great cook. One morning I had blintzes for breakfast, another day sausage cups filled with scrambled eggs, always homemade rolls or muffins. Delicious. I ate off dishes that were the same pattern as Catherine the Great's.

After a very full week, I drove to Bethesda, Maryland, attended a friend's wedding, then drove to Colonial Beach, Virginia, and stayed with my cousin Aila and her husband, Jack. Aila had spent a lot of time with Grandma and told me her memories. We talked about how remarkable Grandma was, so impeccable, such a lady, amazing considering her upbringing, and then look at the choices her brothers Archie and Bill made, both went to prison. At this, Jack remarked in his velvety southern accent, "I always say, Aila, genes will tell. Genes will tell."

"But Grandma had the same genes as her brothers," Aila replied.

CHAPTER TWENTY-FIVE

AILA'S MEMORIES prompted my memories. I quickly wrote them down, fearing if I didn't, they could be as fleeting as the wind and be gone, never to return. Often, as I was falling asleep at night or reading or going for a walk or making dinner or doing laundry, random thoughts about the manuscript would pop into my head, and I would hurriedly jot them down—a way to word something, where to include something. Sometimes it was a full paragraph of inspiration. It was as if the book were out there in the ether, I was getting it in snippets, sometimes rapid-fire snippets, all of it would come in time with patience and hard work. Some days I felt as if my head were going to explode.

I began sorting through all I had collected about the war and tried to make sense of it. I read more books. I noticed that some authors were quite thorough in documenting which divisions faltered while giving short shrift to the divisions that triumphed.

Thankfully James Controvich had a listed phone number. I called and asked about the 362nd regimental history. He said he would send it to me for the cost of the copying and postage. I sent him a check, and soon the regimental history arrived in the mail. It was colorfully written, not at all a drab retelling, but a spirited, personal account, with surreal and humorous anecdotes intermingled amidst the horror. I wanted to depict how gruesome the battles were, not gratuitously so, but to give a vivid sense of what Peter experienced. The soldiers who wrote the regimental history provided much fodder; they did not pull punches.

I was struck by the part about the French officer sitting at a linen-draped table under a tree as the troops readied to launch the massive Meuse Argonne Offensive. He hands the menu to an American officer walking by and invites him to join him. This display of civility in the middle of chaos seemed surreal; yet, if we don't hold on to such civility, where does that leave us?

Though I had a tremendous amount of material telling me what happened, I wanted more, more that was personal, more about what it was like to be at the front with Peter. I found more letters written by soldiers, books by soldiers, unpublished memoirs by soldiers, accounts by war correspondents. I remember a soliloquy in the movie *Foreign Correspondent* about how the word "correspondent" carries a different connotation from "reporter," the war correspondent's account being personal, getting at the essence of things, as opposed to the dispassionate reporting of only who, what, where, and when. While perusing the Forsyth papers, I stumbled across a passage that Irvin Cobb wrote about the war. It was so heartfelt, about the enormity of the war, who could comprehend it? I looked for a place to quote him in the manuscript.

At the Fort Lewis museum archives, I found more letters written by soldiers in Grandpa Peter's division, the 91st. They trained there; it was then called Camp Lewis. R. Barrett, who served in the 316th Supply Train, wrote to Elsie shortly before the division went into battle in France: "We are kept on the constant jump . . The Huns cannot win and they fear our boys like we fear poison . . . When we do have the good fortune of seeing a fair little madam we can't parlez vous so what's the use. . . When the boys get back what a time you girls will have." And in another letter to her: "So you are a businessman these days . . . by the time we fellows get home I suppose we will find girls holding down all our jobs and we will either have to marry the girl so she can support us or go on the bum."

Just before they went into battle in Flanders, he wrote that the uniform is a "mighty fine thing to wear," and "I wouldn't have missed the experience of having been in this fuss, and I wouldn't go home before it was over for $1M—and I could easily use a million too . . . Things look good to me. We don't want peace—give us till early Spring and we will kick 'em to a frazzle and all American officers & men feel the same." I doubt that. Barrett was in the supply train, not at the front of the front experiencing the full brunt of the horrors as Peter was. Only one soldier in the 316th Supply Train died during the war. When deciding which soldiers to quote, I always considered: what unit was he in, was he up there at the front shooting his rifle and being shot at and gassed and jabbed with a bayonet, as was Peter, or was he behind the lines in a support role? Their perspectives would be quite different. William Newland from Massachusetts wrote: "I have been in the trenches eight months & have seen quite a lot of service, am quite willing to go home anytime they want to send me."

While waiting to go home after the armistice, Private First Class O. J. Swanes of the 347th Machine Gun Battalion wrote: "I used to say, when I was up on the front and laying in a shell hole while the Germans were shooting at us, that if I ever got out of this alive I would never worry about anything any more, but it seems we forget very quickly & here I am thinking about the fish business."

By now I had amassed quite a collection of maps, including several large maps of the battlefield, some showing only the 91st, some showing troop movements by day. I spread them out over my dining room table so I could track the progress of the troops as I wrote. I read my notes, studied the maps, read more, studied more, tried to make sense of it until my brain said enough already and I had to stop and go for a walk. Some insight would pop into my head as I walked, and I'd hurry home and investigate it.

The German lines of defense were marked on some of the maps. These had people names: the Brunhilde Line, the Siegfried Line, and so on. I continued to study the maps, write, go back over my notes, read more books. After days, weeks, months, of this, one day out of the blue, Wotan popped in my head. The Wotan Line, Wotan, *The Ring*, Wagner. While doing my homework in college, I used to listen to "Sunday Afternoon at the Met" on the radio. Before the opera, the announcer would summarize the story. I remembered hearing him do so for Wagner's *Ring*, and I remembered Wotan. I remembered the Wotan Line on the map of the German lines of defense. I wondered if the German officers named their lines of defense after characters in Wagner's opera. I had to find out.

Though familiar with the music, I knew next to nothing about the story. I thought, I'll get the CDs for Wagner's *Ring* and read the inserts, they probably list the cast of characters, and then I'll compare them to the lines of defense. I pulled out the map showing the German lines of defense on the Meuse Argonne battlefield and made a list of the names. There was no Wotan Line. Where had I gotten that idea? Well that didn't deter me, I must have seen it somewhere, and I bounded off to the library. (I just looked it up. The Wotan Line was up at the northern end of the Western Front, near Ypres.) I found all but one of the CDs for Wagner's *Ring of the Nibelung*. The cast of characters was listed. The names didn't match the lines of defense. Perhaps the names on the missing CD matched. Not knowing whether I had all the names and wanting to know more about the opera than what was in the CD case, I told the librarian my dilemma, and without a word, he was off and returned with a book—*Opera for Dummies*. Perfect. It told the story and listed the cast of characters. I checked those names against the names of the lines of defense. Some matched, some didn't. Hmmm. I looked in the card catalog and found the book *Nibelungenlied*. Though it is called an epic poem, this was written in story form. The introduction explained that there was more than one version of the story, from Scandinavian sources and from German sources. Wagner used Scandinavian sources. This book contained the German version. I read the book and made a list of the cast of characters. The names matched the German lines of defense. It seems an epic war demanded names from an epic story about an epic past.

The *Nibelungenlied* tells the story of the Huns defeating the Burgundians in 437. I suppose that is why the German officers liked it. Kriemhilde, sister of the Burgundian king, marries the king of the Huns and she provokes the fight, and therefore is responsible for their ruin. So it's their own fault.

I spent two days chasing down and studying the *Nibelungenlied*, for what ended up being a couple of paragraphs in my book, but I had to do it. Something kept tickling at the back of my mind, driving me to do it. I enjoyed writing that part. I hope you enjoyed reading it.

And still I kept reading. *La guerre, toujours la guerre.*

In the accounts I had read thus far about how the war started, every author mentioned that Austria-Hungary imposed ultimatums on Serbia after Archduke Franz Ferdinand and his wife were assassinated in Sarajevo, but none said what those ultimatums were and which Serbia refused and why. I wanted to know. I trotted back to the library on another hunting expedition. No luck.

Over Christmas, while visiting Mom and Dad in Kennewick, I went to their library and parked myself in front of the First World War section and started pulling books off the shelf and looking in the indices. Finally, I found the list of ultimatums in an old book published in 1926. In a nutshell, the Austrians demanded that the Serbs suppress anti-Austria activities, groups, and publications; denounce all anti-Austria propaganda; allow Austria-Hungary to help suppress anti-Austria subversive movements within Serbia; and that Austrian officials participate in investigating and prosecuting co-conspirators within

Serbia. Serbia agreed to do all within international law but did not concede to demands that impinged on her sovereignty. That did not suit the Austrians, and there tumbled the first domino.

This particular author, an American college professor, had many disturbing things to say about how the war started. He blamed France and Russia along with Germany and Austria. He thought they were all up to no good and wanted war for their own selfish gains. He gave specifics about what transpired between France and Russia in the run-up to the war. It was fascinating, full of shadowy intrigue, the stuff of a political thriller, and quite inflammatory, so much so that I thought I better look into it further. I did, and could neither confirm nor negate his allegations and therefore left them out.

As I mentioned before, I wanted to personalize everything as much as possible. I wanted to write about real people doing real things, saying real things. As for the principals involved in starting the war, I named several, but in some instances I chose to name the country instead. When I spoke of countries, I used the traditional convention of the feminine pronoun rather than the vague, lifeless "it." This worked for Serbia and France and Belgium and Britain, but I couldn't see Germany as "she." And yet there is no convention for using "he" in this context. After much mental contorting, I settled on always saying Germany or the Fatherland, no pronouns for Germany.

While researching Irish history, I stumbled upon this line from Kipling: "The dark eleventh hour draws on and see's us sold." Though it is from the poem "Ulster 1912," I was struck by how apt the sentiment was to the start of the First World War. It could be from a poem called "Europe 1914." I tried to find a way to work it into the war narrative, a fitting climax to the part about how the war began, how all those European lands went to war with each other, and so quickly. Instead, I used the first quote that popped into my head: "and they all fall down," which indeed they did. I thought the fact that "they all fall down" comes from a nursery rhyme made it all the more ironic, though for the life of me, I couldn't remember which nursery rhyme.

The other day as I sat writing this, curiosity got the better of me, and the internet now makes such searches so easy. Oh, of course, it's from "Ring Around the Rosy." "Ring around the rosy, a pocket full of posies, ashes, ashes, they all fall down." I remember singing it as a child, we all holding hands and walking in a ring, and at the end, we all fell down. I never thought about there being stories behind nursery rhymes, but apparently there may be for this one. The theory is that the rhyme dates back to the time of the Plague. "Ring around the rosy" signified the red sores from the Plague, "ashes, ashes" because they burned the dead, and they all fell down and died. Learning that magnifies the irony—the First World War, a manmade plague.

SHELBY FOOTE, who wrote an epic history of the American Civil War, advised war researchers to visit the battlefields at the time of year when the battle took place. This way one could see whether there were leaves on the trees that would have impeded the troops' view of the enemy and such things. Though the battles in which Grandpa Peter fought took place in the fall, and I visited the battlefields in the spring while doing my research, I had visited First World War battlefields in that part of France a few years earlier while on vacation, and that trip was in the fall. I remembered wandering through thick, cottony fog, seeing the war memorials shrouded by it, the same kind of fog Grandpa Peter fought through. I pulled out my pictures from that trip. I could see the fog. The more I could get a sense of being there, the more I could put you there.

Christopher Sims at Flanders Field recommended Vera Brittain's autobiography *Testament of Youth*. Vera Brittain was a twenty-year-old student at Oxford when Europe erupted into war in 1914. She abandoned her studies to volunteer as a nurse. Soon she would suffer the horrible heartbreak of losing her brother and her fiancé to the bullets and bombs of the Western Front. Late in the war, her parents summoned her home because they simply could not handle the maid. Her parents were not old. Perhaps the troublesome maid excuse was simply a ruse to get her to come home. Shortly after she went home, the hospital where she had been stationed in northern France was shelled. Nurses were forced to take refuge in the trenches. Some were killed. Her parents may have saved her life.

Some nonfiction books about history are written to teach and be enjoyable to read. These are generally written in narrative form, they are stories, and when well done, are quite readable. Others are written to document everything about a particular subject or person. These books have interesting parts but also much that is seemingly prosaic and ponderous to the casual reader, though quite helpful to researchers. I would say *Testament of Youth* bridged those two categories. Vera Brittain's life was interesting.

She took part in one of the most momentous events in history, the First World War. Though some of the details she documented, in particular the tedious minutia of League of Nations meetings, could be a chore to wade through, for someone seeking a front-row seat to that bit of history, it is quite helpful. History certainly benefited from her writing all that down.

All through my research and writing, I had the sense that the story was big, big in the sense of being important. I felt I had taken on a tremendous responsibility in setting out to tell it. I wanted to hold up the same high standards for writing her story that Grandma set for living her life. I felt I owed it to her. Though I felt this about the entire book, I felt it in a particularly profound way toward the war narrative. I thought of the souls of all those departed soldiers and felt I would have a lot to answer for if I didn't get it right.

I WANTED TO KNOW more about military funerals circa 1937, so I could better describe Peter's. Someone suggested I speak with Colonel Ray Read of the Montana National Guard. I told him about Peter's funeral, how the American Legion processed from the funeral home uptown all the way down to the church, then all the way out to the cemetery, which was several miles.

"What did he do to deserve that?" he asked.

I said he was awarded the *Croix de Guerre* for saving a man's life in Flanders. I asked if that kind of funeral was unusual.

"Yes, but in Butte they'd do it," he said. Then he asked, "If he was awarded the *Croix de Guerre*, why didn't he get the *Distinguished Service Cross*?"

I said I didn't know. I had been puzzled all along that Peter was decorated by France but not by his own country. Colonel Read's comment made me more curious. I read more about medals.

The *Distinguished Service Cross* was "presented to persons serving with the Army who distinguished themselves by extraordinary heroism in connection with military operations against an armed enemy."

The *Medal of Honor* was presented to soldiers who "distinguished themselves conspicuously by gallantry and intrepidity at the risk of life above and beyond the call of duty while in action involving actual conflict with an armed enemy."

The U.S. Army's history of the First World War, *American Armies and Battlefields in Europe*, from which I culled those criteria, included the citations for those decorated with the *Medal of Honor.*

While under heavy fire, Second Lieutenant Albert E. Baesel of the 37th Division attempted to rescue a wounded man two hundred yards from the assault line. Just as he heaved the man onto his shoulder to carry him to safety, the two were killed. For this he was posthumously awarded the *Medal of Honor.*

Sergeant William Sawelson of the 78th Division heard a wounded man in a shell hole calling out for water. Though under heavy machine gun fire, Sergeant Sawelson crawled out of his shell hole and gave the man water from his canteen. He crawled back to his shell hole to get more water and proceeded to crawl again to the wounded man and was shot and killed. For this he was posthumously awarded the *Medal of Honor.*

I pulled out the *Croix de Guerre* citation for Grandpa Peter and reread it. "Near Steenbrugge, Belgium, on October 31, 1918, he went out to the aid of a seriously wounded non-commissioned officer who had fallen in a very exposed place and under violent machine gun and artillery fire, gave him first aid."

I had written that Peter climbed out of the trench and ran to the wounded man and brought him back to the trench and gave him first aid. As I reread the citation I realized that wasn't what happened. It said Peter gave the wounded man first aid "under violent machine gun and artillery fire." So Peter gave him first aid while he was still out on the battlefield, while he was being shot at, in plain view of the enemy, further exposing himself to danger. I corrected the manuscript. I thought more about what the citation said. The man's wounds must have been visibly horrific if Peter felt he had to attend to them right away, before taking him back to the relative safety of the trench. I debated whether to ponder this in the book. I decided not to. It was a dramatic scene. I didn't want to sap the drama out of it with verbosity.

One puzzle as yet unsolved was whether Peter's regiment had artillery support prior to their attack on Gesnes. Some soldiers said yes, some said no. I reread every source I could find to determine which version of events was correct. I read and read but could not definitively say one way or the other. Finally I threw up my hands and concluded, I'll never know for sure. I decided, I'll just write what I know: some witnesses said there was artillery support, some said there was not. The solution was obvious once it finally dawned on me. When faced with two conflicting but equally credible sources, I provided both.

The war hovered over the lives of my grandparents long after the armistice was signed. I considered whether or not to delve into the furor over war bonuses. This certainly affected my grandparents since Grandpa was eligible, and they could always use the money. In 1932, fourteen years after the war ended, during the depths of the Great Depression, veterans marched on Washington and demanded the bonus money. Troops were called out to disperse the crowd. It turned into a tragic and controversial chapter in our nation's history, and included prominent protagonists, namely Hoover and MacArthur.

However, another rule I set down for myself was: the more controversial, the more inflammatory, the more research. It bears repeating: what is thought to be common knowledge can be common mythology. History is not the place to document our personal preconceived notions not rooted in fact. No matter how long a person has been dead or a company gone, a reputation is a reputation; to sully one without garnering all the facts, in context, and thoroughly examining those facts, would be irresponsible. In order to write about the bonus march, I would have to examine all sides, giving the benefit of the doubt to those who appeared to be the villains to see if they were indeed villains, and scrutinizing the actions of those who appeared to be victims, to see if there was more to it. As Mr. Jaggers advised Pip, "Take nothing on its looks, take everything on evidence." It is easy to see one side as all good and the other as all bad. Sometimes that is the case; however, real life is usually not that simple. The truth of the matter can be more complicated, and more interesting, though difficult to ascertain. To be fair to all involved in the bonus march would require a mountain of research, and I decided not to do that and left it out of the book. I followed my intuition on such matters. When something inside tugged at me to pursue a certain subject, I pursued it. If the thought of researching something filled me with dread, I dropped it.

Also, at the part of the book where the bonus march happened, I was so deep into what was happening in my grandparents' lives, I thought, my readers have enough history to set the stage. Now they want to know what is happening with Peter and Aila. What was necessary to the story was that Peter got the bonus money, and how he and Grandma used it. That I included.

I considered exploring the causes of the Great Depression, another subject about which I would have had to do a mountain of research. Some background would have helped set the stage, yet I feared more detail would have diluted the drama at that part of the story, so I didn't delve into it.

There's a cartoon where Snoopy is sitting atop his doghouse, busily writing his great novel. His hero declares to his sweetheart that his love for her is higher than the highest mountain, which is Mount Everest at over twenty-nine thousand feet, and his love for her is deeper than the deepest ocean, which is the Mariana Trench at over thirty-five thousand feet.

Snoopy concludes that his hero is a terrible bore.

One can lose the point in the minutia. More can simply be too much. Where to draw the line between enough and too much, that was the recurring quandary, where indeed.

And yet, I like going to another place and time when I read, and the historical backdrop is what puts me there. Also, detail can add drama. I could have written that Peter saved a man's life. Instead I described what happened, that he ran out of the trench and attended to his wounds while being shot at, demonstrating that Peter didn't just save the man's life, he put his own on the line to do so.

Research can pull the author in many different directions. I realized, I must put a frame around the book; much as when I worked as an engineer, I had to define the scope of the project. It took quite a while for me to impose this discipline on myself, because I found everything so interesting. At the beginning, I saw my book as a precious box in which I wanted to place every treasure I found. As I pieced together this giant jigsaw puzzle, I found many pieces that didn't fit inside the frame. Even so, I never discarded them. I saved them for another puzzle.

I REMEMBER AN afternoon when I had a stack of books about the First World War sitting before me. They were due at the library. I had written that part of the book. It was time to go on. I had to return the books. I felt as though I were saying goodbye to dear friends, and I didn't want to say goodbye. I told myself, I can go visit them later. It's not goodbye forever. It's *au revoir* and not *adieu*.

I became very sentimental about my subject matter.

CHAPTER TWENTY-SIX

ONE OF THE ITEMS on my ever growing to-do list was to learn more about Grandpa Peter working in the linen mill in Belfast when he was a boy. From relatives, I learned that he started out sorting; his sisters were doffers and worked standing in puddles in their bare feet. That was all I knew. What did it mean? Off I went to the library. I found books about fabric, but nothing about the people who made the fabric. Stumped, I put that in my "deal with this later" pile and went on to something else.

As Christmas approached, and I began to receive Christmas cards, one arrived from Honora. She had also worked for Bechtel as a mechanical engineer and had left the company some time ago. Last I heard, she was getting her master's in library science. As I opened the letter, I thought, she must be done with her master's by now, I wonder what she's up to. In her letter, she said she had finished her master's and was now at North Carolina State University working in the textiles library.

I couldn't believe it. I had no idea there were textile libraries. On her letter was her email address. I dashed off a note explaining that I was writing a book. I provided my cryptic clues and asked if she could help. Immediately she wrote back: "Ahh, now I know why God sent me here . . . to help with your book!" A few days later, I received a packet from Honora with the rest of the story. Doffers replaced full spindles of yarn with empty spindles. The yarn was wet as it spun, forming puddles on the floor, hence my great-aunts removed their shoes when they doffed, so their shoes wouldn't get wet. Peter sorted flax fibers by size. Honora even found information about the particular linen mill where Peter and his sisters worked.

I just found another insanely ambitious plan that I wrote for finishing the book. It was dated March 13, 1999. I was going to edit one chapter a day, forty chapters, forty days. This was in notebook number seven. I would fill a dozen notebooks.

That summer of 1999 as I traveled through Montana, I heard much worry about forest fires. The grass was tinder dry.

Auntie Mary and Uncle Ed had just moved into their new house and were still vacating the old. While cleaning out the barn on their old property, Uncle Ed came across a bayonet and gas mask from the First World War, things left behind by the prior owners who were friends of my grandparents. The husband was in the war with Grandpa Peter. Uncle Ed asked if I'd like to have the gas mask and bayonet. I said yes. I was delighted to have artifacts from the war I was researching.

I had my golf clubs with me in a hard travel case, a perfect place to pack an old bayonet and gas mask. Then I got to thinking, I better call the airline, just in case. It seemed odd, bringing a bayonet on an airplane, even though it was in my checked luggage. The man at the airline wasn't concerned about the bayonet; he just wanted to know whether the gas mask had an oxygen canister. It did not. No oxygen for those guys, just filtration.

At the end of one trip to Butte, a wicked squall blew in as I sat on the plane waiting to take off. I was mesmerized, watching the hail and violent wind, a wind so strong it was almost visible along the ground. Living in Las Vegas, I hardly ever see weather. I was relieved when the pilot announced, we'll wait this one out.

As I COLLECTED birth certificates, marriage licenses, and naturalization records and entered these dates on my time line, I soon discovered that I had several different dates of birth for some of my relatives. I used the birth certificate for the actual date, but I still noted the dates from other documents in case it proved significant for some reason down the road. My great-granduncle John Gribben's birth certificate said he was born in Ireland on April 27, 1870. According to the age he provided for the ship manifest, he was born in 1873. On his naturalization papers, he said he was born in 1874. According to the age on his marriage license, he was born in 1877. It was the same for my great-grandparents Arthur and Sarah. A person's year of birth seemed to be a trivial piece of information for my nineteenth-century Celtic kin. At a time when staying clothed, fed, and sheltered were over-riding concerns, who had time for such trivialities?

When culling information from death certificates, I always looked to see who was the informant. Was this person in a position to know the particulars of the deceased's origins? And if he or she was in a position to know, but didn't, perhaps that told me something.

As for census data, other than the fact the person was there— the actual purpose of the census—I often took the rest of the information with a grain of salt, since I didn't know who provided the information for the household. Many households included more than immediate family. If a man was indifferent as to his own age, I can't imagine his being fastidious about remembering the year he immigrated, nor that of the other people in his household, let alone their ages.

ONE OF THOSE THINGS that kept tugging at me and wouldn't let go was to learn more about Father Tougas. Somehow I knew a story was out there, I just had to find it.

The first time I heard the name Father Tougas was when Grandma said, "I was raised to hate the Catholics." I was shocked. I thought she was a cradle Catholic like the rest of us. I asked how she became a Catholic, and she told me about Grandpa Peter quitting his job during the Depression (when they had three little children), and Father Tougas came to the house and brought them food and was so good to them. One day, he said, "Mrs. Thompson, would you like to become a Catholic?" and she said yes, and he gave her instruction, and she was baptized and confirmed.

This was when they lived in Broadwater, outside of Helena. Father Tougas was stationed at the Cathedral in Helena at the time, so I called the parish office. The woman I spoke with said she didn't have any information about him. I wrote to the diocese asking for biographical information. Someone at the diocese sent me a newspaper article that mentioned Father Tougas with regard to renovating the Cathedral after the 1935 earthquake. It said he died in 1946.

Since he died so long ago, I didn't think the current priests could have known him. I mentioned my dilemma to Auntie Mary and she said, "Let's ask Father Butori." Father Butori was the pastor at St. Joseph's in Butte and too young to have known Father Tougas as a priest. I didn't think he would be able to help, but Auntie Mary asked anyway. He said, "Talk to Father Fenlon and Father Ed Moran. Father Ed Moran lives at the Bee-Hive."

First I called Father Moran. He had trouble hearing me and wanted to know for whom I was collecting money. I said I wasn't collecting money. I had quite a time convincing him. He said he'd been ill; he had heart problems. He was very kind, but I felt bad about bothering him if he wasn't feeling well. He seemed to want to talk, so I explained again that I was writing a book and wanted to know about Father Tougas. He said Father Tougas used to go out and visit people. He was a monsignor when he died. He died suddenly and no one was with him.

Next I called Father Fenlon. He mentioned a couple of families who knew Father Tougas. He said I should talk to Father Ed Moran and not to pay any attention if he says he has a heart condition. He also suggested I talk to Father Jack Darragh.

Then he said, "You should talk to Bruce Plummer. He was Father Tougas's associate. He's up in Polson."

Father Plummer officiated at Mom and Dad's wedding. He was pastor at St. Ann's when I was little. Here I was, searching and searching for someone to tell me about Father Tougas, and all along, there was someone right under my nose, someone my family knew, Father Plummer, and he actually knew Father Tougas.

I had seen Father Plummer just a few years earlier, shortly after I moved to San Francisco. Mom and Dad were in town for a convention and invited friends Chuck and Norma to join us for dinner. Chuck was Dad's best man. Father Plummer was visiting and came too.

Delighted with my new lead, I called Father Plummer. He said he was Father Tougas's associate in 1941; it was his first assignment out of the seminary.

I told him that I heard Father Tougas came from money. Was that true?

"There was no family money," he said, "just his salary, but he gave away what he could. People probably gave him money, knowing he'd know who needed it. That could be how the rumor came about that he came from money."

He told me Father Tougas went wild giving Christmas presents; he filled an entire room in the rectory with them. Father Plummer said one day he answered the door and nearly fainted. Before him stood the madame from the brothel, a robust black woman, her cheeks caked with heavy purple powder. She said Father Tougas sent her to collect the Christmas presents for the girls.

He said, "Father Tougas took care of people that no one thought about."

"How did he know?" I asked. "How did he find them?"

"The nuns at the school knew a lot about how the family was doing from what the children brought for lunch," he said.

I asked what Father Tougas looked like. "He was about five-foot-six, he had diabetes, he was very active. One day a week he locked himself in his room (his day off). The next day he was fine."

"Why was that?" I asked.

"The diabetes. He was cheerful on good days. He was serious when he was sick. He fished the Upper Blackfoot. He used worms." He said the part about using worms with a tone of distaste, as if it were almost too embarrassing to mention.

"What was he like as far as his personality?" I asked.

"He was intelligent, well read, interested in everything," Father Plummer said. "He could be abrupt. He was very much in charge of the situation and very organized. He made a large number of converts, some fifty every year. He gave the religious instruction himself. He went out looking for people. He'd pick up old ladies and take them to Mass at the Fort."

He said Father Tougas was a chaplain in the First World War. "His dossier is in the Helena chancery, some of it is private." He encouraged me to ask for it. I didn't mention that I had already written to the diocese.

Chapter Twenty-seven

EVERY DAY I made a list of things to accomplish, items culled from my to-do list. This day it was:

> Call the New York Historical Society for information about Charles Evans Hughes. (Hughes was the governor of New York before he was on the U.S. Supreme Court. Grandma said he was her father's cousin. I wanted to confirm that and find out how closely they were related.)
> Mail request for Peter's birth certificate to the British Public Records Office.
> Call the New York Public library and ask for information about the law firm involved with Arthur's case.
> Call Powell County to see if they have a birth certificate for Sarah's baby.
> Call Father Peter to see if he knows the citation for St. Teresa's "one night in a bad inn" quote.
> Call Montana State in Bozeman to inquire about the vocational congress.
> How did the Cabbage Patch get its name?
> Call the war college:
> — The Germans poisoning the wells—was that a first in the First World War?
> — Did the officers and men eat the same rations?
> Call Fort Lewis to find out about Peter in the boxing match.

Did I complete that list in one day? Probably not, but I kept whittling away at it.

More reading, another book about Butte. What a time in history—war, drought, disease all at once, untold drama packed into so few years, it was as if the world suddenly went mad. I thought about my grandparents, Peter and Aila, and their contemporaries, the "lost generation" who lived through not one but two world wars, two depressions, untold social change—women getting the vote, Prohibition, the map of the world redrawn, and they raised the generation that would go off to fight and win the Second World War.

Back at the Butte Archives, reading old newspapers about trouble brewing on draft registration day in 1917, and at the end of the same week, the Granite Mountain Fire, the worst hard-rock mining disaster in American history, and right after the fire, this in the *Anaconda Standard*: "Governor Stewart today received a telegram from Forsyth announcing that the Cheyenne Indians are holding war dances and threatening violence. They refuse to register for conscription. A big war dance is to be held tomorrow and trouble is feared."

My great-grandfather Arthur was one of the rescuers at the Granite Mountain Fire, one of the "helmet men" as the newspaper called them because of the big, bulky, breathing apparatus they wore. This I needed to research in depth to tell Arthur's part of the story. It struck me as ironic and redemptive—Arthur's risking his life to rescue men from a fire, after what he did in Forsyth.

I found the list of the dead in the newspaper: Irish, Finns, Slavs, Welsh, Cornish, French. Fifteen hundred Serbs took part in the funeral procession. The list of the dead included their addresses. I looked to see if any of them lived at 415 Kemper Street, Sarah's boarding house. It was unlikely since the boarding house was far from the Granite Mountain. Men tended to live in boarding houses near the mines at which they worked. No one from Kemper Street was listed.

One newspaper said the bodies were so swollen that the skin split, and this was because decomposition was hastened by the extreme heat and noxious fumes which eradicated oxygen from the blood. Very vivid. Very dramatic. I wrote that into my manuscript. Then something started tugging at me. That soft, gentle, persistent tug—maybe not, maybe not, better look into it. It made sense that the extreme heat would hasten decomposition, but the noxious fumes? They were dead. They weren't breathing. How could what you breathed cause the body to swell after death? On the face of it, it didn't make sense.

In general, I was careful about what I used from newspapers, but I was particularly careful about articles written about dramatic events while those events were unfolding, such as those written during the Granite Mountain Fire rescue. In the reporter's haste to get the story out, errors could have crept in. A newspaper reported that Mrs. Manus Duggan, the wife of one of the missing miners, went into labor a few minutes after the fire started, and the baby was born while her husband was still in the mine. A later article said the baby was not born yet.

Another newspaper story said the firefighting water became so hot that some of the dead miners were horribly scalded. Were they scalded to death? How awful. How vivid. The juror's verdict from the inquest, which I found in the *Coroner's Register* at the Butte Archives, did not say anything about miners being scalded to death. It said the cause of death was "asphyxiation from gas and smoke from a fire." Could the scalding have been post mortem?

I needed to get a copy of the entire inquest, the official eyewitness account of what happened. Perhaps the authorities questioned some of the rescuers, perhaps Arthur. Oh, to get a quote from Arthur about the rescue, to have a first-hand account of what he witnessed, what a find that would be.

The Bureau of Mines report about the fire, which listed Arthur as one of the rescuers, was quite helpful, but the full transcript of the inquest would be the primary source for what happened. Off I went to the Courthouse to get it. The juror's verdict said the inquest went on for eight days. Inquest transcripts are typed double spaced on legal paper; with eight days of testimony, it must be several inches thick. I figured it must be one of the fattest inquests in the Courthouse. I walked upstairs to the Clerk of Court Office and asked for it. The woman went off to get it. A few minutes later, she returned empty handed. "It's not there," she said. She said nine inquests in a row were missing. Another woman in the office said she had worked at the Courthouse for twenty years and didn't remember anyone ever asking for it. They were astounded that it was missing.

So the inquest for the Granite Mountain Fire, the worst hard-rock mining disaster in American history, seemingly grew legs and marched itself right out of the Silver Bow County Courthouse. I wonder why.

Back at the archives, I told Ellen the inquest was missing and asked if she had a copy in the archives. She didn't. I asked Jodie Foley at the Montana Historical Society Archives if they had a copy. No. I asked Brian Shovers at the Montana Historical Society Library if he knew where I might find a copy. I had read his master's thesis on mining accidents in Butte. He said while working on his thesis, he read the inquests, and the Granite Montana Fire inquest was missing.

"When was that," I asked.

"1987."

I asked Ellen if she had any suggestions as to who might have a copy. I followed every lead she suggested but still came up empty handed.

The newspapers covered the inquest, so I read those articles, hoping to see Arthur quoted. The paper said forty to fifty witnesses were expected to testify. This gave me more encouragement that Arthur might have been one of them. I kept reading . . . what's this? "Looking for Dead Husband Finds Him Dead Drunk." It was a headline in the *Butte Daily Post* of June 26, 1917. This woman's husband didn't come home, so she assumed he was killed in the Granite Mountain Fire. Police Chief Murphy looked into the matter and discovered that her husband's name was not on the list of dead or missing, nor could it be determined whether he even worked at the Granite Mountain. It turned out, he was holed up in jail all this time. Jailer Barney said he'd been drunk a week and was afraid to go home. What the errant husband faced at home must have been fearsome if he preferred the notorious Butte jail. Years ago, a man told Dad that he had seen jails all over the world, he'd seen jails in Turkey, and none were as bad as the Butte jail. It closed in the 1970s and is now a tourist attraction. I've seen it. It's a dungeon.

I called an old codger of a miner, who was very interested in Butte history, and asked if he had the inquest or knew who did. He said he had part of the inquest and would send me a copy. He sent me some interesting papers but not the inquest.

Perhaps another author used it and made a copy. I checked bibliographies and notes. No luck.

I read that concrete bulkheads blocked miners from escaping the fire, in violation of state regulations. I was appalled. That's terrible, terrible and dramatic. I wrote it into my manuscript. Then something started tugging at me: there may be more to the story; I better look into it further. Being an engineer, I knew things are often more complicated than they first appear and at times regulations conflict. I seem to remember a quandary on one of my projects at Bechtel: the environmental regulations said the fuel tank could not be outside, the fire protection regulations said the fuel tank could not be inside.

Dan Harrington mentioned the concrete bulkheads in his report about the fire for the Bureau of Mines. There had been a fire in an adjacent mine, the Modoc, a few weeks earlier, and bulkheads were erected to seal it off from the Granite Mountain. The juror's verdict from the coroner's inquest noted that bulkheads had been erected to contain smoke and gas from the Modoc fire, as did the *Second Annual Report of the Industrial Accident Board*. Rescuers found dead miners near one such bulkhead. Were there locked doors that should not have been locked, bulkheads that should not have been there—other than those isolating the fire in the Modoc? I could not conclusively say one way or the other, so I took it out of my manuscript. If I couldn't be certain of the facts, especially about something inflammatory, I left it out.

The cable that dropped and tore and caught fire in the Granite Mountain was part of a larger modification to install a fire suppression sprinkler system in the mine. How sadly ironic. I wondered whether sprinkler systems were common in mines at that time. Were they required? I looked for mine regulations in effect in 1917. I couldn't find any that listed such a requirement. A Bureau of Mines bulletin from 1915 listed laws from various states and recommended them to all. It said "a mine having only one exit which is covered by a building containing the mechanical plant, furnace room, and blacksmith shop shall have fire protection—water if possible, otherwise chemical extinguishers . . ." This was from a Colorado law. The Granite Mountain had several exits via adjoining mines. Former Butte miner Al Hooper said, in his research into the Granite Mountain Fire, he didn't find any other mines that had sprinkler systems back then. I called one of my former Bechtel colleagues who did fire protection engineering and asked whether sprinkler systems were required back in 1917. He didn't know. I called a retired mining engineer, a graduate of the Montana School of Mines, and asked him. He was quite certain sprinkler systems were not required back then. I called a fire protection engineering professor at the University of Maryland. He didn't know. I gave up. None of the sources I found about the disaster said installing the sprinkler system was to meet a state requirement. Just because I couldn't find such a requirement, doesn't mean there wasn't one. It simply means I couldn't find it.

The newspaper said doctors on the scene gave the stricken miners coffee. I wondered about that. Why would they give them coffee? It seemed an oddly prosaic thing to offer a person who had just escaped death. I hesitated to include that small detail until I could find out why, and yet if true, I wanted to include it. Such familiar details make the story more accessible. Quite by accident I learned that coffee opens the bronchial passages. The miners had breathed toxic fumes, hence they needed those passages opened up to get more good air into their lungs.

Home again, I read, take notes, type them into the computer, now about Butte, now about the war, now Peter's inquest, now again about the war. *La guerre, la guerre, toujours la guerre.* Pages and pages and pages of to-do lists, things to investigate, things to look up.

I headed back to Butte. My flight was to arrive close to midnight. I nodded off as we descended. I awoke and realized the plane was circling. Circling over Butte? Why? The pilot announced that someone had turned off the runway lights, and they were trying to roust someone to turn them back on. Finally someone did, and we landed.

As on prior trips, I spent roughly half my time at Auntie Mary and Uncle Ed's in Butte and the other half at Aunt Aila's in Whitehall. Uncle Ed helped with my ranching questions. He and Auntie Mary and I had dinner one evening at the Peking Noodle Parlor. It's an old Chinese restaurant uptown, a delightful glimpse into Butte's colorful past, with little curtained-off orange booths and the old wire-enclosed cashier cage. In November of 1914, an opium ring was uncovered in Butte, and a Chinese doctor and a Chinese merchant were killed when the bomb they were making for a tong war blew up.

Aunt Aila and I drove down to Twin Bridges to take another look at the orphanage where Grandma and Archie and Patsy lived from 1913 to 1915. We walked past the no trespassing sign, through the gate, and were a few feet down the path when we saw a tall, thin, elderly man with a long, gray beard walking toward us. "We better go," I said to Aunt Aila, thinking he was coming to shoo us off. Instead, he offered to show us around. He said his name was Henry Lockwood. He grew up in the orphanage in the 1920s and 1930s. He said he lived there now.

"So you are the caretaker?" I asked.

"I'm the care giver," he said.

I wondered what he did for plumbing and water and heat in the winter. The place was abandoned in 1975.

He explained which building was the school, which was the hospital, and so on. He led us up the stairs of the huge, magnificent Victorian, and we went inside. That was where Grandma lived with the other big girls. Then he took us inside one of the quaint redbrick cottages where the younger children lived. It was pleasantly cool inside the buildings, even though it was a very hot day. The buildings were in amazingly good condition, considering they'd seen no upkeep in twenty-five years. Henry explained who lived where, what the rooms were used for. In one of the buildings, we saw dear little coat hooks along the wall, about three feet from the floor.

Some of the buildings were obviously newer and much less attractive, designed in an era when the goal of architects seemed to be to "design" the plainest, most eye-displeasing structures they could, leaving a legacy of lifeless boxes.

WHILE READING *The Butte Irish*, I learned that my Irish great-granduncle John Gribben belonged to the Robert Emmet Literary Association. On my next visit to the Butte Archives, I perused the meeting minutes, which had been kept in an old barn. Not knowing how dirty and dusty they might be, I donned an old chambray shirt over my blouse. The Emmets were the Butte wing of Clan na Gael, an Irish American fraternal and political organization that sought an independent Ireland. I found wonderful quotes by Uncle John, who became leader of the Emmets, and by his friend Judge Jeremiah Lynch. The minutes reported that the group feted Uncle Pat when he arrived in Butte; he was Grandpa Peter's brother who was in the IRA. As I studied the membership lists, I never found Pat. Apparently he didn't join. This made me wonder if his IRA involvement was more about excitement and "the gang" than politics, especially since his uncle John Gribben was secretary general of the Emmets, another reason for him to join.

Grandpa Peter didn't join the Emmets either, which fit with what Aunt Aila told me about him—he came to America to be an American. It was also in line with what I read in general about Peter's generation of Irish immigrants—that they were not as invested in Irish independence as were the previous generation, his uncle John's.

Though I knew that troops occupied Butte in 1917 and 1918, it was not clear to me whether the town was under martial law. In 1914, it was clear. I found the governor's declaration of martial law in 1914, but no such document for 1917. Somehow I stumbled onto the Glasser report at the Butte Archives. Ellen must have told me about it. It was a federal report about use of the military to quell domestic disorder. It proved to be a great resource, the best kind, because it contained raw data: reproductions of actual memos, telegrams, and letters. A telegram from a general dated November 2, 1918, said: "Martial law has not been declared in Butte, MT." The troops did not have police powers. Local police would make arrests.

Somewhere along the way, I learned that Enrique Caruso performed in Butte, and I wanted to include that in my description of the raucous town. The contrast between high art and low brow shenanigans was too delicious to pass up. First I needed to confirm that he performed during the time frame I was describing. This proved to be one of the most challenging aspects of my research. I was writing a story about particular people at a particular time in a particular place. The facts had to be correct for the time and place and people. For example, there were contract miners in Butte, but not when my grandfather Peter Thompson arrived in 1914. Contract mining was introduced a few years later. There were first-aid competitions at the Columbia Gardens for Miners Union Day. At first, I included that when I described what was to happen on that day in 1914, Peter's first Miners' Union Day, the year of the riots. Then that little something started tugging at me. Did they hold first-aid competitions that early? It seemed the big safety-first push came later. I called Brian at the Montana Historical Society. He dug into it for me but could find nothing definitive. To be safe, I moved the passage to later in the story when I knew for certain those competitions took place. This was important to include because Peter always played the patient, and then he was one. Now that I think about it, later was the best place for that part all along, just before Peter was injured in the mine.

As I wrote and researched in the fall of 1999, the news was ablaze with reports of rioters vandalizing downtown Seattle during the World Trade Organization meeting. It sounded reminiscent of Butte in 1914. Law enforcement anticipates trouble and wants reinforcements. The mayor says no. It didn't turn out well in Butte in 1914, just as it didn't in Seattle in 1999. The trouble in Butte went on much longer and people were killed and a building was blown up.

Many Hollywood movies romanticize the past; they are, after all, meant to be entertainment, not history lessons. It is easy to think that our current problems are the worst things that ever happened, and whatever happened in the little known past must have been better and easier. It's American optimism at work: if we don't know anything bad about it, it must be good. We take a hermetically sealed tour of a charming European land and assume that life there must be as pleasant as our vacation. The part of life we didn't see must be good. Things are always supposed to get better and better and better, and many things do. We expect it.

I remember my cousin Rosaleen from Belfast asking if something or other ever happens in America. I wish I could remember what it was. It was something so beyond the realm of possibilities, I was surprised by the question. I said no. She said, "Americans wouldn't stand for it."

Every once in a while a sentence for the manuscript would pop into my head out of the blue. I wouldn't even be thinking about that part of the book, and poof, there it was. I'd think, that sounds great, and I'd write it down. Then I'd have to find out if it was true. Grandma said her mother ordered the sheriff after her when she ran off to marry Peter. What popped into my head was Sarah saying to the sheriff, "My daughter has run off to marry that Irishman, and you must go get her and bring her back," and she was saying this to the sheriff who was himself Irish. But was he? He probably was, but I'd have to find out for sure. That was easy, and he was—Sheriff Duggan.

"The towering, no-nonsense Frank Conly," popped into my head about the prison warden. Was he? From my research, I knew the no-nonsense part was accurate. His personality was towering, but was he physically? I had to find out. He was.

I read the Silver Bow County Board of Health meeting minutes to learn how badly the Spanish Influenza hit Butte in the fall of 1918. Very badly. Picture shows closed, dance halls closed, schools closed by order of the board of health. Reported cases quadrupled overnight. Doctors were overworked with no time to report cases. There was no way to know how bad it actually was.

I read the 1918 Butte papers to see what Grandma and Peter's aunts and uncles back in Butte were reading in the newspapers while he was in battle. As the battles raged in France, the Wobblies (the International Workers of the World) were raising Cain at home. Then the influenza hit, and the IWW disappeared from the papers. I kept reading. Still the war, still the flu. Young, healthy adults dying from the flu. Soldiers dying from the flu. Young healthy adults normally do not die of flu. Unheard of. Then by mid December, like a whisper, it was gone.

Rooms for rent for a dollar a day. Lots of interesting slice-of-life tidbits in newspapers.

I looked for casualty lists in the newspaper and found them—for the

American Expeditionary Forces, the number killed in action, the number missing, the number severely wounded, the number who died in accidents, the number who died of disease, the Montana list, the names.

Back home and the mail just arrived. Here's an envelope from Christopher Sims at Flanders Field in Belgium: pictures of gas masks, gas masks on horses, Western Front Association articles that pertain to my research, a copy of the actual coded message sending the 91st from France to Belgium.

CHAPTER TWENTY-EIGHT

I HAD ALWAYS understood that when Grandpa Peter left town, sometimes alone, sometimes taking the family with him, it was because the mines were down. As with everything else, I wanted to corroborate this. At the Butte Archives, I found a table that listed the tons of copper mined in Butte by the Anaconda Copper Mining Company for each year from 1913 to 1949, the exact period of time I needed for my research. (Grandpa Peter arrived in 1914.) However, it listed only copper. What about other metals? And even though the Anaconda was king of the Hill, there were other mining companies in Butte. To get a more accurate picture of how busy the mines were year to year, I needed to know the total ore mined.

On my next trip to Helena, I asked Brian Shovers at the historical society. He walked to the bookshelf and returned with several volumes of *Mineral Resources of the US*. It was published each year by the federal government; there was a chapter for Montana, and within it, a section for Silver Bow County, which was essentially Butte. It stated the amount of ore mined that year. In addition, there were several paragraphs discussing what transpired in Silver Bow County that year vis a vis mining, information I had not seen anywhere else. It said when the mines shut down and for what reason, and what was happening with the price of copper, wages, and the cost of supplies. It said the North Butte Mining Company didn't hazard to state profit and loss for 1931. That was telling. It is one thing to say things were bad, the mines were down, it was the Depression; it's another to say that one of the mining companies couldn't even guess at how much money they were losing. It illustrates the point.

When I returned home, I went to the University of Nevada Las Vegas library and found books for the rest of the years. I went all the way back to 1880, the first year Montana became an important producer of copper. (The first record of copper production, meaning smelting and mining, was in 1868.) Then I jumped to 1892 and recorded data for every year up to 1937, the year Grandpa Peter was killed in the mines. I made a table with three columns: year, quantity of ore mined, remarks. As to whether the mines were down every time Peter left, sometimes yes, sometimes no.

This proved to be yet another example of why it pays to corroborate even reliable oral history. If I had assumed that the mines were down every time Peter left and had not verified it, I wouldn't have looked at those *Minerals Resources* books, and I wouldn't have been able to paint as vivid a picture of what was happening in Butte.

I remembered Grandma saying that Grandpa Peter "worked when he wanted." This I also wanted to confirm. I had the city directory data, but that gave me only a snapshot of one day a year. To begin to fill in the rest of the time, I plowed through the old rustling card books at the Butte Archives. A rustling card was a permit to work in the Butte mines. Once a man had one, he could rustle up work in the mines. At first I thought these books listed only the miners who worked for the Anaconda Copper Mining Company. Later I would stumble across an entry listing the Speculator in 1915, which was a North Butte mine. These were huge, heavy ledger books, about two feet by two feet. We needed to call in a linebacker just to move them. I wondered if the covers were lead lined to make them fire proof, they were so heavy. Even the paper was heavy. The book was divided into letters. The entries were alphabetical by last name, though within a letter, they were not strictly alphabetical. The entries gave the man's rustling card number, the date he applied for work, the date employed, the name of the mine, and the day he left that mine, essentially the man's employment history with the mines. To get to the T's, I grabbed a handful of pages, lifted them up, turned the pages, dropped them down, and poof, up came a cloud of dust, grabbed another handful, lifted them up, dropped them down, and poof, up came another cloud of dust. I skimmed the T's, found Peter, and wrote down his varied employment history. I looked up Arthur and noted his. I looked up Peter's brothers, Grandma's brothers, all in my story who could have worked in the mines, and every time I turned a bunch of pages and dropped them down, up came another cloud of dust. There was quite a pile of dirt on the table when I finished.

After I returned home, I pulled out some engineering paper and drew an x-y graph. Along the vertical x axis I listed Arthur Hughes, Archie Hughes, Bill Hughes, Peter Thompson, Sam Thompson, John Thompson. Along the horizontal axis at the bottom I wrote the years, leaving a grid line for each quarter. For each man, I drew a line from the date he started working until he stopped and wrote the name of the mine above the line. Then a new line when he started again. It was easy to see at a glance who worked steadily, who worked for only short stints at a time, and who had gaps in employment. I noted significant events at the appropriate dates, such as when we were at war, the post-war depression, when my grandparents got married, and so on. Often such events explained employment gaps, though not always.

For Arthur the lines were long. He worked all the time. This corroborated what Grandma said about her father being a hard worker. For Archie and Bill the lines were short, sometimes mere dots with spaces in between, meaning they would work in a mine for one or two days at a time and then not work for several days. For Peter, the lines were long when he first arrived in Butte. After he married, the lines grew short with gaps in between; he jumped around to different mines. I also recorded what the city directories said as to where he worked, in case he was working elsewhere, not in the mines. All told, everything I gathered confirmed what Grandma said: "He worked when he wanted."

Historical research not only helped me set the stage for the story and corroborate oral history, it also helped fill in missing pieces in my family's history. That wasn't my intention in doing it, just another happy accident.

One of the homesteader memoirs I discovered while visiting the tiny library in Forsyth was *Through the Rosebuds* by Margaret Bailey Broadus. She was born the same year as Grandma's sister, Patsy. Though her family still lived on a ranch, Margaret boarded in Forsyth while attending high school. I checked to see how old Grandma's eldest brother Bill was when Sarah bought the house in Forsyth. He was ready to begin high school that fall. Could that be the reason she bought the house, and she and the children moved into town? It was undoubtably one of the reasons. Were there others? Considering what happened later, Arthur burning the house down on the ranch, who knows. There may have been a host of reasons for her move into town, and it could be her moving simply opened up an opportunity for Arthur to run off as he did.

Grandma said her father, Arthur, was separated from his family when he was a young boy. She said he was sent over the mountain to live with his grandparents, and not long after, they died. For some reason, he didn't return to his parents. We understood that he was then sent to the workhouse. To describe that part of Arthur's life, I read books about British workhouses. The 1881 census for Llandovery listed only two Arthur Hugheses close to the right age. Arthur turned ten that year. One boy lived with his parents, who were not William and Mary Hughes, so he couldn't be our Arthur. The other boy worked as a servant for the Morgan family. In *The Workhouse* by Norman Longmate, I read that pauper children in the workhouse could be apprenticed at age nine.

Grandma said her father learned to be a stonemason at a school near the English border. In *The Workhouse System 1834–1929*, M.A. Crowther wrote: "children might go to a pauper school some distance away." Grandma also said it was a Catholic school. Arthur's prison record said he was Catholic.

All this made me more curious about Arthur's mother, this connection to Australia, his being Catholic. Arthur said he was born on the high seas somewhere between Australia and Pennsylvania. His mother, Mary Price Hughes, was the only one of my great-great-grandmothers who learned how to write; she signed the birth registry while my other great-great-grandmothers marked their X. Mary could write, Arthur was Catholic, what's this about Australia?

I didn't attempt research into Arthur's family. I didn't have much to go on. Grandma knew his parents' names but no names of siblings or aunts or uncles. All along I wondered whether relatives of people in the book would surface after it came out. I wondered what became of Colonel Parker, Peter's colorful regimental commander, and hoped I might hear from his descendants. I wondered whether any Thomases might pop up, descendants of Sarah's brothers. Never did I think I would hear from Arthur's relatives, but I did. Through the wonders of the internet, the wife of a Hughes cousin in England learned about *One Night in a Bad Inn* from a woman in California and contacted me. After we exchanged emails, I heard from another cousin in England and one in Pennsylvania. We found enough corroborating evidence to confirm that each had a grandparent who was a sibling of our Arthur. One cousin thought Arthur was murdered by Indians out West. Another thought he was murdered by claim jumpers. I started to wonder, with each new cousin, will I hear a new demise-of-Arthur scenario? Instead of The Third Man, we have The Third Arthur, the one not killed by his wife.

I was also able to confirm that Doris Black's mother, Regina, was indeed

Arthur's sister. Doris was the Welsh woman who wrote to me after I visited Wales.

These cousins had done extensive genealogy research and provided me with what they found.

The story grows ever more curious.

On the 1871 census, taken the month after he was born, baby Arthur and his mother, Mary, were living with Mary's relatives at 16 Cross Lane in Llandovery, in the county of Carmarthenshire, in Wales. Mary's husband, William, was not with them. He was far, far away, with his mother and brother who lived near Leominster, a town of half-timbered houses all the way in Herefordshire, the county in which William was born, which isn't even in Wales. It is in England.

Later, Arthur's parents, William and Mary, moved to the very south of Wales, to Glamorganshire. This we know because his siblings Jane and Albert were born there.

They returned to Carmarthenshire, and in 1881 when the census was taken, William and Mary and all of the children, except Arthur, were living together in Llangadog, about ten miles south of Llandovery. Ten-year-old Arthur was working as a farm servant for the Rees Morgan family and lived on their farm on Cwmynisuchaf Street, in Llanwrda, about halfway between Llangadog and Llandovery.

My mind is swimming with possible plot twists. Arthur's family moves away, his parents leave him behind with his grandmother, his grandmother dies in an epidemic, poor little Arthur has nowhere to go, he is sent to the dreaded workhouse, he is apprenticed to the Rees Morgan family as a farm servant and lives with them. Arthur's family moves back and settles into the little village of Llangadog, just down the road from Arthur. Son and parents live only a few miles apart, but they don't know it.

Yet we know that Arthur did have further contact with his family. My Hughes cousins told me that Arthur's sister Ruth immigrated to the United States. She arrived at Philadelphia aboard the *Belgenland* on New Year's Day 1902. The ship manifest said she was going to see her brother Arthur Hughes in Wilkes-Barre.

Ah, Arthur, if you ever knew how much time your great-granddaughter would spend pondering all this.

CHAPTER TWENTY-NINE

Now to tackle this business about Uncle Archie going to prison for second degree murder.

Grandma told Mom and my aunts that her brother Archie and his friend Roy Walsh went to Renova to rob the store owner. The store owner was shot and killed, and Roy Walsh was hanged for murder.

She contended that Roy Walsh did not shoot the store owner; there was a third man at Renova that night, and he did the shooting. She said he was the son of an influential man in Butte, and his name was kept out of it. She knew the name.

Grandma also said Roy was slow.

That's all I knew.

Aunt Aila gave me two articles she'd been given about the case. One was from *Startling Detective Adventures*, the cover of which showed a startled (of course) Dick Tracy-esque woman holding a pistol in one hand and the phone to her ear in the other. It wasn't clear to me whether the magazine published factual true-crime stories or fictionalized stories based on true crimes. The author interviewed Sheriff John Mountjoy; he was the one who arrested Archie and Roy. The resulting piece was published more than a decade after the shooting.

The other article was from a newspaper, also written long after the shooting.

One might think it goes without saying, but in some quarters it does not, so I'll say it: generally speaking, in the hierarchy of sources, court documents, especially verbatim testimony, trump newspaper and magazine articles. That said, even with court testimony, one must cast a skeptical eye, or as one of my former Bechtel colleagues used to say, ask yourself whether it passes the laugh test. People do perjure themselves. After *One Night in a Bad Inn* was published, I came across the account of a man who supposedly testified in court that he saw miners down in the mine after the Granite Mountain Fire who had worked their fingers to the bone, all the way down to the second knuckle with the bone sticking out, trying to dig through one of those concrete bulkheads to escape the fire.

Perhaps he fancied himself a character in a nineteenth-century French novel. At least Edmund Dantès and the abbé had a wee chisel.

I don't know that it is actually possible for a person to work his finger to the bone, literally. Pain kicks in and stops you. And besides, miners work with heavy tools, such as heavy rock hammers, which they could wield at concrete bulkheads to break them down to escape a fire. In absence of such tools in a gas-laden mine, I think it's safe to say that no miner would stop to pick at the concrete with his fingers but would run off to find another way out, unless he was so delirious that he wasn't acting sensibly, in which case, I suspect the gas would kill him long before he got to the first knuckle. Another man supposedly gave similar testimony. I wondered whether these two even worked in the Butte mines at the time of the fire. I looked in the rustling card books at the Butte Archives, essentially employment records for the mines. I could not find either of them listed.

Getting back to Archie and Roy, I called the Courthouse in Boulder, Montana, the seat of Jefferson County, the jurisdiction in which the shooting took place, and spoke with Marilyn Craft, the Clerk of District Court. She sent me a copy of the court records. The simple cover sheet read:

> Roy Walsh was sentenced to hang by the neck until dead for the crime of MURDER IN THE FIRST DEGREE. This sentence was carried out in the early morning hours of February 14, 1925. Walsh was the last man to be executed in the County of Jefferson.
> Due to the historical significance of these documents, they have been filed, intact, in the vault in the Clerk of District Court's Office. It is located at the end of the insanity drawers.

The court records included everything but the trial transcript, which didn't surprise me since I had been told elsewhere that trial transcripts are generally not kept. I proceeded to wade through the documents.

Oh my—Roy confessed, in detail, and he signed the confession.

Oh my again. Here's a letter from the county attorney to the authorities in Washington state telling them that Jefferson County had captured their fugitive Albert Bell, who now goes by Roy Walsh. Roy was an escaped convict. He had escaped from the Washington State Reformatory at Monroe.

I called the Washington State archives to see what they had about Roy and spoke to Terry Badger. I gave him my clues. A few days later, he called back. He found the file, but it took some doing because of Roy's aliases; he also went by Albert Mason. Soon the file arrived in the mail. The State of Washington kept a lengthy dossier on him. The prison chaplain interviewed Roy and those notes were part of the file. Considering his aliases, I couldn't help but wonder how much of what Roy told the chaplain was made up.

I noted all the pertinent dates on my timeline. Roy escaped from the prison at Monroe on November 24, 1919. Only a few weeks later, the census taker noted him living in Sarah's boarding house at 415 Kemper in Butte. Oh good grief! Roy Walsh was already an escaped convict when he rented a room from Sarah. When Grandma was a teenager, an escaped convict with two gunshot wounds in his leg was living under her roof. It truly was a bad inn.

Sarah was calling herself Anna that year, so two people in the boarding house (that I know of) were going by aliases.

Marilyn Craft in Boulder suggested that I talk to Colleen Llewelyn. Colleen's grandmother was a Mountjoy, the sister of Sheriff John Mountjoy. Colleen's grandfather Johnny Williams was Sheriff Mountjoy's deputy and brother-in-law. I called Colleen; she was very helpful. She said her grandfather Johnny Williams was the one who sprang the trap when Roy was hanged. It bothered him for a long time.

She told me how to get in touch with her uncle Carter Williams, who was in his eighties and still practiced law in Great Falls, and with Sheriff Mountjoy's son Jim. Jim and Carter were boys at the time of the shooting and hanging. Jim told me his father thought "Walsh was a cold-blooded criminal."

On my next trip to the historical society in Helena, I began the tedious task of hunting through issue after issue of the *Boulder Monitor* on microfilm for articles about all this. The shooting happened in June of 1923. I found graphic details about the bandit glaring at Al Johnson through the window. I thought, this is fantastic, it will make the story more vivid. But as I read on and looked at the dates, I learned that the poor victim, Al Johnson, was shot in the larynx and could not speak. Roy had been caught but wasn't talking yet. Colorful details, yes, but I couldn't use them.

The physical evidence showed that whoever fired the gun, fired through closed doors—the solid door and screen door. According to one newspaper story, Roy walked up to the door, knocked, fired a shot through the closed doors on purpose for the heck of it and ran off without robbing the man he went there to rob. It didn't make sense. An accidental shooting, as Roy described it in his confession, made more sense, especially since after the gun fired, both he and Archie bolted and didn't stop to rob Al Johnson.

I should have taken motion sickness medicine before I sat down at the microfilm machine, watching the pages scroll by, scroll by, scroll by, started to make me queasy. I stumbled upon a story about haying season. It said the grasshoppers hadn't been too bad, frequent showers slowed things down. The list of jurors for Roy Walsh's trial showed they were all farmers but one. And it was haying season. That's significant. Very inconvenient timing for those farmer jurors.

One article said Al Johnson was talking with a man in his store just before he was shot. The man's name rang a bell. I searched my "notes. deerlodge" file on the computer. There he was—he was the husband of the married couple in prison at the same time as Sarah and Arthur, the man I called Fred D----. Isn't that curious. The last person to speak with Al Johnson before he was shot did time in prison with the parents of one of the assailants. Could that be a coincidence? I'd have to look into it.

Roy's trial took place only one month after the shooting. That seemed quick. I read about the legal machinations after the trial, about Archie taking the plea bargain. Now into the fall, Roy's sentencing date was set for October, his lawyer planned to make a motion for a new trial. I looked for articles about that. I kept scrolling through the papers, reading the headlines, printing anything promising, until, oh my goodness! Roy escaped! I jumped ahead to find out what happened. He was captured several months later in Missouri. When Sheriff Mountjoy brought him back to Montana, he told all, how he sprang the lock and hid in the attic and slept in the women's cell and poked a hole through the roof and climbed on top and was hanging from the edge by his arms about to drop to the ground when Mrs. Mountjoy came out to hang the wash.

I felt as if I were living in a novel discovering all this. The next relative I saw got an ear full, "You won't believe what I just found out!" and on I went, talking a mile a minute, pouring out this incredible story.

An obvious questions was: did Roy have help? The sheriff thought so. I'd have to find those court records.

These days, I was staying at Aunt Aila's in Whitehall. When the historical society closed, or I was too mentally exhausted to read another word, I'd leave Helena heading south on I-15 and turn off at Boulder and drive through the beautiful Boulder Valley. Pine forests blanketed the massive mountains on either side of the road, looking like the backs of so many giant sleeping bears. As I neared the turnoff to Whitehall, I'd ascend a ridge and all of a sudden, the Jefferson Valley and the Tobacco Root Mountains appeared before me, just as the sun was slipping behind the Continental Divide, casting a golden hue on the already golden Tobacco Roots. What a vista.

I looked for Renova on an old map. I wanted to see which railroad went there. The map showed the railroad but was too general to determine exactly where Renova was. Aunt Aila asked some local old timers where it was and took me to see it. There's no physical trace that it ever existed. It was a railroad stop, I suppose that's the only reason the place had a name at all. The road going east past Renova dead ends before the river, the bridge washed out some time ago—two apt metaphors for what transpired there.

On my next visit to the Butte Archives, I looked for articles about Archie and Roy in the Butte papers. One afternoon, I overhead a man at another table say to his colleague, "This is so fun!" Indeed it was.

Every time I saw the name Walsh or Hughes in a headline, I stopped to read which slowed me down considerably. The Butte papers were full of Walsh and Hughes, but they were Senator Thomas Walsh and Secretary of State Charles Evans Hughes. Our Hughes and Walsh got plenty of newsprint just the same.

In the midst of all this reading, I stumbled across a scandal involving yet a third Hughes, Grandma's brother Bill. He had married yet another underage girl, this one a runaway. Good grief. How embarrassing this must have been for poor Grandma. There were some catty women in her orbit whom she could not avoid. I wonder if they had a field day with this.

I visited Boulder several times to peruse records at the Courthouse. I saw the courtroom where Roy's trial took place. Marilyn mentioned the pronounced tick-tock of the clock in the courtroom, and that the windows made a creepy sound when the wind blew. Those would be great details to use to set the scene. While waiting for the verdict, an eerie wind made the windows shudder, as the tick, tock, tick, tock, of the clock slowly marked time . . . But I didn't know if it was the same clock, and I didn't know if the wind blew during the trial, so I couldn't use those details.

Auntie Mary came along on one of those visits to Boulder. We went to see the old jail where Archie and Roy were locked up and from which Roy escaped. It is now Justice Court. The facade was kept when it was expanded and converted into offices. We spoke with Deb Rennie and asked what it looked like on the inside when it was the jail. She suggested I speak with her dad, Dick Rennie, a retired highway patrolman.

Dick described the jail for me in detail. I told him about Archie and Roy going to Renova to rob Al Johnson and then the gun went off and they ran. He said the gun could have gone off by accident. They were probably nervous and shaky. Roy could have squeezed the trigger by accident. He said he had a rifle with such a hair trigger that he could lay it on the floor and drop something, and it would go off. He wouldn't let anyone near it. I asked about the gun Roy was carrying, a 30-30 rifle. Dick said that was a saddle gun. He said Archie and Roy were probably both so scared when the gun went off that they didn't know what happened.

CHAPTER THIRTY

By now I had so much information, so many stories, so many anecdotes. Compelling though the material was, the trick was how to knit it all together into a smooth narrative. Not an easy task. Coming up with segue ways between family anecdotes and historical backdrop proved to be a real brain teaser. It would have been easier had I done a little research and filled in the blanks with my imagination, but I didn't want to do that. I liked being bound by the facts. Had I fictionalized it, you wouldn't know what was true and what was made up. I wanted you to know it was true. That was the power of the story. Sticking to the facts certainly made it more challenging, but that was much of the fun. It was as if I'd been told to prepare a gourmet dinner using only what was in kitchen. In my case, the pantry and refrigerator were full.

As I pieced snippets of stories together, much as Grandma stitched together fabric remnants to fashion one of her cozy quilts, I began to see Grandma emerge as a person apart from being my dear grandma T, and my admiration for her grew immensely. For years, I had heard fragments of stories here and there, each dramatic, but when I laid out all those stories in one place, in a book, the whole was so much more dramatic than the parts. Seeing the whole picture made her strength of character and poise and grace all the more vivid, and her example more powerful. It made me realize how truly remarkable she was. She was no longer just my sweet grandma T. I still can't get over how she overcame all she did, and yet, had you met her, she would have focused her attention on you, and called you dear, and you would think this sweet, pretty, tiny woman never had a care in her life.

She was an inspiring enigma. I think when she came to be, God kissed her on the cheek and shed a tear, for He knew she'd wear a crown of thorns; the kiss bestowed the special graces to overcome it.

WRITING IS LIKE music in that it has a beat, a tempo, a pace, a cadence which helps set the mood and tone. In one place you have an allegro, in another a lento, in another an adagio. The lively spirit of a Scott Joplin rag, the velvety elegance of a Chopin waltz, both are beautiful, yet so different, each have their place.

A different tone, a different cadence, a different pace, seemed appropriate for the different parts of the book. There were things I wanted to use but left out because it would have disturbed the tone or rhythm I was seeking for a particular passage. The start of the war was swift, I wanted the writing to mirror that. I wanted it to be rapid, to fly. In the homesteading narrative, I took a more even-keeled pace. In the part about my Irish relatives, it seemed Aunt Brigid's lyrical voice was in my head as I wrote. In parts about Grandma T, I sought a gentle touch to mirror hers. In telling Butte's colorful history, I took a lighthearted tone in some parts, a somber tone in others. The stories about the War of the Copper Kings and Montana's nineteenth-century election shenanigans are hilarious in retrospect, though they must have been horrifying at the time. The lively futures market in vote buying during those early senate elections, when the state legislators elected U.S. senators, if not nonpareil, deserves at least dishonorable mention in the annals of election chicanery. Imagine an envelope full of one thousand dollar bills stuffed into the hands of a politician—in 1899.

As my knowledge of the story grew, the text evolved. What seemed to belong in part two now seemed better suited to part four. I did much juggling and rearranging. What belonged where wasn't always obvious. There were many priceless gems for which I couldn't find the right spot. Those went into my "Don't Know Where to Put" file.

YEARS AGO, Mom gave Grandma the book *The Best Loved Poems of the American People*. After Grandma passed away, the book went back to Mom, and she gave it to me. "I thought you might like to see which poems Grandma liked," she said. Grandma had left several markers in the book. I left all the markers in place and put it on my bookshelf, and there it sat. Now that I was researching her life, I pulled it down from the shelf and looked at the marked pages. One of the markers was a few pages from a little pamphlet size copy of the *Rubáiyát* of Omar Khayyám. Aunt Brigid said Peter's last words to his father were from the *Rubáiyát*. I thumbed through the pages. Next to several stanza's, Grandma had drawn a huge asterisk. Oh, my gosh, it's about Peter after he died. It was as if she were directing me. *Here you are, dear, you might like to use this.*

I did.

ONE EVENING while helping make dinner at Mom and Dad's, I ask Mom, "What did Grandma trade her ration coupons for during the Second World War?"

"I don't remember," she says. "Ask Auntie Mary." Then as an after-thought, she says, "Grandma never had enough money to use all her ration coupons."

Wow, that is significant. Rations evoke want, and yet Grandma didn't have enough money even for rations. I have to find a way to include that in the book. I jot it down.

I call Auntie Mary; Uncle Ed answers the phone. "Mary, it's Murder She Wrote," I hear him yell. Auntie Mary comes to the phone laughing. She answers my question about the rations (I should have known Grandma would have traded them for butter) and that makes her think of something else about Grandma. I listen and take notes. I try not to interrupt and ask questions. I try to listen and go back to questions later.

Chapter Thirty-one

As I shut my suitcase, I listened to news reports of Hurricane Floyd walloping Manhattan. My flight to New York was the next day. Oh, well. I had two reasons for going to New York City to do research: it was where Arthur fled as a fugitive and was captured, and Peter's brother Denis died in an accident there.

Mom and Dad joined me for that trip, which made it more fun. They arrived several hours after I did. Seeing the cab situation at Newark, I tried to warn them not to take a gypsy cab but wasn't able to reach them. They unknowingly took a gypsy cab but thankfully arrived safely at the hotel.

Armed with clues I had gleaned from the depositions over Arthur's state of aliveness and from the letter the lawyer wrote describing how Arthur was captured, we set out to see where all of this took place. The old stone building on Maiden Lane, which housed Charles Hayes's law office, was still there. Charles was the husband of Sarah's friend Jennie, the one who told all about Arthur being alive and digging up the body and burning the house down. His office was in Lower Manhattan, which was where most of the events surrounding Arthur's capture took place. I would need to find pictures of what the area looked like back in 1913.

Off I went to the historical society to see what I might find there. The fellow working at the information desk looked at me askance, as if I must be up to no good. He was not particularly helpful.

My reception at the New York Public Library was quite the opposite. I discovered the room devoted to books about New York City and told the librarian what I was researching, and before I knew it, a stack of books appeared before me. I found the historical background and pictures of Lower Manhattan that I needed.

Undeterred by the odd reception at the historical society, I went back to do more research. One afternoon as I walked along Central

Park making my way back to the hotel, I stopped, transfixed by what was going on across the street. A tall, thin man on roller blades, who with the skates looked to be about seven feet tall, was standing in the middle of the road with arms out-stretched, stopping traffic as a stooped, elderly woman with a walker inched her way across the street. I don't think I'd ever seen anyone move so slowly in my life. I thought, good for her, she's out and about. No one honked as she inched along, inched along. Once she was safely across the street and on the sidewalk, he skated off. Traffic resumed.

I visited the Seamen's Church Institute in hopes of learning what life was like for Arthur working that voyage to Buenos Aires in 1913. Before my trip, I tried to research this at the library. I found many books about ships and seafaring, but nothing about the seamen who worked aboard those ships in that era. Much history is written about stuff and institutions. I wanted to know about the people. The stuff interests me only as it pertains to people. I also wanted to know what the Seamen's Church Institute was, and to try to figure out why Arthur went there. The director of the institute was generous with his time. I found a book about the institute but nothing about the life of the mariners around 1913.

The letter the lawyer wrote detailing how Arthur was captured said the *World* article of October 4 contained errors and that was the reason for the letter. It wasn't immediately obvious to me what the *World* was. It was the *New York World*, owned by the Pulitzer family, and was one of the major newspapers of the day. Even if it contained errors, I was curious to see what it did say about Arthur. The New York Public Library had the old papers on microfilm. It didn't take long for me to find the article about Arthur. It was on page eight. Hilarious. I didn't think to look for an article in the *New York Times*, but later after I was back home I did. The *Times* also ran an article, also on page eight, and also hilarious. I pictured these reporters in a Park Row saloon, downing a few beers, writing their copy, and the story growing ever more colorful with every swig, and they chuckling over each clever new line. Both stories were lighthearted fiction based on fact. The essential elements were correct, the fill-in details were made up. One reporter said, when the authorities walked into a saloon and saw a man with a hand as big as a ham encircling a glass of beer, they knew they had their man. Hand as big as a ham, what a wonderful simile. The reporter knew that something about Arthur's hands distinguished him, and he made up this hand as big as a ham encircling a glass of beer story. It was entertaining, but it wasn't how or where the police apprehended my great-grandfather.

Aunt Brigid had given me Uncle Denis's address in Brooklyn. Presumably Grandpa Peter lived with him when he worked in New York. I asked a cabby to take us there, but he didn't want to. I didn't press the issue.

CHAPTER THIRTY-TWO

MY NEXT TRIP to Helena was later in the year than I would normally go to Montana, one never knows when winter will hit, but my list had grown so long, I needed to go. I decided to stay there rather than commute from Butte or Whitehall. I found a bed and breakfast across the street from the Cathedral, an easy walk to the historical society. It was in a beautiful, old, restored Victorian in a neighborhood full of beautiful, old, restored Victorians. When I checked in, I asked the owner about the history of the building. He said it was where the priests from the Cathedral used to live. "You mean this was the rectory!" I exclaimed. "I'm writing a book and a person in my book lived here!"

The next morning was Sunday. I went down to breakfast and had a nice visit with the owner and other guests, and then went back up to my room to finish getting ready. I planned to meet my cousins in East Helena for Mass. I glanced at the clock in the room. I had plenty of time. As I put on my watch, I noticed the time was different. The clock in the room was slow. I'd never make it to East Helena in time. I finished getting ready and scurried across the street to the Cathedral.

Though I had a long list of things to research during my stay in Helena, Father Tougas was not on it. I figured I had exhausted my sources in finding out about him. As I sat there at Mass, I remembered that my paternal grandmother was baptized at Sacred Hearts Cathedral in Helena, yet this was St. Helena's Cathedral. After Mass, I waited to speak to the priest to ask him why there were two cathedral names. I waited until the crowd cleared and then approached him. He was Father Darragh. After he answered my questions about the Cathedral, these words unintentionally poured out of my mouth: "Do you know anything about Father Tougas?"

"Yes," he said, "I know stories about Father Tougas. There's a woman here you should meet. He brought her into the church," and as he said this, he ushered me back inside the church. "There's her daughter," he said, "she's the bishop's secretary," and he steered me to the side door where he introduced me to Paula House and her mother, Mrs. Rachac. Mrs. Rachac told me about how Father Tougas brought her into the Church and how he used to visit them. She had terrific stories. Paula said she worked for the diocese and had biographical information about the priests.

First thing Monday morning, I called her. Paula gave me Father Tougas's dates—birth, ordination, death. She said, "The diocese now has an archivist," and before I could say thank you, she transferred me to Sister Dolores.

I scurried over and spent the rest of the day in Sister Dolores's office. Father Tougas wrote many letters while serving as a chaplain in the First World War, opening yet another window for me into the war. As I read, I heard the voice of an eager young man at the beginning of a budding career. As time wore on after he returned home, a more sober, mature man emerged, one who clearly had no time for Church politics.

When I met Father Darragh at the Cathedral, he offered to tell me what he knew about Father Tougas. I made an appointment to see him at his office. Father Bud Sullivan also joined us. They told me about Father Tougas buying presents for the girls in the brothel. One of them said, "He was well liked by everyone, even his fellow priests." He emphasized "even his fellow priests," as if that were of particular note. That struck me as an odd remark; yet, the Catholic Church is, if not the oldest, one of the oldest bureaucracies on earth, and the older the bureaucracy, the more political.

I told them how Father Tougas brought Grandma into the Church and saved the family from starvation during the Depression and how good he was to the family. Father Darragh said he was glad to hear that someone was writing a nice book about a priest. He sounded relieved.

Father Sullivan stood up and walked to the phone. "You should talk to Joe Maierle," he said as he thumbed through the phone book. "Father Tougas did his wedding. His wife, Clare, is from Boulder."

Boulder!

Oh, my goodness—Boulder! My mind jolted from Father Tougas back to Archie and Roy.

As soon as I returned to my room at the B&B, I called the Maierles. Clare answered. I explained that I was writing a book, and understood they knew Father Tougas, could they tell me anything about him. "Joe," she yelled, "she wants to know about Father Tougas." Then to me, she said, "He doesn't know anything."

"Do you remember a young man named Roy Walsh who was hanged for shooting a store owner at Renova?" I asked.

"Oh, I remember," she said and went on and on about it as if it happened yesterday.

After those very welcome research detours, I set off for the historical society to attack my lengthy to-do list. As I walked through the neighborhood, I saw a doe sitting on the front lawn of one of the houses. I thought, is that a life-size deer yard ornament? She turned her head. Nope, she's a real deer. She looked as if she owned the place, as if she were the family pet.

At the historical society, I checked the penal code for 1923 to see if the punishment for murder had changed during the intervening years between Sarah's arrest and Archie and Roy's. As I suspected, it was still death or life in prison. It also said if someone was killed during the perpetration of several named felonies, including robbery, this was murder in the first degree, and the prosecution need not prove the killing was deliberate in order to sustain a conviction of murder in the first degree. In other words, an accidental shooting during the perpetration of a robbery resulting in death would constitute first degree murder.

One of the archivists did a word search for me on the various names in my book, and lo and behold, up popped Sarah Hughes. She was mentioned in a letter a woman wrote reminiscing about growing up in Forsyth. The woman was a teenager at the time of the fire. She wrote about Sarah's trial. It was clear that she did not have first-hand knowledge of what she wrote, but I wanted to include some of it in my manuscript. After much thought as to how to couch it, I wrote, "According to gossip outside the courtroom . . ." People gossiping about Sarah and Arthur was certainly part of the story, I just needed to be clear that was what it was.

Next I went through the governor's files for 1923 to 1925, the period of time when Roy Walsh was tried and hanged. One of the newspapers said Roy's lawyer, John Elliott, collected a petition of people requesting clemency for Roy. I was interested to see who signed it and how many names were on it. I figured it would be in the governor's files. As I pulled each folder out of the box and went through every page looking for the petition, I found several letters requesting clemency for Roy, and the governor's prompt responses. It hadn't occurred to me to look for such letters, but there they were. Mrs. Joanna S. Grigg of Butte wrote that Roy should be punished for "sins indulged while conscience slept . . . that conscience had never been awakened by the voice of love." Referring to Roy's first prison break, Miss Marie Smith wrote: "with child like insubordination he longed only for escape."

Others said leave his sentence be.

One of the letters was addressed to Albert Schoonover. Who was he? My goodness, he's Roy. That was his real name, not Roy Walsh, not Albert Bell, not Albert Mason. The letter was from his aunt.

As I sat there reading all these letters and papers, I heard a loud ruckus outside. I looked out the window. Clouds were galloping over the city. I sat there, mesmerized and watched. Soon they were gone. I resumed reading.

By far the longest letter requesting clemency for Roy was from Deputy Johnny Williams of Boulder. He wrote twice. His first letter was dated February 7, 1925. Governor Erickson responded two days later. I was struck by how quickly the mail moved and was dealt with.

This business about a third man at Renova kept coming up. Miss Marie Smith mentioned him. I called Johnny Williams' daughter Wanda to ask if she knew Marie. She said she did, and if Marie said something, she knew what she was talking about. Marie pointed to the man I called Fred D---- as the third man. So did Johnny Williams. He said Al Johnson was afraid of Fred D----.

Fred D---- was the horse thief ex-con who was the last to speak with Al Johnson before he was shot. He was on the witness list for Roy's trial but was never called. Sheriff Mountjoy questioned him at the scene. From what I could find, he had no alibi.

Fred D---- and his wife were the married couple in prison at the same time as Sarah and Arthur. His wife, whom I called Mildred, was the one convicted of rape. Later I obtained the court file from the Madison County Clerk of Court in Virginia City and learned that Mildred was convicted of aiding and abetting the rape of her own twelve-year-old daughter. The rapist pled guilty. (Mildred's lawyer was Lyman Bennett, who later became a judge and presided over Roy's murder trial.) I wondered if there was another connection between Mildred and Fred, and Sarah and Arthur, other than the four being in prison at the same time. Did Mildred and Fred live in Butte? Did they live with or near the Hugheses? I looked in the city directories and found Fred D---- working at the Original Mine in 1918. His wife wasn't listed, even though she had been paroled by then. Arthur had worked at the Original, but in 1918 he was working at the Pennsylvania Mine. Other than living in Butte at the same time, I didn't find anything to connect them. Of course, absence of a record is simply absence of a record. It doesn't tell you anything conclusive one way or the other. The city directories and census provide a snapshot of one day. What went on in between, who knows.

As I continued to read page after page in the governor's files, most of it having nothing to do with my research, I stumbled across a familiar name—Grandma T. She wrote to the governor on Archie's behalf after he was paroled.

Though I found much of use in the governor's files, I found no clemency petition. I even went through Governor Erickson's wife's papers. She left a diary. I thought perhaps she might have mentioned something about Roy. She didn't.

Someone told me, since Roy's case was appealed to the Montana Supreme Court, the trial transcript might be in the state supreme court file at the state law library. Off I went to find out. The woman there found it and sold me a copy of the microfiche. I think it cost a dollar.

That day at Father Darragh's office, Father Bud Sullivan suggested I visit Joe and Clare Maierle and said he would make the arrangements. When I called him, his voice on the answering machine said, "I'm busy counting my blessings. When I'm done, I'll call you back." He did and made arrangements for us to meet at the Maierles. They lived across the street from the governor.

When I met them, Clare was ninety, and Joe was a bit older. Joe cofounded Morrison-Maierle, an engineering firm in Helena. Clare said she and Joe dated when they were young, married others (Father Tougas officiated at Joe's first wedding), and after they raised their families and both were widowed, Joe looked her up, they started dating again, and got married.

She asked if I'd like something to drink. I said, sure, I'll have some orange juice. She slapped Joe on the leg and said, "Joe, go get her some orange juice."

Clare was a McCauley from the Boulder Valley; her grandparents were among the first settlers to stay put there. I got the impression that she knew everything that went on and never forgot a thing in her life. Did she ever have stories. I could barely keep up with her. Well he was a McSomebody and he married a McWhatever and they moved to California and he did thus and so and they had five children and one of them did this and that and he got sick and they moved back and on and on. She spoke with no punctuation, no pausing to find her words, out it came like a gusher, and ninety years old.

Clare was a teenager when Roy was hanged. She said everybody blamed Sarah Hughes. "People in Boulder thought she was Roy's mother and that it was all her fault," she said. She remembered watching the men erect the gallows.

She remembered Sheriff John Mountjoy being affable and easy to know. She thought Deputy, later Sheriff, Johnny Williams was a wonderful man. I asked if she heard anything about a third man being involved in the shooting. She said no. I said Johnny Williams wrote a letter to the governor saying he believed someone else was involved and had not been brought to justice.

"If Johnny Williams said there was a third man there, I'd believe him," she said.

It was strange how Fred D---- managed to identify the make of a speeding car on a rainy night with no moon and no outside lights and himself an ex-con with no alibi. All this about a third man being at Renova that night coincided with what Grandma said, though the name she gave was not Fred D----. She said what business this third man's father was in.

As I sit here writing this, I can't help but think of the mysterious third man in Graham Greene's Vienna, though that story was written long after our third man mystery at Renova.

Grandma T's life was like something out of a novel, particularly a Dickens novel. As in David Copperfield's event-filled life, when things really got desperate somebody popped up to help her. Like young Pip in *Great Expectations*, she was "raised by hand" and unwittingly found herself in the company of convicts. Like Oliver, she lived in an orphanage, and couldn't get away from a cruel cuss named Bill, and found herself under corrupting influences, which she resisted, even though they came from her own mother.

Sarah was indeed a cross between Auntie Mame and Fagin.

So much of the story seemed like something out of literature. Though I knew about Calpurnia's dream, it wasn't until I was watching the television mini-series *Julius Caesar* that I made the connection between Grandma T and Calpurnia. At the scene where Calpurnia warned Caesar not to go to the Senate because of her dream foretelling his imminent demise, it struck me like a thunder clap: it's like Grandma T! Grandma warned Grandpa Peter not to go to work that day. Something bad was going to happen to someone in the mine, she just knew it, and she was right.

And there were those names, real names, names a clever novelist would pick. Of all places, Sarah was living in the Hesperus Lode when she died. The *Hesperus*, a shipwreck—her life was a self-made shipwreck. Judge Crum certainly acted like one toward Sarah—sending a mother with five children to prison for bigamy after all those months she spent in the county jail charged with a crime that never happened.

And we had people struck by flood, drought, and pestilence, and Moses was there too—he was the sheriff. I was well into the book before that one dawned on me.

In the middle of my two weeks in Helena, I drove to Butte for the weekend. Halloween was that Sunday. Uncle Ed had booby-trapped the front door to entertain the trick or treaters. I approached each time with trepidation. On Saturday, we drove around town to look at the decorations which were quite elaborate. Halloween day, I drove to Whitehall to have dinner with Aunt Aila and Mary Jane, and then drove back to Helena. I took the familiar beautiful route through the Boulder Valley, always on the lookout for deer about to dart in front of my car. It was dusk as I pulled into Boulder. I took a brief detour to drive past the Courthouse. Behind the old jail, I saw a large tree silhouetted against the darkening sky, its long branches bare and bent. It looked like a hanging tree. I shuddered. I thought of Roy. Below I saw little ghosts and goblins scurrying across the street.

The next morning, back at the historical society, I combed through everything about the First World War and the Granite Mountain Fire. The file for the war contained Powder River Gang newsletters. The Powder River Gang was the 362nd, Grandpa Peter's regiment. One of the articles included a day-by-day description of the battle experience of one of the battalions, and it just happened to be the Second Battalion, Peter's battalion. I also found an article about the passing of Winks Brown, the soldier who helped Peter pull the wounded man into the trench in Flanders. Winks died after he was back home of a gunshot wound incurred during the war.

And, yes, Winks was from Philipsburg, just as Uncle Sam had said. That detail may sound inconsequential but any corroborating evidence helped give me a better sense of the reliability of my sources, in this case, my cantankerous uncle Sam.

I read the transcripts of oral histories by veterans of the First World War, hoping for some tidbits about Peter's regiment. It turned out, many of them were not living in the West when they went into the army and, as such, were not in Peter's division. One of these soldiers, Samuel Billings, was from Massachusetts. He said while out on patrol, the Germans shelled them with poison gas and high explosives. He stopped to help a wounded man before putting his gas mask on. After the war, his doctor recommended that he go west to build up his constitution, his health having been compromised by being gassed. The doctor thought work in the factories in the East would not be good for him. There was not enough ventilation. He followed the doctor's advice and moved to Montana in 1924. As for the war, he said he enlisted right away, when he was only eighteen, and was assigned to the First Division. He said, "Bullets, shells, gas whatever, one thing hurts as much as another. They're out to kill you, and you're out to kill them. In war, if you have to go, use whatever you've got." He said the war matured him. "I was no longer a kid."

While reading old issues of the *Madison Monitor*, the Twin Bridges weekly, hunting for anything about the orphanage, I stumbled across the poignant and prescient editorial about the war that I included in *One Night in a Bad Inn*, again showing the benefit of doing my own research. Gems abound, but I had to be around to see them. It's like sending someone out to look for gold, and they—not knowing you'd also like those other pebbles—leave them lying on the ground, the red ones that turn out to be rubies, and the blue ones that turn out to be sapphires. Though I was reading the 1914 papers, I didn't think about it being the year the war started. I was simply hunting for clues about the competition Grandma won which led to her college scholarship.

A November 1914 paper said the British government declared copper to be absolute contraband.

I looked in the Montana code to find out what the beneficiaries of a man killed on the job in 1937 received, what we now call workman's compensation. Peter left six beneficiaries—his widow and five children under eighteen. Grandma would get sixty-six and two-thirds percent of the wages he was receiving at the time he was killed, for four hundred weeks. This was subject to change when the number of beneficiaries decreased as the children grew up. Four hundred weeks was 7.7 years. The safety report from Peter's accident, which I found at the Butte Archives, said 2800 days, which is 7.7 years. Peter was earning $5.75 per day, according to the safety report.

While reviewing my time line, I saw that around the time the settlement money ran out, Grandma received her regular appointment at the post office and her salary went up considerably.

I read the Montana Industrial Accident Board report for the year Grandpa Peter was killed in the Tramway Mine. These reports provided another window into what was happening in the community, as did the Montana Department of Labor and Industry reports. I decided to read all the reports for the years applicable to my story. It was in the *Fifth Annual Report of the Industrial Accident Board*, for the twelve months ending June 30, 1920, that I learned when contract mining started in Butte and why. The report also said: "Butte still has the biggest pay-roll on record for a city of its population." I had read such in other sources, one being the delightful and informative book *Copper Camp* which said in 1905, "In proportion to population, Butte claimed the largest payroll in the world."

Aunt Aila drove up to Helena one day. I had told her that the old rectory was now a bed and breakfast and thought she might like to see it. She saw the spot where she used to sit in the kitchen and eat her lunch when she was a little girl. This was after she had been sick, and Father Tougas insisted she eat lunch at the rectory. We drove out to Broadwater and she showed me the dreary little houses they lived in when she was a child. Their little log house still stood, it survived all these years, it even withstood the 1935 earthquake while magnificent granite edifices crumbled. It strikes me as another metaphor for Grandma.

The next time I went to Helena, the little log house was gone.

Back at the historical society, I resumed reading the Industrial Accident Board reports, now the prison warden's reports, now the warden's correspondence, now the meeting minutes for the Board of Prison Commissioners (the parole board). This is odd. Arthur and Sarah were treated differently from the other prisoners regarding parole and release. I wondered why. Arthur was recommended for parole, not paroled, then released outright before his sentence ended. I read the minutes over a period of several years encompassing the time when Sarah and Arthur were in prison. Every time the board deviated from the warden's parole recommendation, the reason was noted in the minutes—every time except for the cases of Arthur Hughes and Sarah Hughes. There has to be a story.

I went through the governor's files for anything about Sarah and Arthur, something that might unlock the mystery around their parole. No answer there.

The prison logbook entry for Arthur said: "Expiration of sentence reduced by Rule 119." What was Rule 119? After much hunting, I found the definition in the "Laws, Rules, and Regulations" for the prison. Regulation 119 said: "Prisoners who are employed outside the prison walls as Trusties, in road building, or other work, shall be allowed ten (10) days good time allowance upon each month of their sentence in addition to that provided for by statute for good conduct." Did that mean each month of their total sentence, or each month of their sentence minus good time? Did it depend on how long they worked outside the walls?

I proceeded to go through the prisoner logbooks and wrote down the circumstances for each convict for whom Rule 119 was noted. Mr. A. in for forgery. Mr. B. in for grand larceny. Another Mr. B in for burglary. I recorded each prisoner's sentence and time served, calculated good time allowed (time off for good behavior), and calculated the deficit that could account for Rule 119. I plotted this on a graph and studied the data. I was looking for a pattern. I spent an insane amount of time on this. The pattern I found was—there was no pattern. From what I could gather, Rule 119 simply gave the warden discretion as to when to recommend parole.

And yet why deny Arthur parole and then release him outright, meaning no parole? And why no explanation in the minutes?

Months later, in an entirely different context, Auntie Mary remarked, "Grandma said Charles Evans Hughes was very good to her father."

"Did she say in what way?" I asked.

"No," she said.

A light went on. If Charles Evans Hughes helped Arthur get out of prison, Grandma wouldn't have mentioned it because she never told us that her father went to prison. When I returned home, I ordered the late supreme court chief justice's papers from the Library of Congress.

I also wanted to confirm how he was related to Arthur. The index showed genealogical data in his papers. When the microfilm arrived, again

I parked myself at the reader at the Sahara West Library. I found a letter complaining about Huerta, the Mexican dictator, but nothing about Arthur, and no genealogy that could confirm or negate that Charles Evans Hughes and Arthur were related.

Coming up empty with his papers, I read published biographies. Charles Evans Hughes was born in Glen Falls, New York. At his own request, he was tutored at home, what we now call home schooled. His father, David Charles Hughes, was a Welsh immigrant; his mother, Antoinette Carter, was American born. His father used to tell him, "Be nice to your mother, she won't be with us much longer." It reminded me of what Grandma used to say to her children: "You children need to learn how to do this, because I won't be with you much longer." She always thought she was going to die soon.

Fellow Republican Teddy Roosevelt convinced Charles Evans Hughes to run for governor of New York. Once elected, Hughes refused to heed party requests for political appointments; he thought they should be based on merit. He distrusted organizational politics. Sounds like Grandma.

President Taft appointed him associate justice to the Supreme Court in 1910. He left the court to run against Woodrow Wilson for president in 1916. Grandma told me that during the election campaign there was talk in the family that he was not born in this country.

After Wilson won, Hughes resumed his law practice, then served as secretary of state, then as a judge for the World Court. In 1930, President Hoover named him chief justice of the U.S. Supreme Court.

Now to print the transcript of Roy's murder trial. Off I went to the UNLV library. I sat down at the machine, slipped the microfiche into the reader, slid the reader around to find the first page, pressed print, waited, moved to the next page, focused, pressed print, waited, moved to the next page, pressed print, waited, put more money in the machine, focused, pressed print, . . . hours of that, 152 pages of that.

The next morning, I began my forced march through the trial transcript. It was 304 pages long, with two pages on each 8½ by 11 inch page. The print was very small and blurry. I had to study it closely to make out some of the words, so tedious, so very, very tedious, as legal proceedings tend to be. Gems were tucked away in there, I just knew it, I just had to persevere to find them. It's like mining—there's a valuable commodity buried in the dirt, but you have to dig through a tremendous amount of muck and waste rock to find it. Patience, patience, reading, note taking, more reading. At times, I shook my head in frustration at what I was reading. I wanted to reach through time and grab Roy by the shoulders and shake some sense into him. *Roy, will you please stop talking!* "I think I understand what a felony is," he says. He thinks he understands? I wanted to scold his lawyer: what were you thinking putting a chatterbox ding-a-ling defendant like Roy Walsh on the stand? Here you are giving him the spade. Here you are helping him dig his own grave. Here you are helping him pound nails into his own pine box. Now don't get me wrong, Archie and Roy did wrong and should have paid for it. They went there to rob a man, and they were armed. Roy's confession told us he was not innocent. Even so, he still deserved a rigorous, competent defense. All evidence pointed to an accidental shooting—when the gun went off, they both ran and didn't stop to rob Al Johnson.

I thought about how Roy described what happened and tried to visualize it. Roy said as he approached the side door, he heard a noise and jumped into the hop vines along the store and the gun went off. Roy was crouched down along the side of the store, not in front of the door, and yet the bullet went through the door and hit the only person in the house. The holes in the screen door and solid door showed that the bullet ranged upwards, which is consistent with Roy saying he was crouched down. Even so, Roy must have been holding the rifle at a strange angle, and Al Johnson must have been standing in an odd spot as he locked the door—it would seem to the side of the door rather than in front of it—for the trajectory of a bullet fired from Roy's gun to hit him in the neck. The more I think about it, the more bizarre it is. They had to be the two most unlucky men on earth that day.

Whenever I had the actual words of people in the story, I wanted to use them as much as possible. Personalities are revealed in their words. Since I had the actual trial transcript and Roy's signed confession, I had a plethora of quoted material. I had to strike the right balance between providing enough but not too much. I didn't want the story to become tedious, and yet I didn't want to leave out any salient detail else I confuse you. I didn't want to cut muscle, just the fat. The delineation was not always clear.

I decided to take testimony from the court documents, in particular Roy's confession and the trial transcript, and put those events where they happened in the story, as I had done with the Forsyth murder mystery part. I was careful how I worded what happened the night of the shooting. Roy contradicted himself as to whether his gun went off, which one could dismiss as a young troublemaker saying anything to save his own skin after he discovered he had confessed to murder. But considering the bizarre angle at which the bullet had to travel, and all the scuttlebutt about a third man, and an ex-con with no alibi at the scene, I still wondered, was it Roy's gun that went off? Was someone else there? I wrote, there was a shot, Roy ran, and Archie ran. Of that I am quite certain. All evidence I found corroborated that.

In early drafts of *One Night in a Bad Inn*, I included my reactions to what happened at Roy's trial, as I did here a few paragraphs ago. All through the writing, I struggled with whether to include my reactions or hold back and let you react without my prejudicing your reaction. In Roy's trial, I decided to leave the reactions to you.

The dilemma, as always, was where to draw the line between what to spell out and what to leave unsaid. Silence need not always be filled with chatter, and so it is on the page. I wanted to walk you right up to that fine line and stop, and let your mind fill in the rest, give you just enough to jumpstart your imagination.

Early in my research, I read Robert Graves's autobiography *Good-Bye to All That*. He was a British officer in the First World War. I remembered a scene in his book where a soldier ran out into no man's land to help a wounded soldier. Those back in the trench watched in disbelief. He could be easily shot. At least that's how I remembered it. It sounded much like what my grandfather did when he saved that man's life in Flanders. I thought, I'll look back at what Graves wrote and possibly quote him. I found the passage in the book and discovered that he did not say those in the trench watched in disbelief. I was watching in disbelief. I was there in the trench with those soldiers. He walked me right up to that fine line and left me there, and I filled in the rest with my imagination. I was engaged in the story, a participant as it were, not merely a spectator. I wanted to do that in my book.

As I wrote, and read what I had written, I realized that Roy was becoming the protagonist of this part of the story. The victim's story ends with his death, right when the criminal's begins a new chapter and becomes more interesting. As time passes, one fades from memory, the other can gain sympathy if he is an amiable, likable fellow, such as Roy Walsh. I could see this happening to me and to the people in the story. I had to make a deliberate effort to bring poor Al Johnson back into it, lest he be forgotten.

As I mentioned earlier, I had decided to split the book into four parts, each with a title. Now I decided it should be six parts. It made sense to make the Archie and Roy debacle a separate part of the book; it was a complete story in and of itself. But what to call it, I needed a title. I thought Shakespeare, something from Shakespeare, or something that sounds like Shakespeare, a play on words. Archie and Roy, two men, *Two Gentlemen of Verona*. I could have called it "Two Knuckleheads from Butte," but that sounded flip, and after all a man was killed. *Two Gentlemen of Verona* kept floating through my mind, Verona, Renova, Al Johnson was a merchant, *The Merchant of Venice* . . . "The Merchant of Renova." That's it. And it put the focus on Al Johnson, the victim, which was where I wanted it.

To fill out the story, add texture as it were, I decided to research the tertiary characters, even those who made mere cameo appearances. I thought having some background on them would make them more real. I found a memoriam for Howard Johnson, the county attorney who prosecuted Archie and Roy; it provided biographical information and listed the names of his sons. I tracked down his son Keith in Butte. Keith was a perfect resource in that he was very careful about what he said, no conjecture. I found his father, Howard Johnson, intriguing, this young, newly elected county attorney, trying his first major case, a murder case. What Keith told me about his father's experience as a pilot at the end of the First World War, and all he accomplished before he was elected county attorney, helped me draw the picture of a very ambitious young man. It added to the setting.

While in the throes of writing about Archie and Roy, at the end of a visit to Kennewick, I was sitting in the airport waiting for my flight, visiting with Mom and Dad, when all of a sudden our attention was diverted to a young man walking through the airport, flanked by two guards. He was a tall, skinny, scary-looking kid with long, light brown dread-locks. He was heavily shackled, feet manacled, hands manacled. A modern day Roy Walsh, I thought. So sad.

I couldn't help but think about the contrast in choices made by Grandma and Archie.

All of this research about crimes and prisoners and the prison made me think a lot about the situation of prisoners and about capital punishment.

In my hunt for old prison records, just finding the names of the prisons took some work. Though the one in Deer Lodge is still called the Montana State Prison, in many places, they aren't called prisons any more; instead, it is the Washington State Reformatory at Monroe, Missouri calls them correctional centers, elsewhere they are called penitentiaries, and they are run by the Department of Corrections. Lofty, admiral goals are imbedded in those names, but what if the convict doesn't want to be reformed, what if he is not penitent, what if he doesn't want to be corrected?

The argument for paroling those convicted of violent crime is that the convict can be rehabilitated, corrected, reformed, which assumes he is penitent. The trouble is, a person may not want to be rehabilitated, corrected, or reformed. When it comes to behavior, a human being is not a machine that can be overhauled and repaired and restored to normal working order. We cannot send a person off to be corrected, as we put a car in the shop to be fixed. It is not a matter of *can* the criminal be rehabilitated, but does he *will* to be, does he choose to be law abiding. It is his decision. Others can guide him, can encourage him, can cajole him, but ultimately he must decide, decide to do good and avoid evil. No one else can do that for him. This is the realm of the will, and when we enter the realm of the will, we enter the realm of soul, the realm of the spiritual.

I don't think Archie and Roy intended to kill anybody. However, they did attempt armed robbery, and even if it didn't happen at Renova, if they kept that up, sooner or later somebody was going to get killed, themselves or somebody else. From everything I learned about Archie, he straightened up after prison. I can't help but wonder whether his buddy being hanged shocked him into it, or was it the nine years in prison, or both.

I felt I was getting to know these people. I found myself talking about them as if I knew them. I had to convey this in the book.

In December of 1999, I flew to Mom and Dad's for Christmas. While boarding the flight to Salt Lake, I heard someone cough. A sense of dread swept over me, not my normal reaction to hearing someone cough. I took my seat and didn't give it another thought.

Mom and Dad had invited several people over for dinner the next evening. I now had a bit of a cough. There were nine of us at dinner. Chuck had done research in Antarctica, and we were interested in hearing all about it. After dinner we watched a documentary about Antarctica.

While watching the katabatic blow and blow across the snow and ice, I got a sudden chill. I thought it was from watching the wind blow over the snow and ice.

During the night, my cough grew much worse. I was leaning over the edge of the bed coughing and coughing so badly I thought I'd choke to death. I was achy, my skin hurt. All I could think about was the people at dinner. I hoped I didn't give them whatever I had.

By morning, I felt miserable and weak, and was still coughing a deep, gut-wrenching cough. Mom got out the thermometer. I had a fever. Dad said I better go to the doctor. Mom took me. "It's influenza," the doctor said. Influenza? I had done all that research on the 1918 Spanish Flu. Cough, fever, sudden chill, I knew those were symptoms of the flu, but it didn't occur to me that I could actually get it. The doctor gave me a prescription for Tamiflu. I didn't know there was medicine for flu. Tamiflu was fairly new then. We stopped at the pharmacy, filled the prescription, and went back to Mom and Dad's. I lay in bed and moaned. Soon, the symptoms diminished. Thank God for Tamiflu.

I know I said I wanted to steep myself in the times and places in my book, but the flu I could have done without. However, it did give me a greater understanding of what happened in 1918 and colored how I wrote about the influenza pandemic. Shortly after I came down with the flu, Dad got it, then Mom got it. We all recovered, thank God. In 1918, people didn't.

CHAPTER THIRTY-THREE

ON ONE OF the tapes of Grandma talking about her life, when asked why she and Grandpa Peter got married in Pocatello and not Butte, she said, "Because there was a depression on when we got married. We were very foolish to get married at that time. People should not make a drastic move when there's a depression on. There was a depression on, and he had this good job in Pocatello, Idaho."

That doesn't fully answer the question. They could have gotten married in Butte before Peter went to Pocatello, but they didn't. They eloped. I never thought of it that way until I began to scrutinize their lives and decisions. Grandma said her mother tried to send the sheriff after her to stop her from running off to marry Peter. She was almost twenty years old, so there was nothing the sheriff could do. He probably sympathized with her.

Grandma also said her mother tore up her clothes to prevent her from going away to college. There were several reasons to elope.

As for what Grandma said about Peter working elsewhere because there was a depression on, I knew this wasn't the Great Depression of the 1930s. Grandma and Grandpa married in 1921. I needed to learn about this other depression.

The depression of which Grandma spoke happened right after the First World War. The war was a jolting, brutal, colossal government intrusion into lives and economies, something neither recovered from easily. The War Industries Board took control of sale of copper during the war. As a result, when the war ended in November of 1918, the mining companies were left with enormous stockpiles of unsold copper. The price of copper plummeted from a war-time high of twenty-six cents per pound down to fifteen cents by March of 1919, a forty-two percent drop. The peace conference began in January of 1919 and would go on for months. The author of the 1919–1920 Montana Industrial Board report called the debate over the peace terms a "political football," and said the delay created uncertainty in the markets. This clearly affected my family in Butte. Europe had formerly purchased sixty percent of American copper.

Markets do not like uncertainty, it causes them to freeze up, and there is no uncertainty like not knowing what your government is about to do in a big way. As the victors gathered in Paris to decide how to punish the vanquished and redraw the map of the world, many Europeans waited and watched in anticipation, not knowing which country they would be living in when it was all decided, whose laws would govern. This uncertainty cascaded onto countries trading with them, such as us. How do you write a contract if you don't know whose laws will govern? Once all was settled and the borders redrawn, the markets would thaw, but when? How quickly? Yet the economy did recover quickly, and my grandparents spent the roaring twenties back in Butte.

I wondered why the Great Depression of the 1930s lasted so much longer than the depression after the First World War. I did more reading. As for the severity of the post-war depression, from 1919 to 1921, unemployment tripled. From May of 1920 to June of 1921, wholesale prices collapsed, a whopping fifty-six percent drop. The depression of 1920–1921 was the worst economic contraction on record up to then, worse than after the Civil War, worse than after the War of 1812. Though quite deep, it was short. We came out of it quickly. And yet, the Great Depression went on and on and on. Why? For one thing, the politicians reacted quite differently. In 1920 we were essentially without a president. President Wilson was incapacitated by a stroke in the fall of 1919, but this was kept quiet. He stayed secluded. When Harding took office in early 1921, he pushed for cutting taxes and cutting federal spending, which Congress did, the thinking being, if Americans must tighten their belts, so too must government. After the 1929 stock market crash, the politicians did the opposite, and a panic morphed into a long, long, long depression. To say more about the differences in these two depressions, one short, one horribly long, would have required a mountain of research. I decided not to pursue that thread. The place to address the differences would have been when the Great Depression started, and I thought delving into it at that point could be a distraction, too much extraneous detail at a dramatic part of the story.

Some subjects cry out for a metaphor. The Great Depression struck me as one such subject. I thought of the economy as a ship. Ships are timeless.

They seem almost animate, we call them by name. I became attracted to the ship as metaphor by Tolstoy, in *Anna Karenina*, when Anna said the count wanted to "burn his ships," and when Levin feared he had burned his. I had always heard that metaphor about burning bridges. The ship in that metaphor struck me as more vivid, more radical, more final. I thought of Cortes. If a bridge burns, there may still be a way to get across, though difficult. After burning your ships, there's no going back short of building a new one, which may be impossible.

As I reviewed the data I had collected on how much ore was mined in Butte, and watched it drop year after year after 1929, I realized the worst of the Great Depression did not happen overnight. From 1929 to 1930, mine production in Butte dropped forty-five percent; the next year, another twenty percent; the next year, sixty-five percent. I thought of a massive ship slowly starved of fuel, she sputters, she slows, the engine dies, but she does not stop on a dime; there is too much weight, too much motive force.

First I wrote, "A massive ship that is the U.S. economy does not stop on a dime." Something didn't sit right. Then I thought about a ship heading for the falls, if the captain doesn't change course, catastrophe looms. That didn't seem right either. After much pondering, I settled on "a massive ship does not stop on a dime," and followed that with sputtering and slowing and stopping, as a massive ship starved of fuel slowly glides to a listless stop, as did our economy in the 1930s.

Speaking of metaphors, I still needed to find the exact quote by St. Teresa of Avila from which I culled the title, *One Night in a Bad Inn*. The priest I heard use the metaphor might have been paraphrasing her, and my memory might have paraphrased him. I wanted to use Teresa's exact words as an introductory quote.

St. Teresa of Avila lived in Spain in the sixteenth century. As a young woman, she joined the Carmelite order, which had grown lax, the nuns more devoted to gossip than prayer. In Teresa's words, "the convent was not founded on a strict observance." After a prolonged illness, Teresa embarked on reforming the Carmelites. She founded the Discalced Carmelites, discalced meaning without shoes. They were cloistered in their monastery, lived in silence, and devoted their lives to prayer.

Teresa was a mystic, and she wrote much. My hope was to find someone familiar with her works who could lead me to the bad inn quote. I couldn't remember which priest used the metaphor, or even where I was living when I heard it. I asked my parish priests. "Wasn't me," said Father Joe. "It wasn't me, but I like it," said Father Tom. I tried to find Father Peter, a Dominican whom I heard give a talk about Teresa, but no luck.

I picked up a book of Teresa's writings and started to thumb through it. The publisher was the Institute for Carmelite Studies. I thought, I'll call them. Surely there's a St. Teresa scholar there, and he can help me. I called and told the receptionist, I would like to speak to someone about St. Teresa of Avila's writings, and explained about my book and the title. She said I had to ask for a specific person. If I didn't have a name, she couldn't help me.

Then I remembered that a couple I knew when I lived in Maryland were Third Order Carmelites (lay people who are members of the order). I wrote to Marge. She sent me the passage and source.

I was surprised to see that "one night in a bad inn" was an exact quote, according to the translator, validating my earlier bold editorial decision to change the title from *A Night in a Bad Inn* to *One Night in a Bad Inn.* While reading the rest of the passage, I found my introductory quote: "The bad inn lasts only a night."

NOW TO RETURN to researching felons. In the back of my mind, I remembered something about William Hughes being charged with burglary or robbery in Forsyth in March of 1914. Naturally I thought he might be our Bill, Grandma's eldest brother. I wanted to find out.

Aunt Aila said there was a reform school for boys in Miles City. I thought since Bill was sixteen, perhaps he was sent there. I called Jodie at the Historical Society. No luck.

I pulled out the papers and books I had collected about Rosebud County history. As I perused *They Came and Stayed,* searching for clues about the robbery, I also looked for biographical information on tertiary characters from that part of the story: Sheriff Moses, Judge Crum, Coroner Booth, and the lawyers. I found nothing about the robbery, but I did find information about Coroner Booth. I looked for Sheriff Moses but didn't find him. I called Brian at the historical society in Helena and asked if there was a biography of William Moses in the "mug book," a collection of Montana family histories. No Moses.

I remembered that Liz Cole had given me an article about Judge Crum. I dug it out of my Forsyth file and read it again. Judge Crum's grandchildren said he spoke in CAPITAL LETTERS. How vivid. I pulled up the part of the manuscript where Crum IS SCOLDING ARTHUR AND SARAH AND PUT HIS DIALOGUE IN CAPITAL LETTERS. My sources for his words were the trial minutes and newspaper stories.

This business about William Hughes being charged with burglary or robbery kept tugging at me. I looked it up in my notes on the computer. It wasn't William Hughes, and it wasn't 1914. It was Fred Hughes. He and an accomplice broke into a pool hall in 1930. Could he be the long lost baby Sarah was carrying while in jail? I found his prison records. From his age, he couldn't be our Sarah's child.

I still had this idea in my head about a William Hughes being accused of something in March of 1914. I called Liz at the Rosebud County Courthouse. She checked the court records. No William Hughes. Still I was convinced there must be. Something kept tickling by brain, and it was not going to stop.

I thought, I'll look at the Forsyth newspapers.

Sitting at the microfilm machine, armed with a roll of dimes and my notebook, I began to read more old issues of the *Forsyth Times-Journal*. For some reason I decided to start in June and work backward. I have no idea why. Rewind a page, glance over the headlines, rewind a page, refocus, glance over the headlines, rewind a page, page after page after page, June . . . May . . . April . . ., "US Marines killed in Open Fight with Mexico." Hmm. What's that about. The April 23, 1914, paper said four were killed and twenty wounded in a fight against the Huerta government. Hmm. I made a note. The April 2, 1914, paper said Attorney General Kelly ruled that under Montana law, a girl under sixteen cannot consent to marriage even with parental approval. It may be apropos to Bill's illegal marriages. I printed it and made a note. Rewind a page, glance over the headlines, rewind a page, glance—Moses. What's this? It was one of those notices to creditors when someone dies. The man who died was Sheriff Moses. Being the sheriff, his obituary should be a full article. It would no doubt yield helpful biographical information and possibly a picture too. It would be great to see what he looked like. I jumped back to find it. Rewind, rewind, check the date, rewind some more, oh, too much, now forward. Advance, advance.

Oh—my—goodness.

On January 22, 1914, exactly one year after Arthur dug up that body, the *Forsyth Times-Journal* headline read: "Sheriff Wm. Moses Shot and Killed." I couldn't believe it. I read on . . . shot and killed . . . by his own deputy . . . The deputy was charged with murder. I about fell off my chair. I felt like Jennie Hayes when she found out Arthur was alive.

It seemed every time I turned over a stone, the story became more dramatic. Behind every person who touched my grandparents' and great-grandparents' lives, there was a story. Nothing in this story, I mean in the entire book, was plain vanilla. Nonstop drama, my brother called it. Who shot the sheriff? The deputy. The deputy? I figured the assailant would have been a bad guy he was chasing down, not his own deputy, not a deputy he had known for years. Oh, my. I've got to get the rest of this story. I started going forward in the microfilm and forgot all about the mythical William Hughes robbery of 1914, this time just stopping at the front pages, figuring a story this big would always be front-page news. Here they are, the articles about the trial. How could I have missed them? Oh, it's because Moses's name was not in the headlines for the trial. And it was moved to Custer County. Not guilty? How can that be? Deputy John Burgess shot Sheriff Moses several times in front of several witnesses, and he is found not guilty? He claimed self defense. He shot his own wife in the melee. Dr. Huene recovered three bullets from Sheriff Moses's body, all from John Burgess's gun, one through the back of the neck, according to the newspaper.

Earlier in my reading about the history of Rosebud County, I learned about the Bitle murder. Undersheriff Bitle was staking out suspected cattle rustlers, a gun battle ensued which ended with Bitle shot dead. That trial was also moved to Custer County. The county attorney charged the shooter with first degree murder. The jury found him guilty, but only of manslaughter, and he was sentenced to ten years in prison. In both cases, a Rosebud County peace officer was shot in the line of duty, and the trial was moved to Custer County. In one case the shooter was convicted of a lesser charge; in the other, the shooter got off scot-free.

I was struck by the sharp contrast between those cases and Roy's death sentence. Justice is blind as she holds the scales, yet she wears no halo and claims no infallibility.

Apparently Sheriff Moses's trouble started right after he carted my great-grandparents off to prison. Deputy Burgess said he "didn't think Moses was in his right mind from the time of the Hughes trial." Further testimony showed that Burgess and Moses had quarreled for a long time, and the two had threatened to kill each other. From reading the newspaper accounts of the trial, it sounded as though Sheriff Moses's wife's leaving him put him over the edge. It's easy to turn the victim, who is dead and can't defend himself, into the bad guy. I wondered about Deputy Burgess shooting Moses three times, once through the back of the neck. It sounded outrageous, how could the jury find him not guilty? Could there be more to the story?

I obtained the court file from Custer County. Unfortunately, the trial transcript wasn't available. I asked if there had been an inquest, thinking the doctor who performed the autopsy would have testified. No inquest. I called Liz at the Courthouse in Forsyth. No inquest there either. All I had to go on about the bullet being fired into the back of his neck was the newspaper. I included it anyway with a note saying I was not able to confirm this elsewhere. I didn't find anything in the court records that was contrary to what the newspapers reported. In all my research, I did not observe flights of fancy on the part of reporters at the *Forsyth Times-Journal*.

I must admit, when Jennie Hayes said in her deposition in New York that Arthur told her he had to get away from Montana because the sheriff wanted him dead, I dismissed it as an exaggeration. Then when I learned all this about Sheriff Moses and John Burgess, I thought perhaps I shouldn't be so hasty to jump to such a conclusion about my dear great-grandfather. But even if it were true that the sheriff wanted him dead, he could have simply moved his family to another county—they had already sold the homestead. If he wanted to leave Sarah, he could have just run off, he didn't have to fake his own death. Yet this way, if Sarah got the life insurance money, he might feel he had provided for his family, and as such, assuage his guilty conscience in a most bizarre way.

While eating breakfast at a bed and breakfast in Helena, one of the men at the table asked about my book. I told him about the fire on the ranch, about finding the dead body and the murder charge.

The man asked, "Did it happen in March?"

Surprised, I said, "Yes, what made you ask that?"

"Because if I lived on one of those ranches out in eastern Montana back then, by March I'd be ready to do something crazy."

Thinking about Sheriff Moses and his deputy threatening to kill each other, and then the deputy actually doing it, and Judge Crum cussing out the county attorney and pulling his revolver on him, and Arthur going to all that trouble to dig up a dead body so he could disappear, one could conclude they got a bit cranky.

After I wrote this into my manuscript, I got to thinking about Sheriff Moses being shot and killed only a few months after he arrested my great-grandparents and carted them off to prison, and about Coroner Booth being in a serious auto accident while Sarah was in jail awaiting trial for killing Arthur, and a few years later, the Yellowstone overflowed its banks and flooded Forsyth and destroyed Coroner Booth's store, and a terrible drought hit eastern Montana, and the prison warden who had charge over Sarah and Arthur was removed from office not long after they left prison, and Judge Crum was impeached. Quite a string of bad luck for people involved in Sarah's arrest and imprisonment. Strange.

Now as I review my old notebooks, I see it right here in my notes: a criminal petition against William Hughes on March 14, 1914. So specific. Why did I write that? Why wasn't it in the computer? And yet, the crazy circuitous route I took chasing a ghost led me to Sheriff Moses and his deputy shooting him.

Chapter Thirty-four

Mining questions were collecting on my to-do list, questions about working conditions that were too specific for the books I'd read. For answers, I called a former Butte miner and professional curmudgeon. After answering my questions, he started complaining about the IWW (the International Workers of the World) and out of the blue said, "It was our crew who blasted the hall," meaning blew up the Miners' Union Hall in 1914.

"Why?" I asked. "To get rid of the IWW?"

"Yes," he said.

"Were they afraid the IWW would take over the Union?"

"They already had."

"Was Riley IWW?" Riley was head of the union in 1914.

"I don't know about him."

This man was only a toddler when all this happened, so he obviously heard about it from someone else. Colorful though it was, it was hearsay.

Early in my research, I read the *Encyclopedia of the American West* article about Butte which said the miners "made the highest wages in industrial America; indeed, by 1905, in proportion to population, Butte had the largest payroll in the world." Quite a bold and telling statement, I was delighted to find it. I quoted it in my manuscript. Later, as I mentioned a few pages ago, I found statements about Butte having the largest payroll per capita in the world in other sources: in the book *Copper Camp* and in an Industrial Accident Board report. It made sense, if the miners were earning the "highest wages in industrial America," and the miners made up the lions share of the workforce, Butte could easily have the largest payroll per capita.

Then one day, tucked away in a drawer at my parents' house, I found old newspapers Mom had kept that included articles about Butte history. One was the April 7, 1979, *Montana Standard* which quoted a 1888 newspaper that said Butte wages were the highest in the West. Bricklayers earned $6 to $7 per day. Carpenters and stonemasons earned $4 to $5 per day. Miners earned $3.50 to $4 per day. I was baffled. This would indicate, at least in 1888, that bricklayers earned a higher daily wage than miners. Granted, the *Encyclopedia of the American West* reference was for 1905, not 1888. Relative wages could have changed. I was interested in the period of time when my relatives arrived, the early twentieth century.

This new information cast doubt in my mind as to whether I could make the "highest wages in industrial America" claim. I decided to look into it further.

The encyclopedia article said "in industrial America." Were carpenters and stonemasons lumped with miners as industrial workers? I understood carpenters and stonemasons to be craft workers. Even if they were a different category of workers, this piqued my interest in finding out what wages were for the crafts in 1905—my Irish great-granduncle John Gribben was a carpenter, and my great-grandfather Arthur was a stonemason and bricklayer. I thought it would be interesting to know how their wages compared to the miners at the time the miners were the highest paid workers in "industrial America," according to the encyclopedia article.

I already had day's pay data for the miners. I remembered seeing wages for craft workers in one of the Montana Labor and Industry reports. I dug those reports out of my files. When I read the reports the first time, this wasn't something that interested me, another reason to keep copies of documents and buy books; I never knew in how many varied directions my research would take me nor how many times I might want to revisit a source. The *Fourth Biennial Report of the Department of Labor and Industry* said on July 15, 1919, the mining companies granted a pay increase of a dollar a day, bringing day's pay for miners, first class engineers, mill, and smeltermen to $5.75 per day. Journeymen of all crafts would receive $6.50 per day.

That was the case in 1919. But the statement about earning the highest wages in industrial America was for 1905. How had things changed in the intervening years? There had been a world war. There had been a miner's union in 1905. There was not in 1919. The hunt continued. Even though the Labor and Industry report distinguished miners from craft workers, meaning what I found did not negate the statement about earning the highest wages "in industrial America," I still wanted to know how wages for miners compared with craft workers in 1905.

Again I called Brian at the historical society. He searched but couldn't find craft wages circa 1905. I looked in my notes and saw that another book made a similar claim about Butte miners being highly paid. I never did find that author's source for the highest wages claim, nor could I refute it, though I did stumble across evidence tending to support the claim. I wasn't comfortable using such definitive language without being able to confirm it solidly with a primary source, so I softened the language in my manuscript, saying instead that they were *among* the highest paid industrial workers in the country.

I am wary of definitive absolute statements claiming the highest, the most, the worst ever. Early in my research, I came across a source that made a worst ever statement, which I interpreted to be as of today. Upon further inspection I discovered that the information had been culled from old newspaper headlines. What may have been the worst ever at the time the headline was written may not be now.

For the Granite Mountain Fire, I easily found a list of all hard-rock mining disasters in the United States and how many men were killed in each and could confirm that, yes indeed, the Granite Mountain Fire was the worst hard-rock mining disaster in American history.

Another such statement was that the Meuse Argonne was the bloodiest battle in American history. I understood bloodiest to mean the most casualties. I figured there must be a book somewhere that gives casualty numbers for all wars in which our country was involved. But where to find such a book? I know, I'll call West Point. I called the reference librarian at West Point, and right off the top of his head he recommended *Warfare and Armed Conflicts* by Michael Clodfelter. I found it at the UNLV library and compared casualty numbers. The Meuse Argonne was indeed the bloodiest battle in American history and still is.

Clodfelter also said the U.S. military saw 70,000 flu cases at home and abroad, thirty-two percent were fatal, and most of the non-battle deaths in the First World War were from the 1918 Spanish Influenza. That comes to 22,400 deaths from the flu. All those men passed the physical, meaning they were otherwise healthy. The equivalent of an entire division, dead from the flu.

As I RESUMED writing the manuscript, my great-grandfather Arthur seemed to be fading away. He was fading from Grandma's life. She said he left and came back, left and came back, three or four times, then he left for good.

CHAPTER THIRTY-FIVE

ARTHUR FADED AWAY to Portland. Grandma found him there, so I went there too.

At the historical society in downtown Portland, I found out where Arthur lived and where Grandma and Grandpa lived. I read about the neighborhoods. Portland seemed to have a much quieter history than Butte.

One item still staring up at me from my to-do list was to confirm that Arthur was in the Spanish-American War. His death certificate in Oregon said he was; his second wife Eunice was the informant. I had already pursued several avenues to confirm this with no luck. The National Archives did not have military records for him. I found nothing in Wilkes-Barre to confirm his enlistment, which was where he was living during the war. I thought I'll try here in Portland. The man at the information desk said he could do a search to see if Arthur received a pension for being a veteran of the war. As he typed away on the computer, I stood at the counter and waited, feeling bleary after a full day of research, not thinking of anything in particular, my mind drifting as I idly gazed out the window at a large stone structure. The thought floated into my head, that looks like an old church, the church where Arthur worked.

Could it be? I checked. It was.

The man found no record of Arthur receiving a pension for being in the Spanish-American War.

As I poked through more records, I stumbled across the obituary for Eunice's first husband. It said he was a Spanish-American War veteran. Perhaps she was confusing husbands.

IN THE SUMMER OF 2000, I planned to make another trip to Forsyth. I suggested to Mom and Dad that they come too, so Mom could see her grandparents' ranch and where her mother lived as a child. Dad said, "While we're out there, let's go to Mount Rushmore." I said, "Okay, and let's go to Deadwood." Liz had mentioned taking her grandmother there.

First I flew to Pocatello to see where Grandma and Grandpa got married, and from there drove down to Soda Springs to see the remnants of Conda, the tiny mining community built by the Anaconda Copper Mining Company to house workers at the phosphate mine. Grandma and Grandpa lived there right after they married. Grandpa Peter worked as a motorman at the phosphate mine.

Then I flew to Billings and drove to Forsyth. At the museum, I read more diaries. At the Courthouse, I did more digging into the criminal and civil records. That evening, I joined Liz and her friends at the country club for a round of golf. As we played, I could hear the occasional crack of a rifle at the firing range off in the distance. One of the women hit her ball into the rough and wandered over to find it. Another warned her that so-and-so bludgeoned a rattlesnake to death with his pitching wedge over there the other day.

Whenever I mentioned the address of Sarah's house in town, the response was, "That's south of the tracks," as if that meant something. I was hesitant to approach a strange house uninvited after what happened in Wales. I wasn't worried about the people, just the dogs. After we finished our round of golf, Liz and I went to the house, Liz leading the way, undaunted by possible dogs. An elderly man opened the door and invited us in. He said he was renting it. I asked if he had come across any old letters or papers left by previous owners. He hadn't. I tried to contact the owners of the house to find out if they had. No luck.

The next day, I went to the library. After explaining about my book, the librarian directed me the local interest section. Then she opened a cupboard and took out a large box and said, "This might be helpful too." I sat down at a table and started going through the contents. This was starting to feel like an archeological dig. I never knew what I would unearth. In the box, I found a short, typed manuscript written by Elizabeth Newnes June. It was about her life, and it was marvelous—another peek behind the curtain of history at everyday life from days gone by. She wrote about how they harvested the ice, and collected rain water in a cistern, and made soap, and about how two of her brothers joined the army in the First World War and were shipped off to France and lived; a brother who stayed home died of the 1918 Spanish Flu.

People such as Elizabeth, who write diaries and personal histories and donate them to a library or museum or archives, do a tremendous service to history. They may never realize how valuable those simple artifacts are to researchers. They are gold.

"Is Elizabeth Newnes June still here?" I asked. The librarian told me she passed away a few weeks ago.

I went to see Mignon Tadsen again, the woman who grew up on the ranch across from my great-grandparents. She went to school with Grandma and her brothers. Mignon was now living in a rest home. I found her sitting in the multipurpose room with curlers in her hair. I explained that I was Aila Hughes's granddaughter and asked what she remembered about Mrs. Hughes.

"That Mrs. Hughes," she said, "she was a character. She'd cuss out my grandfather. He'd say, 'You don't know anything about anything,' and that would get her going. They'd cuss each other out. My grandfather enjoyed it.

"She'd come riding up in her buggy with two horses at top speed and get to the house and *whoa*!" and Mignon motioned pulling back on the reins. "Why she could get in and out of that buggy faster, well, faster than I can get in and out of a car. Then she'd yell and we'd all come into the house and have coffee. There was always coffee on the stove."

"Did Mrs. Hughes speak with an accent?" I asked.

"No, not that I remember," she said. Then she added, "My grandfather had great respect for Mrs. Hughes's knowledge."

"What do you remember about Mr. Hughes?"

"I don't remember anything about Mr. Hughes," she said. Then she paused a moment and declared emphatically, "I *liked* Mrs. Hughes! I didn't believe those things people said about her. People and their gossip."

The way she said "people and their gossip," she sounded like Grandma T.

"What did they say?" I asked.

She looked around and said, "If she doesn't get here soon, I'm going to cuss." I was baffled by that. I thought maybe she meant the woman who was supposed to remove her rollers and comb her out.

I asked what Aila and Bill and Hector were like (Grandma and her elder brothers). She said Aila was quiet. Bill was quiet and a know-it-all. Hector was more talkative and friendly. "I liked Hector the best," she said.

She told me about riding to town in the buggy with her grandfather. He'd stop the buggy at the edge of town then gallop the horses into town.

"Do you remember the first time you saw an airplane?" I asked.

"Do I!" she said. "We saw this plane flying, it was up there, up there, and then it was down. There was a big write up about it in the newspaper."

"Was it open range where you walked to school?" I asked.

Mignon laughed. "When it was really cold, my grandfather would come in the buggy and get us."

"What animals roamed around?"

"Bobcats, coyotes, foxes in the chicken house. I liked those days, all was open. Where is she? If she doesn't get here soon, I'm going to cuss."

I asked if she ever went to the Hughes house. She said yes.

"What was it like?"

"It was very clean."

"So you were born in 1898, the same year as Bill," I said.

"Yes."

"Wow, Mignon, 102, that's great."

"I don't see what's so great about it," she said. "I think I've lived too long."

She would be around for another five.

I DROVE TO BILLINGS and picked up Mom and Dad at the airport and returned to Forsyth. I took them out to the old Hughes homestead. Whit and Elsie still lived there. I tried to rouse them but couldn't. I had been warned their hearing wasn't good. I walked over to the corral to look at the horses. As I approached, the colt sauntered toward me, looking curious and friendly. The mare stomped and scraped the ground angrily with her hoof. Even with the fence between us, she was intimidating. I backed away.

We left Forsyth and drove to Miles City. I wanted to see the Olive Hotel where Sarah and Tom stayed back in 1913, and to retrace their steps through town and take pictures. As we entered the wood-paneled lobby of the Olive, I imagined it looked much the same when my great-grandmother Sarah marched across it eighty-three years earlier to register herself and Tom. I asked the woman at the front desk if she had old registry books from 1913. She said no.

Next, we set off for Deadwood. As we drove south, gone were scatterings of ponderosa pines and cottonwoods, just pale green sage and sparse brown grass and desolation as far as the eye could see, as if we were on the road to the end of the earth. I saw several antelope running, as they always seem to do. Cattle must have been out there, way out there. I didn't see any.

We passed hardly any cars. Mom's Irish cousin Sam said, when he told his travel agent in England that he wanted to go to Montana, the travel agent exclaimed, "Montana! Nobody goes to Montana! Even the Americans don't go to Montana!" It did seem to hold true that day.

At Broadus, I saw the sign for the Powder River. I was delighted—the Powder River Gang was the nickname for Grandpa Peter's regiment. I hadn't studied the map enough to realize we'd be crossing it. We stopped to get a better look. As I leaned over the railing of the bridge, down below I saw two boys playing in the river. They looked like modern incarnations of Tom and Huck and waved enthusiastically once they saw us. We waved back. As I raised my camera to take a picture, they snapped smartly to attention.

Though quite by accident, I was able to confirm that the Powder River was nothing more than a contiguous collection of puddles, at least the day I saw it.

As we approached the Black Hills, the sparse brown grass and pale green sage gave way to deep green pine trees and vivid red rock. The beautiful contrast of bold colors made the place feel less desolate. We pulled into tiny Deadwood and easily found our hotel on Main Street.

Deadwood is definitely on the road to nowhere, but if you are ever going that way, don't miss it. It's a must-see, as is Mount Rushmore. Deadwood is an Old West town restored to its Old West charm. We wandered down Main Street and happened upon Calamity Jane cracking her bull whip. A little farther down Main Street, I heard a familiar sound harkening back to my childhood. I turned around to see two little boys decked out in cowboy garb, firing cap guns.

The historic preservation that has gone on in Deadwood is impressive. I thought of the opportunities in my hometown of Butte. Butte has so much more history, so many more colorful stories and characters, and it's on two interstates. It is on the road to everywhere.

WITH EVERY ITEM checked off my to-do list, I added more questions. I seemed to be drawing from an infinite well.

I still had much research to do in Butte that summer of 2000. I delayed scheduling my trip as I followed the news about the forest fires. The highway between Butte and Helena was closed. Family and friends said the smoke was horribly oppressive and made the sky dreary. "Ash fell like rain," Aunt Aila said. "You could taste it in the back of your throat." They were essentially living in the middle of an enormous camp fire for weeks.

Once the fires were under control, I went. Aunt Aila and I drove down to Twin Bridges again. We stopped at the Old Hotel for lunch. Henry Lockwood, the man I met at the orphanage, was also there having lunch. Twin Bridges is the kind of place where you can bump into everyone you know in a matter of minutes.

After lunch, we drove over to Uncle Sam's house. He wasn't there. Aunt Aila said he'd be down at the Lost Cabin. That would be a good name for a book about Uncle Sam: *Found at the Lost Cabin*. And we did indeed find him there, sitting at the bar. I asked for a cup of coffee. "This is a bar," the barmaid said.

After a short visit, we went back to Aunt Aila's and I spent more time visiting with her and Mary Jane and hearing their stories about Grandma, and stories Grandma had told them. After dinner, Aunt Aila handed me a book she was reading, *Nightmare Town, Stories by Dashiell Hammett*. The introduction said, when Dashiell Hammett was a Pinkerton detective in Butte, somebody offered to pay him five thousand dollars to kill Frank Little, the IWW rabble rouser. He declined. (Frank Little was lynched in Butte in 1917.)

I GOT TO THINKING about one of those newspaper articles I stumbled across when looking for articles about Archie and Roy. It said Sarah testified as a defense witness for two men charged with robbery. I inquired about the case at the Courthouse. These two had been arrested for a wide assortment of crimes—burglary, vagrancy, robbery. In this particular case, they were accused of mugging a woman.

The names of the defendants kept rolling around in my mind. They had a familiar ring to them, like Butch and Sundance, Bonnie and Clyde. I asked my parents if the names rang a bell. They said no. I asked Uncle Joe. No. I asked my aunts. No.

While staying at Auntie Mary and Uncle Ed's on this trip, I asked Uncle Ed. He told me about a man with the same name who knew his grandmother, and it turned out to be the same man. This man was also mixed up in tracking down Bill's second illegal wife, the runaway from the girls' home in Helena. Small, small world in Montana.

Later that evening, Auntie Mary and I tried to call Aunt Aila to make arrangements to get together with her the next day. No answer. We called again several times. No answer. It was getting late, but we tried again. No answer. We were puzzled. Obviously she's out late, and Mary Jane too.

In the morning, Mary Jane called. Uncle Sam had died.

CHAPTER THIRTY-SIX

MY NEXT RESEARCH trip to Butte coincided with Mom's class reunion. Mom and I dropped Dad off at the golf course and then drove uptown to the Courthouse.

This time I was searching for information about the mysterious Mr. Rigley, Sarah's third husband if we don't count Tom. I found no marriage license and no death certificate for James Rigley in Silver Bow County. I also looked in Madison County, since Sarah lived there for a while, but found nothing. Yet her name was Rigley when she married Daniel Sheehan.

Thinking about Bill and his two illegal marriages and Sarah and all her husbands, I thought, I should look for all marriage licenses for anyone named Hughes and anyone with Sarah's other last names: Mitchell, Rigley, and Sheehan. I might have looked at Elliott too, I don't remember. I sat down with the marriage index. H, Hughes, Aila. Aila? Grandma T. I was stunned. My grandparents married in Pocatello in 1921. The records in Butte said Aila Mae Hughes and James Eveline Winston were issued a marriage license on February 20, 1920. There was no marriage certificate. They never married. I showed Mom. She didn't know anything about it. I told my aunts. They didn't know anything about it either. What happened? Why didn't they get married? Was he killed in the mines? I looked for a death certificate. No death certificate. Was he incapacitated in a terrible mining accident? I looked at the accident reports at the Butte Archives. Nothing. I went back to Helena and read the Industrial Accident Board records. Nothing.

That name was familiar, Winston, Winston, then I remembered, of course, the law office near the Courthouse. I walked over and told the two men there the story. They said their ancestors came later than 1920. If there was a connection, they weren't aware of it.

Though I had learned plenty about my notorious relatives, I still wondered: could there be anything else out there? I proceeded to look for all of Sarah's surnames in the civil and criminal records.

In the criminal records, I found only Bill: the robbery case and the perjury case.

Then I proceeded to look at the civil cases.

Oh my. Lawsuit after lawsuit with hurricane Sarah at the center.

The biggest lawsuit, in terms of paperwork, was the battle between Sarah and Mrs. Dougherty over ownership of the boarding house at 415 Kemper Street. Who would have thought that court filings for the contested ownership of a house could be so entertaining. With my great-grandmother Sarah at the center, it had to be. It sounded as though eccentric old woman number one were suing eccentric old woman number two, except they weren't old.

Mrs. Dougherty says she's going to take the place back, Sarah threatens to burn it down. Mrs. Dougherty says if Mrs. Hughes hadn't wasted her money on dissolute living, she could have paid her bills.

Sarah said she replaced the locks in the boarding house; when Mrs. Dougherty filed suit, the locks disappeared. Sarah said she replaced the windows, now said windows were broken. And the list went on. Almost line for line, each thing Sarah had replaced or fixed was now gone or destroyed, now that Mrs. Dougherty was suing her.

Mrs. Dougherty said the furnace was dynamited.

The court issued a restraining order forbidding Sarah from doing damage to the house.

I get the impression that my great-grandmother Sarah thrived on drama. My grandmother did not.

Tucked away in that well-documented verbal warfare, I found another gem—a detailed description of the boarding house and an inventory of everything in it. Using this and what Grandma said and what Auntie Mary's friend Sylvia said, I was able to describe the boarding house in detail, which helped me paint a vivid picture of everyday life in this raucous early twentieth-century mining town. Had Sarah not gotten into all that legal trouble, I wouldn't have had so much detail.

I found it interesting that Sarah bought the house in Forsyth, and Sarah was buying the boarding house in Butte. Not Arthur, not Arthur and Sarah, just Sarah.

This thought just occurred to me: could it have been Sarah who insisted that Grandma and Grandpa's house be in Grandma's name only.

The 1920 census showed that Sarah had seven boarders. The court records said the boarding house had twenty-three bedrooms. That's quite a high vacancy rate—further evidence of the hard times during the post-war depression.

It is amazing that Sarah started making payments on this enormous boarding house in July of 1916, just a year and a half after she was paroled. She and Arthur certainly bounced back quickly after prison.

(The interest rates for the two mortgages were eight percent and ten percent.)

As I continued my trek through the civil records, I found litigation over the promissory note Sarah used to buy mining claims in the Tobacco Roots Mountains, across the Divide, east of Butte. The promissory note was for mortgages on the boarding house and the furniture, which she was buying but did not yet own. I have to believe Richard Richards, the man who sold her the mining claims, came up with this promissory note idea and didn't care that it was worthless, because he in turn sold the note to someone else who sold it to someone else. Doesn't that sound current as I write in 2009.

I found a lawsuit involving a woman named Mrs. Mary E. Hughes. To ascertain whether she was Sarah using an alias, I had to find corroborating evidence. I wasn't able to find any for that case and had to conclude she was not our Sarah.

I kept looking.

An annulment? For Sarah? When she was seventy-five years old? She did thrive on drama.

There was too much just to take notes. I needed to make copies of the records. Mom and I went into the little copy room, I inserted the pages, and the machine whirled away copying all this. As we waited, a man walked in who appeared to work there. We introduced ourselves. He said he was the assistant county attorney.

Then he asked one of the strangest questions I have ever been asked: "Do you know where Evel Knievel is?"

Do I look like someone who would know where Evel Knievel is? I could see Mom was as puzzled as I. The odd thing was, we did know.

"We were just at the country club and someone said he was playing golf there," I said. Then I thought, why does the assistant county attorney want to know where Evel Knievel is? I didn't ask. I didn't want to know.

I HAD READ about the Anaconda Road riot, which happened at the entrance to one of the mines during a wildcat strike in April of 1920. I was interested because Great-grandpa Arthur, Great-grandpa Sam, and two uncles were working in the mines at the time. The author wrote that Thomas Manning was shot and killed in the melee. He quoted a sarcastic headline from the *Butte Bulletin*, a labor paper, clearly unhappy that the coroner's inquest determined that a Person Unknown killed Manning, the implication being that something nefarious had gone on to protect the guilty. Knowing that Butte's colorful history was peppered with all manner of shenanigans, it wasn't a stretch to believe it.

Then that little something started tickling my mind and wouldn't give me any rest until I looked into it further.

The footnote listed a Montana Department of Labor and Industry report, which I found and read. The report provided interesting details from the coroner's inquest. Naturally I wanted to read the inquest myself, so I trotted back to the Silver Bow County Courthouse to get it.

Missing.

Just like the Granite Mountain Fire inquest, it grew legs and marched itself right out of there. I asked for the inquest over the man who was shot and killed at the Miners' Union Day riot in 1914. It was also missing.

Perhaps someone will be cleaning out an old house someday and unearth all those inquests. I hope so.

I went back to the archives and looked up the juror's verdict in the *Coroner's Register*. It said there was "no testimony to show or tending to show where Thomas Manning was when shot," which is what the Labor and Industry report said.

Chapter Thirty-seven

Back home again, asking police officers my forensic questions—could the bullet that killed Al Johnson have mushroomed when it hit the door, what about the types of guns used. I wrote more of the Archie and Roy debacle and thought about what happened. Grandma mentioned somebody named Kelly. County Attorney Howard Johnson brought in the former county attorney, James Kelly, to prosecute Roy. Could that be the Kelly of whom Grandma spoke or was there another Kelly? I was curious about Smith, the man charged with helping Roy escape. Two out-of-town lawyers defended him. One was James Kelly, the same James Kelly who prosecuted Roy. That seemed odd. The other lawyer was Matt Canning of Butte. It appears the two out-lawyered Boulder's young county attorney, calling into question the wording of the law, that it said it was illegal to help a prisoner escape but did not specify from *legal* custody. I can't imagine the legislature ever contemplated making it illegal to free a kidnap victim.

Clever lawyers, indeed, I was curious to learn more about them. It turns out Matt Canning was the top defense lawyer in Butte. James Kelly's brother, Dan, was counsel for the Anaconda Copper Mining Company and, prior to that, was the Montana attorney general.

As I dug into this, I stumbled upon a big brouhaha between Dan Kelly and U.S. Attorney Burton Wheeler during the 1918 wildcat strike in Butte. Apparently, a letter explained what the fuss was about. I asked Ellen at the Butte Archives where I might find the letter. She recommended Burton Wheeler's autobiography, *Yankee from the West*. What a find it turned out to be. Wheeler provided a marvelous snapshot of the town as he discovered it in 1905, which was around the same time my relatives were discovering it. I found no evidence that Wheeler or his co-author researched the historical aspects of his book; in want of such evidence, I assumed he did not. Therefore I used only his personal observations, things of which he had first-hand knowledge. Some of what he wrote of a historical nature piqued my curiosity to do more research. He said the chimney sweeps in Butte were organized when there were only two of them. I thought, that is hilarious, what a delicious illustration of Butte being the "Gibraltar of unionism"—two guys and they have a union. I needed to confirm that it was true before using it in my book. Was it scuttlebutt, a Buttism, or fact? I spent an insane amount of time and energy trying to verify it but couldn't. I still wanted to use it in the book, but how? The solution was obvious once I thought of it. I wrote, "According to one prominent lawyer and politician of the time . . ." Scuttlebutt, gossip can be helpful and illustrative. I just had to be clear that was what it was. A refreshingly honest headline in the March 7, 1925, *Boulder Monitor* read: "News and Gossip in the Montana Legislature." We do want to know the gossip when it comes to what our politicians are cooking up, but we want it distinguished from fact. I felt as long as such things are not damaging to a particular person, it can be helpful to include the scuttlebutt of the time, just as long as it is characterized as such.

Wheeler said the way you got elected in Butte was to go into every saloon and buy drinks for the house as often as possible. He claimed he managed to win his seat in the legislature in 1910 without a "rain of gold across the bar." He also said, back then the job of Silver Bow County sheriff "was reputed to be worth $40,000 to $60,000 on the side." This was at a time when $5000 was a good year for a lawyer. I wanted to use that, couching it as scuttlebutt. True or not, it was what at least some people thought at the time, which is telling. I ended up not using it because it broke the flow of the passage where it would have fit. As I said before, prose is like music, it has a rhythm. Adding more can just be more and become background noise, an unwanted distraction. Once I made the point that Butte was a wild and woolly place, there was no need to belabor it, no matter how irresistible and plentiful the examples were. At first it was painful to take anything out of my manuscript or not include some anecdote that I really liked. Toward the end, I became ruthless. If it didn't work, it had to go.

Wheeler went on to be elected to the U.S. Senate. When asked what he thought of the greatest deliberative body in the world, he said, "It reminds me of the city council in Butte."

He also wrote that "the people who can buy you and thereafter have you in their pocket have no respect for you." I'm sure he's right. No matter what price a man puts on himself, he sells himself cheap. You can't put a price on integrity.

Another happy accident in finding Wheeler's book was reading what he had to say about the September 1918 wildcat strike against the mines in Butte. This happened right when Grandpa Peter and the rest of the Wild West Division were making their way through eastern France to begin, what was then, the biggest offensive in American history. The copper mined out of the Rockies was vital to supporting the war effort. A book I read earlier in my research said during this wildcat strike, men were rounded up and held without charge, and Wheeler was appalled. However, when Wheeler wrote about the wildcat strike and people being arrested, he didn't say anything about being appalled or about anyone being held without charge. I decided to look into it, which was quite easy since I had a name—William Dunn. I wrote to the Silver Bow County Clerk of Court and asked, do you have any record of William Dunn being charged with anything in 1918? The staff promptly sent me the information. He was charged with sedition. There was a writ of *habeas corpus*, so presumably he was not charged immediately. The *Anaconda Standard* of September 15, 1918 said: "The charge against Dunn is urging, by publication, the curtailment of the production of copper necessary to carrying on the war with intent to cripple and hinder the United States in the prosecution of the war."

Were others held without charge? Who knows. Since Wheeler's own words contradicted what I read in that other book, I corrected my manuscript.

I found many gems in Wheeler's book but no letters between him and Dan Kelly, which was my original purpose in reading it. Later, I stumbled across something that said the letters were printed in the newspaper, yet another hunt, and I found them.

IN AUGUST OF 2001, I joined Mom and Dad for a trip to Banff to sightsee and play golf and then spent a few days with them in Kennewick. My flight home was on September 10. A friend from the Maryland suburbs of Washington, D.C., was flying to Las Vegas for a visit on September 11. Mom kept trying to get me to stay in Kennewick longer. She had never tried to get me to change my plans before. I kept saying, "Mom, Marion is flying in. I need to buy groceries and get ready for her visit."

As planned, I flew home on September 10.

The next morning, I was still in bed, just starting to wake up, when a friend called from Denver. She was hysterical. I dashed into the living room and turned on the television.

I hurriedly checked Marion's schedule. She was scheduled to fly out of Baltimore later that morning.

In 1914, the actions of a violent secret society, that required a death oath from its members, sparked a world war, a war massive and brutal in heretofore unfathomable proportions. An end to innocence. Now in 2001, a different violent secret society, different aims, another war, another end to innocence.

Imagine if the terrorists had printed ads in the newspapers in Washington and Boston saying they were in a state of war and all air travelers could be in peril. Now imagine reporters flocking to airports asking travelers how they felt about the threat. Then it happens. That's what happened in May of 1915. The German government printed such an ad in New York City newspapers just days before the *Lusitania* set sail. As she neared Ireland, a German U-boat captain fired on her and sank her—crew, passengers and all. Many notables were on board, further personalizing the tragedy. One of the Vanderbilts was last seen fastening a life vest to a woman holding a baby.

The *Lusitania* wasn't the first or the last passenger ship to be torpedoed and sunk during the First World War, just the most famous.

I thought about airport security and people being afraid to fly. I figured, if we change our behavior out of fear, we've declared defeat, and the bad guys won. I thought about my great-grandfather Sam Thompson and my paternal grandfather Anton Leskovar. They knew the U-boats were out there, it was not a theoretical threat, it was a fact; yet, they and other intrepid passengers got on those ships anyway.

Chapter Thirty-eight

As for the war, though I didn't plan to delve into weaponry, I did want to address one of the unique horrors of the First World War, namely the use of poison gas. The helpful staff at the U.S. Army Military History Institute in Carlisle gave me a bibliography on gas warfare which included a puzzling note about peach pits and gas masks. The bibliography listed a book on the subject, which I found at the UNLV library, or I should say, in the UNLV library catalog. Though I looked for it repeatedly over the course of a year, it was perpetually checked out. I found other books about chemical warfare but nothing about peach pits. I kept looking. At long last, I found the answer in *Chemical Warfare* by West and Fries published in 1921. Peach pits and nut shells were burned to make charcoal, which was put in the gas mask to filter the gas out of the air.

As so often was the case, in chasing one minor item, I stumbled across much more, including the eyewitness account of Reverend Watkins about seeing the first French soldiers who had been gassed. Grisly.

In this and another book I sought for yet another reason, I learned that German soldiers warned British and French officers of German plans to use poison gas. The officers didn't believe them, and consequently when the Germans did use it, Allied soldiers had no gas masks, no protection whatsoever.

One of the poison gases the Germans used was phosgene, which killed by causing the lungs to fill with fluid. I remembered what I had read about the 1918 Spanish Influenza. In its most virulent form, it caused the lungs to fill with fluid.

Messrs West and Fries also helped me fill in the blank on a completely un-related part of the story. I had wondered what was behind Hector's mile long name, Grandma's second eldest brother: Hector Osiris Dundonald Warren Hughes. Sarah said she named him after a military officer. Reverend Johnson told me the Welsh often took names from literature for their children. That made sense for Hector. Osiris was the name of an Egyptian god, a king and judge of the dead, usually depicted as a partially wrapped mummy. I cannot imagine attaching such name to a baby. Warren is a fairly common name. That left Dundonald. When I asked Mair in Llandovery, she thought it sounded Scottish. Then while reading *Chemical Warfare* by West and Fries, I found him. On page two, it said Admiral Lord Dundonald was "perhaps the ablest sea captain ever known, not even excluding Lord Nelson."

NOW BACK TO thinking about what happened in Forsyth. I thought more about Sheriff Moses being shot and killed by his deputy. I wondered why he left South Dakota. Was there a story? I tried to find a phone number for the historical society but had no luck, so I called the library in Belle Fourche. I asked if there was a historical society or archives and said that I was looking for information about a man who was sheriff there around 1910.

"You mean Moses," the woman said.

"Yes," I said, surprised. "How did you know?"

"He's the most famous sheriff around here," she said.

"Why is that?"

"I don't know. I see his name all over the old newspapers."

She said they had just closed for redecorating, so she wouldn't be able to get to this until next week. She asked for my name and number and address. After hearing my address, she said, "What's some woman in Las Vegas doing asking about Billy Moses?"

I explained that I was writing a book about my great-grandparents who homesteaded in Rosebud County. William Moses was the sheriff, and they knew him. I couldn't bring myself to say they knew him because he arrested them. I never did hear back from her and didn't pursue it. Perhaps someday I will.

IN JANUARY OF 2002, I received an email from Christopher Sims in Belgium. He said to commemorate the seventy-fifth anniversary of Lindbergh flying across the Atlantic, the city of Waregem was planning an exhibit about Lindbergh and the First World War. They wanted to profile a soldier who survived the battle and asked if I had pictures of Peter they could use. I sent Christopher a brief biography of Grandpa Peter and several pictures. When I told Mom there was going to be an exhibit in Belgium featuring her father, she said, "Let's go!"

So we did.

In May of 2002, Mom and Dad and I flew to Amsterdam, spent a few days in that beautiful city, ate wonderful meals in little restaurants on side streets off the canals, visited Anne Frank's house, were sated with Rembrandt at the Rijksmuseum, and then drove to Antwerp and spent a night and a day there. From Antwerp, we continued driving south. The idea was to see Waterloo and arrive at our hotel in Bruges in time for dinner to celebrate Mom's birthday. At the outer reaches of Brussels, I mistakenly exited the freeway rather than follow the ring road around Brussels to go to Waterloo. I couldn't figure out how to get back on the freeway, and I couldn't see a place to pull over and stop and consult the map. Not seeing any other choice, I drove all the way across Brussels. We arrived in Waterloo much later than I had planned, but we still had time to see the battlefield and make it to Bruges (Brugge in Flemish or Dutch) in time for dinner.

I had booked rooms at the Die Swaene in Bruges. The staff sent me directions. Turn right at the church, the directions said. I did. After the fish market on the left, turn left. We didn't see a fish market. Not knowing what to do and seeing no place to pull over and ask for directions, we commenced driving aimlessly around Bruges in hopes of finding the Die Swaene. Bruges is a lovely old medieval city. Streets built for ox-carts now must accommodate cars and are one way and some change direction in the middle of the street. There didn't seem to be any rhyme or reason to how the streets were laid out as far as I could tell. It was a maze. Either wherever the cow happened to walk, there became the road, or drunks laid out the streets back in the days of unsafe drinking water, when it was beer for breakfast, beer for lunch, beer for dinner, or so I'm told. As in Ghent, I asked for directions and was told the same thing: I can tell you how to walk there, but I don't know how to drive there. Finally, on yet another loop past the church, I saw a little sign pointing to where to turn for the Die Swaene. Had we been looking for that little sign, we'd have found it quickly, but we didn't know to look for it, and the little sign was on the right, and we were looking for the fish market on the left. Sadly we arrived too late for our lovely dinner at the hotel.

Needless to say, we left the car in the parking garage for the remainder of our stay in Bruges.

The Die Swaene was well worth the trouble to find. It was quite a good inn, a lovely inn, nestled on a quiet, leafy street along one of the canals. The rooms were decorated with white lace canopies, crystal chandeliers, golden cherubs. Outside the windows were little wrought-iron railings from which hung planters overflowing with blossoms. The place brimmed with charm. It looked like the place where the beautiful fairy princess went to live happily ever after with her handsome prince.

The entire town appeared to have been plucked from a happy fairy tale, with those wide canals, narrow streets, cobblestone bridges, everything clean, painted, and polished. Bruges had been named the cultural capital of Europe that year. The town was wearing her Sunday best.

We took the horse-drawn wagon tour and the canal boat tour, both with excellent guides telling us the history of Bruges. The young woman driving the horse told us about the Battle of the Golden Spurs and defiantly proclaimed, "And that is why we do not have to speak French!" We visited the basilica in which resides the Relic of the Precious Blood, brought back from the Holy Land by the Count of Flanders.

We asked the concierge if there were other tours. He arranged a private walking tour for us with a friend of his, a local historian.

In between tours and wandering around, we enjoyed delicious meals in tiny restaurants with linen-draped tables, always with white asparagus on the menu since it was in season. After several days in delightful Bruges we departed for Ypres (Ieper in Dutch), the sight of horrific battles in the First World War in which my great-uncles Denis and John fought in the British Army.

The hotel I had booked in Ypres turned out to be depressing and dismal and not clean—quite a step down from the Die Swaene. Dad scouted out one that was quite nice, we settled in, had dinner, and walked to the Menen Gate for "Last Post."

Every evening at eight o'clock, a bugler sounds "Last Post" at the Menen Gate. Ypres was a walled city, and this was one of the entrances. It is now a war memorial. Carved into the stone walls are the names of 55,000 missing British soldiers from the Ypres salient in the First World War, almost the same number as on the Vietnam Memorial. That's just the missing, for just the British, in only one part of the Western Front, and it doesn't even include all the missing British soldiers from the Ypres salient. There wasn't enough room. The rest are listed on other war memorials. The citizens of Ypres have been honoring the fallen British soldiers in this way since 1928, the only interruption being during the Second World War when Ypres was occupied by German soldiers.

The next day we visited the In Flanders Fields Museum at Cloth Hall. I walked along, reading the displays which did not spare the gore of the war. I tried to concentrate over the din of a large group of rambunctious British high school students. It was as if their teacher had called recess in the middle of the museum. I read how Ypres was flattened during the war, a medieval city of medieval stone buildings, flattened by massive artillery shells. The Allies defended it to death, as the Germans pummeled it to death, for four long years of bloody stalemate. I read how the huge tower of Cloth Hall, under merciless bombardment, burned, crumbled, and collapsed. I saw the pictures. I was struck by how familiar it seemed, as we, just a few months earlier, had watched our own towers burn, crumble, and collapse.

After the war, Ypres was rebuilt, brick by brick, stone by stone, to look just as it did before the war.

I picked up several brochures and made arrangements for a battlefield tour. Our guide, a knowledgeable young Englishman, took us through the battlefields on which Uncle Denis and Uncle John fought (Grandpa Peter's brothers). As we rode along, I saw cows lounging lazily on the thick green grass, now a long red barn, now a farmhouse, now a concrete pillbox left over from the war.

We stopped at a massive British cemetery. I walked among the graves, reading the stone crosses: A Soldier of the Great War Known Unto God, A New Zealand Soldier of the Great War Known Unto God, An Irish Soldier of the Great War Known Unto God, A Canadian Soldier of the Great War Known Unto God, and in between those, Private H. Moses, Royal Irish Fusiliers, 16th August 1917; Lance Cpl W. Gihon Royal Irish Rifles, 16th August 1917; and on they went, row upon row upon row of white crosses.

A chill wind blew. I cinched my hood tighter.

We stopped at the German cemetery. It was dark and somber to evoke the Black Forest. Our guide said the Belgians gave up land for British, French, and American cemeteries but were not too keen on giving land to the Germans. As such, the German dead were gathered into one cemetery, many in a mass grave. A young Canadian woman remarked scornfully,

"Isn't that rather grotesque?" I saw a twinge of pain in our guide's eyes. I winced.

Back at the hotel, I thumbed through the brochures I had picked up at Cloth Hall. One was for a pub museum. What is that? Mom and I went off to find out.

Actually, it was called the Ramparts Museum, but I will forever remember it as the pub museum.

We followed the map on the brochure and easily found it. It was one of those small, dark, European pubs where you walk in and everybody turns around and stares at you. I walked up to the counter and explained that we wanted to see the museum. The man told me how many euros, we paid, and he led us out the back door into a tiny courtyard and then to an open doorway on the left. Inside the doorway we could see a turnstile and, beyond it, complete darkness. He slipped two tokens into the slot. Immediately we heard artillery blasts and saw flashes of light coming from the darkness. He motioned for us to go in. Had I been alone, I don't think I would have. Together being brave, Mom and I went in. We walked through a narrow labyrinth on the sides of which were life-size displays of soldiers in the trenches. One was peering through a periscope type device to see over the top of the parapet. With the flashes of light and sounds of artillery blasts and the narrow walkway, it felt as if we were in the trenches. The air was even musty, as it must have been for the soldiers, with exploding bombs hurling dirt up into the air over the top of them over and over and over.

The next day we drove to Waregem to see the exhibit at city hall about the war. Walls of sandbags led to the entrance, simulating a trench. The exhibit was much larger than I expected and impressive, definitely museum quality. As I rounded a corner, there was my grandfather, Peter Thompson, an entire panel dedicated to him.

After touring the display, we followed Grandpa Peter's footsteps across the battlefield, so I could take notes and pictures.

On Sunday, we attended the Memorial Day service at Flanders Field American Cemetery in Waregem. Though we arrived early, there was no parking to be found. There were so many people there, hundreds of Belgians. An American major hopped to when he heard we were next of kin and escorted us into the cemetery. He turned us over to a Belgian officer who escorted us to our reserved seats in the front row. A few seats away sat an American woman dressed all in black, wearing a black hat and dark sunglasses, even though it was a cloudy day, looking like a stand-in for Lana Turner in an old movie.

The ceremony began. The colors were presented, followed by an invocation and prayer. An American general with NATO spoke. The *burgemeester*, Yolande Dhondt, gave an eloquent speech. She recalled the First and Second World Wars. Twice in half a century Europe was devastated by war. Cynicism took hold. Hope was vanquished. Then came fifty years of relative peace. Then came September 11.

Her speech got me thinking. The Belgians and French took the brunt of the First World War on the Western Front, as far as destruction to their homes and livelihoods. Entire towns were obliterated by the shelling. I thought of the citizens of Ypres watching in horror as the majestic tower of Cloth Hall, there since the Middle Ages, burned, crumbled, and collapsed. Two decades later, they were overrun again. Both times, jocular young men from across the sea, the doughboys and then the GI's, sailed to their shores and fought to liberate them. Then to see their liberators attacked, and our towers burn, crumble, and collapse. As many of us thought we were impregnable, much of the world thought we were, too. No one wants to see their bulwark battered.

Assembled before us stood about fifty Belgian children. A guitarist began to strum softly, and the children began to sing: "Oh say, can you see, by the dawn's early light, What so proudly we hailed at the twilight's last gleaming, Whose broad stripes and bright stars . . ." Each child gripped a tiny American or Belgian flag which they raised and held high as the tune swelled.

Belgian children have been learning our national anthem and singing it for Memorial Day since 1922.

A soft mist began to fall. Umbrellas opened.

More speeches, a wreath laying. The children were dismissed into the cemetery. Each planted his or her flag at the grave of an American soldier.

A plane flew over and dropped poppies, just as Lindbergh did during the Memorial Day service in 1927.

The American ambassador presented us with a flag that had flown over the cemetery.

The ceremony ended, the crowd began to disperse.

I still hadn't found the Spitaals Bosschen, the woods Peter's division took on the first day. I asked Christopher's friend Patrick where it was. He pointed. "Right there." I was looking right at it.

Christopher walked over and said, "Somebody wants to talk to you." He led me to a man in a wheelchair and introduced me to Ivan. Ivan said he understood that my grandfather fought there in the 362nd Regiment. I said yes. He then presented me with a plaque on which stood a tiny American soldier, saluting with his right hand, and packing a rifle in his left. On the base was printed: SG P THOMPSON, 362 INF 91 DIV. How thoughtful! I couldn't get over it. I thanked Ivan profusely. He said all he wanted in return was a postcard from where I lived. I said I'd be delighted to send him one. He said he made the statue out of shrapnel found in the Ypres salient. I said, "My grandfather's brothers fought in the Ypres salient with the British Army!" He hurriedly said something to his wife in Dutch. She handed him a little plastic box which he gave to me. In it was a little statue of a British soldier on horseback, which he also made from shrapnel found in the Ypres salient.

Christopher and his wife escorted us to the champagne reception. There I met General Moffett, the second in command of the 91st. I couldn't help but notice how much General Moffett looked like Uncle Sam in his younger days. I told him about my book. He gave me several signal corp photographs of the battlefield and a 91st Division coin and 362nd Regiment pin. I asked if he had any idea why my grandfather was decorated by the French government but not his own government. He shrugged and said, "Who knows. Maybe the paperwork got lost."

He said there was one surviving member of the 91st. "He lives somewhere around Seattle." He'd have his staff send me the man's name and address.

CHAPTER THIRTY-NINE

SHORTLY AFTER I returned home, I heard from Colonel Mollica on General Moffett's staff. The soldier's name was William Lake, and he lived in Yakima, Washington, which is only a hundred miles or so from Kennewick, where Mom and Dad live. He was 107 years old. I wrote to him and asked if I could visit. He wrote back: "Busy picking peaches and pears. It is very warm. We are having really nice weather." And, yes I could visit him.

Over Thanksgiving, Mom and I drove to Yakima. Not only was Mr. Lake in the 91st Division, he was in Grandpa Peter's regiment, the 362nd, and he was from Montana. He was born in Lewistown in 1895, the same year as Grandpa Peter. He was in the machine gun battalion and didn't know Peter (I brought a picture to jog his memory); nevertheless, I was very interested in everything he had to say about the war.

He said he caught the measles in New York but didn't let on because he didn't want to be separated from his unit. Once on board ship, he couldn't hide it and spent the voyage in the infirmary. He was left behind in England when the rest of the regiment went on to France.

I mentioned what I had read about the train crash in France and about how the machine gun battalion took the brunt of it.

"Did measles save your life?" I asked.

"Oh, yes," he said. "My best friend in the regiment was killed in that train crash." He said he caught up with the regiment in France the day before they went into battle in the Argonne.

"How did you get there?" I asked.

"I walked."

"How did you know where to go?"

"They gave me a map."

"But how did you find your unit once you got to the Front? Did you just ask people, where's the 91st?"

"Yes."

I still can't get over that. Two hundred thousand men massing to go into battle, and here's this young private from Montana on foot, wandering around, and he's supposed to find his unit. And he did.

We took him to lunch at a restaurant he recommended. Then we went back to his home, which was small assisted living place, essentially a boarding house for elderly people. After we visited a while longer, he said he wanted to walk to the drugstore. We went along. To get there we had to cross Yakima Avenue, a busy five-lane thoroughfare through the heart of town, the kind of road I dread crossing on foot, especially with no light. Mr. Lake appeared undaunted. He said he went there every day. A spry young 107-year-old indeed.

THOUGH I HAD whittled down my to-do list considerably, I had not exhausted all my curiosity. There was still more to investigate. I wanted to learn more about Uncle Denis being a prisoner of war. Aunt Brigid told me some stories, and I had copies of the postcards he wrote to his mother from the prisoner-of-war camp. I wanted more. Off I went to the library and stood at the First World War section and started pulling books off the shelf and looking in the index of each for prisoners of war. I found next to nothing. As with every other part of my research, I didn't want to know about prison camps in general, I wanted to know about the particular prison camp where Uncle Denis was imprisoned and what life was like for him. I kept looking, more books, more books. Then it occurred to me to look up the name of Denis's prison camp, Limburg, which was on the postcards he sent to his mother. I found it in Martin Gilbert's book *The First World War* and learned that Limburg was a special camp for Irish prisoners of war; the purpose of which was to turn the Irish soldiers against Britain. At home I looked in *Ireland's Unknown Soldiers*, the history of the 16th Irish Division. There was Limburg in the index.

I asked Christopher at Flanders Field in Belgium if he had come across anything about the treatment of British prisoners of war. He sent me an essay by Senator Jeremiah Beveridge published in the book *The Last Magnificent War: Rare Journalistic and Eyewitness Accounts of World War I.* Senator Beveridge toured German prison camps prior to our entering the war. He spoke freely spoke with English, French, and Russian prisoners using his own interpreter. He wrote that as of February 1915, Germany had approximately 700,000 prisoners of war, roughly the equivalent of increasing Germany's population by one percent in only a matter of months. He said Germany was preparing to receive many more prisoners.

Christopher also sent me a prisoner's pass to go for a walk. It said in effect, on my honor I won't run away, and if I do, I know I'll be shot.

A little here, a little there, now I had a good bit about Uncle Denis in the prison camp. Now how to present it in my manuscript. Where to put it. The war story was about Grandpa Peter, but I wanted to include what was happening with his brothers Denis and John, but I had to find a way to do that without interrupting the flow of the story about Peter. I didn't want to distract from the drama of the battles. Much writing, then reading what I wrote, then rearranging, reading, rewriting, rearranging. Not easy.

I read more newspapers from the war years, 1917, 1918, more time at the microfilm machine at the Sahara West Library, more rolls of coins to print pages. I stumbled upon many interesting tidbits—two feet of snow at the Columbia Gardens at Easter (the delightful amusement park that used to be on the mountain above Butte), humorous quips about men registering for the draft, Lloyds of London laying odds on when the war would end. I wonder what insurance companies are predicting today about current events.

I reread some of the books I had read early on, thinking new things might strike me. I read many good books to research *One Night in a Bad Inn*, books that flowed smoothly, were clearly written, and interesting. Admittedly, a few were a chore to read. One in particular was jumbled and fractured, like the ore veins under Butte, fraught with apparent contradictions never explained. I felt I was staring through gauze trying to read it. Others were flat-out boring. My job as storyteller was to read such books, plumb the pertinent interesting parts, and present what I learned coupled with my own original research in an interesting and compelling way. Not an easy task.

There seems to be a prejudice in some quarters, no doubt going back to our Puritan past, that something we do *not* enjoy must be better than something we *do* enjoy. If we enjoy reading a book of history, it must not be good history. Good history must be a chore to read. This is nonsense. History is a fascinating tale of intrigue and surprise, heroism and catastrophe, cruelty and goodness. It contains all the elements of great literature:

beauty, truth and goodness, which shine out against a backdrop of deceit, wickedness, and evil. As Henry David Thoreau said: "Wherever men have lived there is a story to be told, and it depends chiefly on the storyteller or historian whether it is interesting or not." It is up to the storyteller to tell an interesting story in an interesting way. In the wrong hands, even an interesting story can be reduced to dullness.

Chapter Forty

Now I set about polishing my oeuvre. I had written the entire manuscript, but I was by no means done. The material I had was gold. My challenge was to write a story equal to the subject matter. I still had miles to go before I could sleep.

I set a goal of working on two pages a day. I had finally learned that writing a book is not a sprint—it's a marathon. Best to pick up one little piece, polish and perfect it, then go on to the next little piece.

When I slipped back into feeling that sense of urgency, that I had to finish the entire book right now and would become paralyzed by the thought, I reminded myself, I have to work on these two pages today, just these two pages, that's all, tomorrow another two pages, and the day after that, another two pages. When I was learning to play golf, I thought I had to hit the ball so hard because the hole was so far away. I learned to just hit it and not worry about how far away the hole is. Just write.

Something about the first chapter wasn't working. I couldn't figure out why. I worked on it and worked on it but still wasn't satisfied. As I re-read and re-read my manuscript, always tweaking and re-writing and re-arranging as I did, I imagined myself reading the story aloud, and sometimes did read parts aloud. Often this helped in tossing out the wrong words and finding the right ones.

More questions. Did Peter play soccer at the Columbia Gardens? When was John Denis born, Aunt B's first child who died? Did hawthorn grow in Butte? Where was Race Track? More newspapers requested through interlibrary loan, articles about Father Tougas building St. Helena's Church in Butte, *Jefferson Valley News* articles about Archie and Roy. More hours at the microfilm machine. More gems. More notes. More to work into the manuscript. I felt I was digging into a bottomless well and finding an infinite treasure trove. I wanted to use everything, but I couldn't. Several anecdotes are interesting. Too many strung together can become tedious. Where to draw the line. Where indeed.

Grandma told me how she and Grandpa met. They were on a double date. Grandma was with Frenchy, one of the boarders. She brought a friend to be the date for Frenchy's friend, Peter Thompson. At the dance, they switched partners. Not long after, Frenchy and Grandma's friend got married. I wanted to include the part about Frenchy and Grandma's friend getting married, but I couldn't figure out how. The drama was, they switched partners, and that's how my grandparents met. It was another case where more would have diluted the drama.

Cousin Bridgeen and her son came to visit from Ireland. Bridgeen asked for copies of the pages that mentioned her grannie, my great-aunt Brigid. After she returned home, cousin Rosaleen called from Belfast. She had a couple of corrections, which I appreciated getting. I had written that "the men drank whisky" at the wake of a relative in Ireland. She explained, "Whisky without an 'e' is Scotch whisky. Whiskey with an 'e' is Irish whiskey. My grandfather used to say, 'Irish whiskey is for men. Scotch whisky is for women and young boys.'"

I made the correction.

As I PONDERED events in the story, I couldn't help but think of the stark differences compared to today. Grandma used to say, "There was nothing good about the good old days." She didn't elaborate, but now I understand at least some of what she probably meant—the days of her youth, of washing sheets, towels, clothes in a tub with a clothes stomper, of hanging said wash on the line outside and having it freeze solid and having to be careful not to break those precious sheets and towels and diapers when taking them down, a time when simple household chores were back-breaking, all-consuming tasks.

I was struck by how late life was back then. Ranching families in Rosebud County gathered for dances, they put the children to bed in the wagons when it got late, and the parents continued the party until dawn. As a teenager, Grandma T hosted a party in the middle of the week and served refreshments at midnight. This I know because it was written about on the society page. Life did not adhere to an 8:00am to 5:00pm work schedule with weekends off. Roy's murder trial began at 8:30pm on a Friday night and resumed Saturday morning with only Sunday off. The trial ended at 8:30pm the following

Friday evening, the jury deliberated and handed down a guilty verdict at 11:20pm. And all this happened only one month after the shooting.

So many tasks are accomplished much faster and easier today, and yet much of life is slower. In 1905, Arthur and his neighbors in Rosebud County did not spend hours, even days, deciphering complicated tax rules. That would soon change. I found a 1925 political cartoon in the *Jefferson Valley News* showing a very exasperated man leaning over a crossword puzzle with the title "Income Tax Return." He is trying to think of a four letter word expressing "contempt."

"Our life is frittered away by detail," Thoreau chastened. But I digress.

It struck me how much singing was part of my grandparents' social lives. Grandpa Peter sang for family and friends at parties. Each day at the Vocational Congress, Grandma and the other girls sang in assembly. The soldiers sang as they marched through the French countryside. They were participants in their own entertainment.

I thought about the Irish fraternal organizations to which my kin in Butte belonged. This was not unique to the Irish; other ethnic groups had their own fraternal organizations. These organizations provided sick and death benefits, their own private safety net. In nineteenth-century Wales, they were called friendly societies. Once the government and employers began to take over this role, the need for friendly societies eroded, and they have since diminished in prominence or gone away all together.

FROM THE VERY BEGINNING, I thought a lot about writing. I don't mean in terms of procrastinating and not doing it, but in how to do it. I read books and articles about writing, though there came a point when I realized, a person can overdo that. It is possible to be over coached. It is possible to edit the life out of my own work. I certainly didn't want to do that. I thought about Corporal Rendinell, the marine who wrote about his experience at Belleau Wood. His story was rough and lively and so much him, and that made it wonderful and unique. An overzealous editor could have edited his personality right out of it and left it flat and lifeless, bleaching it to blandness.

As I read and thought about writing, and observed what I liked about the writing of others, I wrote down writing tips for myself on index cards which I kept on my desk. I referred to them frequently.

Author and historian Shelby Foote advised releasing things about the characters as you go. That made sense. It's how we get to know people in real life. We don't learn everything about a person all at once. It is over time that we get to know people. I thought, I will release things about the people as I discovered them, and in that way I hoped you would get to know them as well as I did. I worried that since I knew Grandma, I would overlook things I needed to tell you. There might be things I took for granted and would neglect to mention. I wanted you to know her as fully as I did.

Mom said Father O'Connor taught her at Carroll College that writing should be "precise, concise, and specific." Our minds latch onto the specific more easily than broad generalities. Rather than simply saying, Peter and Aila went to parties at Aunt B's, I wanted to describe such a party. Another phone call to Aunt Aila to ask more questions.

I listened to many lectures about history and thought about why some grabbed my attention while others left me cold. I realized the speakers who held my attention talked about specific people, rather than generalities, and quoted them. The quotes made the people real. I tried to work quotes into my manuscript as much as possible. Between the court transcripts and the tapes of Grandma T, I had a tremendous amount of quoted material, yet how to include more quotes while keeping the flow of the narrative. I couldn't toss quotes in at random just for the sake of quoting people.

I thought about books I liked and scrutinized why I liked them, apart from the story. I pondered what it was about the writing that made these books appealing. When Dr. Van Helsing was chasing the evil count by land, knowing Dracula was traveling by ship, Dr. Van Helsing hypnotized Mina periodically to find out where Dracula was. One time she said, "Darkness, creaking wood and roaring water." With those simple words, I was in the scene. Roaring water, the ship was moving fast; creaking wood, I could hear it; it was dark, all the more sinister. Great writing need not be verbose. Another time, Mina said, "Lapping waves and rushing water." So simple, yet with those few words, Bram Stoker put me on the ship, I was there, that was all I needed, and I knew the evil count had not yet arrived.

St. Francis de Sales wrote: "To speak little—a practice highly recommended by ancient sages—does not consist in uttering only a few words but in uttering none that are useless." The same is true of writing. If it takes three lines to describe an artillery blast, the writer has sucked all the drama out of the scene.

While reading books by Charles Dickens and John Steinbeck and Charlotte Brontë, I felt as though they were sitting with me telling me these stories, and they came across as good company. That was also the case with Somerset Maugham. I always had the sense that Somerset Maugham was telling me a true story about real people, though I knew he wrote fiction. This made his stories all the more engaging. In his introduction to the movie *Quartet*, made from four of his short stories, he said he drew heavily from the experiences of people he encountered and from his own experience. He said fact and fiction were so interlaced in his fiction, it was hard for him to remember which was which.

Whether the way these authors came through in their work was part of the fiction, I don't know. It is impossible to know how much of the novelist is in his or her writing, though I suspect there is always some. Writing is personal. I thought about the advice Rafael Alvarez gave me: "If a part of the real you isn't in your book, you are cheating the reader." I wanted my book to have engaging feel, as if I were sitting down with you telling you this story, or writing you a letter. I wanted it to have a warm familiar tone.

Something else I liked about my favorite novels was the authors gave me something to ponder, nuggets of wisdom, passages that made me reach for my pencil and underline a sentence or two and turn down the corner of the page, such as Annie in *David Copperfield* saying, "There can be no disparity in marriage like unsuitability of mind and purpose." Dickens' novels are deeper than young-boy-in-peril stories. The theological discourse between the characters in Steinbeck's *East of Eden*, indeed the story itself, illustrate the truth: we have free will— "*thou mayest.*"

I continued to struggle with how far to take the story, where to stop and let you draw your own conclusions and thereby become more engaged in the story. When I read *David Copperfield*, though Dickens never says it, I knew David shouldn't marry Dora. I knew they weren't right for each other, and I knew Aunt Betsy knew it, though she never said so. David wanted Dora to become someone she wasn't, someone she never could be. I found myself urging David, don't do it. How does an author do that? He is showing without telling. In doing so, he engaged me in the story.

Gene Kelly said dance should look so easy that the audience thinks they can go home and do it themselves, otherwise it isn't dance. He made it look effortless, yet his dancing was incredibly athletic. All the hard work was behind the scenes, it was invisible. I think the same holds true for good prose. The best prose reads as though it were effortless, not forced, never contrived. It can be a lot of work to make something seem effortless.

As I read my "Don't know where to put file," and struggled over where to put this anecdote, or that one, what to keep, what to leave out, I thought about what John Steinbeck wrote in *Journal of a Novel*: "There is one purpose in writing that I can see, beyond simply doing it interestingly. It is the duty of the writer to lift up, to extend, to encourage. If the written word has contributed anything at all to our developing species and our half developed culture, it is this: great writing has been a staff to lean on, a mother to consult, a wisdom to pick up stumbling folly, a strength in weakness and a courage to support sick cowardice. And how any negative or despairing approach can pretend to be literature I do not know."

St. Paul put it another way: "Say only the good things men need to hear, things that will really help them."

Does that mean I must ignore the untoward in my writing? Obviously not. Paul didn't. Steinbeck didn't. It's a matter of emphasis and balance. It's a matter of context. The untoward isn't the whole story. Showing only the darkness is pointless, vapid, and boring. Showing only the light gives the light short shrift. In a dark room, a lit candle draws our eyes and brightens the place. In daylight, we hardly notice it.

Or as Mrs. Brown said to Mr. Brown: "What is the meaning of goodness if there isn't some badness to overcome?"

Barbara Tuchman believed that the increase in nonfiction reading and decrease in fiction reading since 1964 was the fault of the novelist. She said while depravity is part of life, it isn't the point of life, as some novelists seem to think it is; many modern novels don't make you want to turn the page because you really don't care what happens to the person. "Certainly the squalid and worthless, the mean and depraved are part of the human story just as dregs are part of wine, but the wine is what counts."

Those books enamored with the squalid, blind to the good, are what my brother calls "bummer lit." Pray tell, what is the point?

Recently I read about an enormous seven figure advance going to an author for a particular novel. When I read what the book was about, it sounded pessimistic, dreary, and disgusting. I thought who on earth would want to read such a thing? The answer turned out to be hardly anybody here. The American public didn't buy it.

Americans are not a pessimistic people.

Will Durant wrote: "For Michelangelo art was the selection of significance for the illustration of nobility, not the indiscriminate representation of reality." The same holds true for writing, even more so for writing history, especially when faced with a plethora of source material. The writer must choose, and choose wisely. The writer must distinguish the important from the unimportant.

When an American bishop expressed distress over the large number of lapsed Catholics, Pope Benedict replied: "Has your preaching lost its salt?"

Good writing must have salt.

What is most important about writing is what is conveyed. William James wrote: "Why should we think upon things that are lovely? Because thinking determines life." Thinking also determines writing.

Great art expresses beauty, truth, and goodness—the transcendental goods. When it comes to literary works, the novel is the medium to illustrate metaphysical truth; narrative nonfiction is the medium for facts. Though I was writing narrative nonfiction, the subject matter was replete with metaphysical truth, the most important being that each of us is captain of our own ship with regard to character. We have free will. That was the point of the story.

From the beginning, I had the sense that the story was big, it was timeless, it contained many timeless themes: the ageless battle between good and evil, the indomitable human spirit overcoming tremendous odds and holding out for what is right. The heroine, my grandmother, never courted adversity, but faced it nobly. Because the story was timeless, I wanted to use timeless words. One exception was in the part about the stellar legal team hired to defend the man accused of helping Roy Walsh escape. I wrote: "In short, Smith's legal team had juice." Juice was the first word that came to mind, the only word, and the perfect word, a bit of slang for emphasis.

As I LISTENED to news reports of Spain pulling out of Iraq, I thought about Russia pulling out of the First World War right after we got in it, which had a much bigger impact on the war than Spain pulling out of Iraq, orders of magnitude bigger. I rewrote that part of the manuscript to make the enormity clear.

THE TROUBLESOME first chapter still wasn't working. I worked it and re-wrote it, I don't know how many times, and I still wasn't satisfied. It had been my albatross from the beginning. After the first chapter, the story seemed to tell itself. What to do, what to do. I wondered who the patron saint of writers was. I needed all the help I could get. I looked it up. It's St. Francis de Sales. I had read one of his books years ago and loved it. I read a little about his life. He was bishop of Geneva around 1600. His birthday was August 21, the same as Grandma T, isn't that interesting. It was January; his feast day was coming up. I decided to make a novena.

At the end of the nine days, in the middle of the night, actually in the early hours of his feast day, January 24, I awoke with a start—I knew exactly what I needed to do. I had to let it breathe. That's what I had to do. I had to let the story breathe.

From the beginning, I felt an obligation to be as objective as possible, to write as a fair journalist, to try to see all sides, give everyone the benefit of the doubt, not gloss over things. I felt an obligation to the truth, to tell the story straight. I had written the first chapter delivering the plain facts. There are many ways to present the facts. I now realized I needed to let those facts breathe. Somehow I knew intuitively what that meant and went on an all-out writing binge. I had to get it down fast. I wrote and wrote and wrote. When the family was going out to the homestead, originally I had written: "It was a slow eight miles. After several hours, Arthur turned the wagon off the dirt road toward the south." I changed it to: "It was a slow eight miles, plodding along on that dirt road, pulling a heavy load of furniture. After the Indians, they probably didn't see another soul the whole way. They certainly saw plenty of cattle and horses and sheep grazing and, quite likely, the white bottoms of frisky antelope leaping across the prairie." I knew from my research that ranchers on those particular ranches raised cattle, horses, and sheep. I had seen the frisky antelope. I had read where the Northern Cheyenne camped. Small changes, yes, but they added texture. More detail can distract from the story or enrich the story, the juggling act is deciding which is which.

While watching a play I'd never heard of by a playwright I'd never heard of, I found myself bored. I could have cared less what happened and started glancing at my watch fifteen minutes into the performance. I asked myself why. As I thought about it, I realized the playwright had thrown a whole bunch of characters at us all at once. Since I didn't get to know any particular character, I wasn't curious as to what was going to happen to any of them. It was as interesting as sitting in an airport with nothing to do for three hours.

I thought more about my first chapter. I thought, I'll begin with Arthur, with his story, let my readers become interested in him, and then Sarah, and proceed accordingly. Back I went to the computer to rejig that first chapter, which meant painfully reordering it. I say painfully, because I was enamored with one particular sentence, and the entire first chapter revolved around that one sentence. Self-editing takes discipline. I had to force myself to be dispassionate, even ruthless. I finally came to the conclusion, that wonderful sentence had to go. And with a surgeon's scalpel, I cut it. It was painful, like cutting off an arm, but it had to be done.

The first chapter was better now, but something still wasn't quite right. I had included much about Wales. It did help to set the stage, and I liked Wales, I wanted to write about it. Be that as it may, lovely country that it is, in a book, the parts must serve the whole. Writing requires self-possession. Does this lovely paragraph, this splendid sentence, serve the whole? If not, lovely though it is, it must go. All that about Wales was interesting, and yet I had this dead body lying about. How long was I going to leave him there and keep you wondering? Cut, cut, cut, all that gone. Bye bye, dear paragraphs, but I say *au revoir* and not *adieu*. I will stow you away in a safe place for another day when perhaps I will find a use for you elsewhere.

After boldly gutting much of the first chapter, I split it into two. The passage about going out to the homestead appears in the second chapter of the book, whereas, prior to my epiphany, it had been in the first chapter.

So in searching for the right words, at times I concluded: there are no right words. It did not work. It had to go. Other times, when a particular sentence wasn't working, I concluded the sentence was fine the way it was; it simply needed another sentence before or after it.

IN THE MIDST of polishing my oeuvre, while on a flight to Seattle, the man seated next to me asked, "What made you decide to write a book?"

"When I found out my great-grandmother was accused of murder."

"Wow!" he said. "I have to hear this!"

From his wildly enthusiastic reaction, I realized—that has to be the opening line of the book. I also realized that the way I talked about the book was different from the way I had written it. As for content, I had to think like an assiduous journalist; in approach, I needed to imagine myself telling this story to someone at a dinner party or on an airplane.

I READ MORE of what famous writers had to say about writing. I think it was Flannery O'Connor who recommended adding another sense to help put the reader in the scene. What did it smell like, what were they hearing, was it hot, was it cold, was it damp?

I thought about Arthur digging up the body.

I thought about Arthur picking up dead bodies in the mine after the Granite Mountain Fire.

The newspaper said when the rescuers found the bodies of the dead miners, some were so swollen that the skin had split, and this was due to the extreme heat and noxious fumes. Gruesome. I didn't want to be ghoulish for the sake of being ghoulish, but I was telling that part of the story from Arthur's perspective. He was one of the rescuers, and I wanted to describe what he was seeing, but was all that true? Certainly the extreme heat down in the mine would hasten decomposition, but I still wondered about noxious fumes. On the face of it, it didn't make sense. I trotted off to the library and looked for books on forensic pathology. My question was too specific. I couldn't find the answer. I called the Clark County Coroner's office here in Las Vegas and explained that I was writing a book and what my question was. The woman said, "You need to talk to Dr. Telgenhoff." I got his voice mail and left a message and he called back. I explained about my book and about the Granite Mountain Fire, and that many of the Butte mines were very hot even without a fire. I told him what the newspaper wrote about the heat and noxious fumes accelerating decomposition.

"Is that possible?" I asked.

He said the heat would cause the bodies to swell and turn black and green.

"Could they swell to the point that the skin split?" I asked.

He said that was possible.

What about the noxious fumes? He said noxious fumes might have contributed depending on what they were.

I said, according to the newspaper reports, some of the miners were delirious when the rescuers found them. What would cause that? He said lack of oxygen. How obvious, and yet it hadn't occurred to me. The *Coroner's Register* said they died of asphyxiation. Fire depletes oxygen creating carbon monoxide, carbon monoxide means no oxygen. Of course they would be delirious. So much to think about, so many things spinning around in my head, at times I could miss the obvious.

I told Dr. T about Arthur digging up the body in Forsyth. It was January in Montana, very cold, and the body had been buried four days. When I asked about the condition of the body, he said, "He would have been just like when they planted him."

I explained about the second disinterment, when County Attorney Beeman had the graves dug up to see if there had been a grave robbery. I said this time it was August in eastern Montana, it can reach one hundred degrees Fahrenheit in the summer, and the body had been buried for several months. He said, considering Montana's wet and cold and then dry and hot weather, it probably looked pretty messy.

I told him about the sheriff finding the burned body the morning after the fire. It was a cold day in March. Would it have smelled foul? He said no, burned hair can smell pretty bad, but not burned flesh.

CHAPTER FORTY-ONE

I HAD ALWAYS ASSUMED, since Grandpa Peter received a French medal, he must have saved a French officer. Now I knew that was not the case. The man he saved was a noncommissioned officer in his own regiment. Mom encouraged me to find out if Peter could be awarded an American medal for saving that man's life. I planned to look into it after I finished the book; however, Mom happened to see her congressman and mentioned this to him, and he said his staff could help. I called his office, and a woman on his staff sent me the paperwork to send to the army. Soon I discovered that the only way Peter could be decorated was if one of his commanding officers had recommended he be decorated. Such paperwork would be at the National Archives.

I called the National Archives and spoke with the First World War specialist, Mitch Yockelson. I explained about the medal and about my book. He said, "You need to come here." I thought I was done with the war narrative. I told him I had already done quite a bit of research at the Military History Institute in Carlisle. Mitch said there are materials at the archives that are not in Carlisle. I needed to make a trip to the National Archives in College Park and do more research. I must admit I was a bit disheartened by this news, but I quickly came to my senses. Of course Mitch knows I need to go there to do research. For Pete's sake, he's the First World War specialist at the National Archives. I called the airlines and booked the first flight I could. I planned to spend a week there. Mitch thought that would be enough time.

Several years ago, our nation's archives outgrew the space in the National Archives building on the Mall in Washington, D.C., where we go to see the Declaration of Independence and the Constitution. Archives for the First World War and later are now housed in a large facility in College Park, Maryland, in the Washington, D.C., suburbs. That is where I went.

Why, you might ask, did I spend so much time and effort and money researching the war narrative? To know my grandmother Aila and what she was up against, you had to know her parents, Sarah and Arthur, and her husband, Peter. To know Peter, you had to know what he went through in the war. To leave out his war experience, or gloss over it, would be akin to writing the biography of a fireman who risked his life rescuing people from the World Trade Center on 9/11 and skipping over what happened to him on 9/11. Being in combat has got to be a seminal event in any man's life. The war itself was a seminal event in my grandparents' lives. On those tapes, Grandma said, before the First World War thus and so, after the First World War thus and so, just as I find myself remembering things as before 9/11 or after 9/11.

And if I was going to tell Peter's war story, his role in one of the most momentous events in history, I was under a tremendous obligation to get it right.

When I arrived at the National Archives that May of 2005, Mitch already had several boxes of archives waiting for me. The way the National Archives works is, you find the record numbers for the boxes you need and submit a request. The boxes are pulled at intervals throughout the day. It was a big help that Mitch had submitted a request for me the day before. I wasted no time waiting. And of course, Mitch was right. I needed to go there. Nothing I found negated what I had already written, but I found much more texture, more first-hand accounts, which helped me add a deeper, more personal dimension to the story. I wanted to do more than simply present the plain facts of Peter's war experience; I wanted to put you there with him. To do that, I needed ground-level details and I found them, some in Carlisle, some in Helena, some at Fort Lewis, some came from Christopher in Belgium, and now more at the National Archives, many, many pieces to create a vivid whole.

I found blunt letters written by Peter's division commander, General Johnston, expressing his frustrations—ambulances weren't getting through in the Argonne. Peter's brigade commander, General McDonald, wrote blunt operations reports expressing his desperation—the troops were exhausted, pushed to the limit. No complaining, just the facts, and the facts were grim.

General McDonald said they were hit by their own artillery several times in the Argonne. I knew about one incidence. I needed to find out about the other times.

All along, I wanted to know the name of the man Peter saved and what became of him after the war. From the medal citation, I knew Peter saved him on October 31, 1918, so that gave me the day he was wounded. As I went through box after box of archives for the 362nd Regiment, I came across lists of wounded. Wrong dates. I kept looking. October 31. That's it. I knew from the medal citation that the man was a noncommissioned officer. I went down the list looking for noncommissioned officers in Peter's company wounded on October 31. There was only one: Sergeant Arnold Pratt.

As for his wound, it said GSW. What is that? Oh, of course, gun shot wound—or wounds. It may have been several.

Mitch suggested that I look at correspondence from the division's officers solicited by those writing the U.S. Army's history of the war. From the research I had already done, Peter's regimental commander, Colonel John Henry Parker, had emerged in my mind as a larger than life character, a cross between Teddy Roosevelt, Henry V, and George Patton. HE WROTE HIS ENTIRE LETTER IN CAPITAL LETTERS WHICH GAVE THE IMPRESSION THAT HE WAS YELLING ALL THE TIME. I felt, if I didn't get the war story right, I'd spend eternity listening to him straighten me out.

The more I read about what happened at Epinonville, the first town Peter's regiment took in France, the more bewildered I became. Eyewitness accounts varied from, they didn't advance at all on the second day, to they took the town and held it on the first day. Chances are they were all correct. Two battalions were advancing, each with about 750 men. What one officer described was no doubt accurate for his part of the battlefield, and what another officer described was no doubt accurate for his. I had to figure out, where was Peter? Which account most accurately described where he was? What was he seeing and experiencing? I wanted to tell the story through his eyes. Being that specific to time and place and person makes research difficult. The battlefield was so chaotic between the fog and smoke and gunfire and the erratic movement of people, compasses didn't work because of the all the metal, and the constant deafening artillery blasts, and the gas calls, masks on, masks off, with masks on they could hardly see. How could a person even think straight much less give an accurate account of what happened?

Security at the National Archives was very strict. I couldn't bring in a bag or purse, just a small change purse. No zippered coats or sweaters were allowed. As I left each evening, security guards examined all my notes and papers. Cameras watched over us in the reading room.

As I plowed through box after box of archived letters, memos, reports, and messages written by the participants, I broke this source material down into three categories.

The first were immediate: field messages and field orders sent across the battlefield by the officers, daily operations reports written by General McDonald, intelligence reports.

The second were written shortly after the events, a few days or weeks later: summary of operations written by General Johnston and Colonel Parker, letters written by soldiers.

The third were written after the troops returned home, and some long after: the regimental and division histories, General Pershing's book, correspondence between officers wanting to set the record straight, letters written to help the army write the army history.

The intelligence reports were written by the intelligence officer, Lieutenant Carlos McClatchy (later documents identify him as Captain McClatchy). I thought, what a quintessentially American name—a Spanish first name and Irish surname. I have to find a way to include him in the story, just so I can say his name.

Around the time *One Night in a Bad Inn* came out, I read a news story about McClatchy buying Knight Ridder. Naturally it piqued my curiosity. Was it the same family? I did some investigating. It was. I wrote to the family via the company, and Carlos's son James called me. He had been going through his father's papers and sounded delighted to hear about my book. He said his father started the *Fresno Bee* from scratch after the war. He remembered his father's army friends visiting. He said his father had a hard time emotionally from the trauma of the war and died young, at age forty-two (the same as Grandpa Peter). He also told me Carlos was not his father's given name. He had changed his name to Carlos. A few weeks after we spoke, I saw the obituary for James in the newspaper.

In my quest to learn more about Sergeant Arnold Pratt, in particular what he did after the war, Mitch suggested that I look at the troop ship manifest; it included emergency contact names and might give me a lead. As I read the manifest looking for his name, I saw that someone had marked in red who had been disciplined or was sick and couldn't go. This corroborated what I had read elsewhere about the measles outbreak in the regiment while they were in New York waiting to ship out. I was surprised by how many soldiers had been disciplined and were sick. I wondered if whatever they were doing to warrant being disciplined was also how they got sick. Peter was neither disciplined nor sick, nor was Sergeant Pratt. I looked for other familiar names. It was tedious work because as with other lists of names in that era, they were sort of in alphabetical order but not completely. I had to read every name on every list.

When I mentioned Colonel Parker to Mitch, he said the name sounded familiar. He went back to his office and found a reference to him being called Gatlin' Gun Parker. He suggested I look at Colonel Parker's pictures in the photo archives. Sometimes biographical information was noted on the pictures. Another great lead and off I went.

I decided to look for pictures of all the officers in Peter's chain of command. The woman at the information desk asked which war. I said the First World War. She led me to a bank of file cabinets containing the card catalogs for the picture archives. The sign said World War II. I said, I'm looking for the First World War. She then led me to the Civil War files. I said, the First World War. Apparently she didn't get many requests for those pictures.

Descriptions of the pictures were noted in the card catalog. I found the numbers for pictures that sounded promising and filled out my request. As with the paper archives, the photo archives are pulled at regular intervals.

At the appointed time, I returned to the photo archives. The woman gave me white cotton gloves to wear while handling the pictures. The pictures were taken by the signal corp, and each was mounted on a large white card. Colonel Parker looked just as I thought he would, complete with confident smirk. On the card it said: "Known as 'Gattling Gun' Parker who describes himself as an 'artist with a machine gun.' He has been wounded in action three times . . . Only officer in U.S. Army known to have gone into battle on horseback in this war."

I looked for pictures of Peter's regiment. I found one, taken as they boarded the troop ship. It was taken from the back, so I couldn't see any faces. I hoped to find some battlefield pictures, but no luck.

After finishing in the photo archives, I resumed my trek through box after box of paper archives. Some multi-page documents were held together with small nails woven through the upper lefthand corners of the pages. When I needed to separate them to make copies, I took the papers to one of the staff members, and he or she gingerly removed the nail. The papers were becoming so brittle. Some I barely touched, and the paper broke.

At last, I found the file of letters recommending soldiers in Peter's regiment for medals. As I began to skim them, looking for Peter's name, I found myself reading each medal citation. They were quite detailed and provided a vivid picture of the battlefield. I went back and read all the medal citations for men in Peter's regiment and took copious notes.

A letter to General Penn of general headquarters, dated November 27, 1918, discussing recommendations for the *Distinguished Service Cross* and *Distinguished Service Medal* said: "It is very difficult to see just where your Board draws the line. Some cases disapproved are almost identical with one case approved."

Though I found several letters recommending soldiers from Peter's regiment for the French *Croix de Guerre* and the Belgian *Croix de Guerre*, I never found the letter recommending Peter. At the time, I figured the letter could have gotten lost or was misfiled. We have the medal, we have the citation from the French government, I hoped the letter recommending him might have additional information.

I found another memo that mentioned Sergeant Arnold Pratt. It said he was sent to a hospital after being seriously wounded, and the division lost track of him.

As I thought more about Sergeant Pratt, and about Peter being decorated by the French government but not the American government, I wondered, since Peter's division was under the command of the French army while in Flanders, Sergeant Pratt could have been sent to a French hospital when he was wounded. Colonel Parker was sent to a French hospital all the way down in Bordeaux after he was wounded in the Argonne. Howard Johnson, the county attorney who prosecuted Archie and Roy, spent more than a year in army hospitals after his airplane crashed in France. Sergeant Pratt could have spent months in the hospital. Perhaps he never was reunited with the 91st. Perhaps he couldn't tell American officers what Peter did to save him. Perhaps he told someone in the French hospital and the medal recommendation made its way up through the French chain of command and there never was a recommendation from the American army. Perhaps the American army never knew what Peter did. Peter would not have told anyone, not in a million years.

Also, the day Peter saved Sergeant Pratt's life was even more chaotic than usual. It was the same day their company commander, Lieutenant Closterman, was killed before he could return with the orders for the day. The troops jumped off into battle with no orders.

AFTER I RETURNED HOME, while retrieving my mail I saw my neighbor Alan. He asked how things were going on the book. I told him I was ninety percent sure I had found the name of the man my grandfather saved during the war. I said I still had a little more to do to be one hundred percent sure. Alan said, "Isn't ninety percent good enough?"

I thought, what if the man Peter saved died of his wounds. I pulled out the regimental history and read the descriptions of how each man in Peter's company was killed. As with the medal citations, these were detailed. Each included dates and circumstances of the man's death. If he was wounded and died a few days later, that was noted. I found no noncommissioned officers from Company E who died of wounds incurred on October 31. Sergeant Arnold Pratt remained the only possibility.

The descriptions of how each man died in action and the medal citations proved to be tremendous sources for those ground-level details I included in the battle narrative.

I still wasn't done with Sergeant Pratt. I wanted to know what became of him after the war. His emergency contact number on the troop ship manifest was a woman in Pueblo, Colorado, so I called everyone I could find named Pratt in Pueblo, Colorado. No luck.

Perhaps Sergeant Pratt did spend months in a French hospital recovering from his wounds, and while there fell in love with the lovely French nurse taking care of him, and after he got out of the hospital stayed in France and married her. Who knows.

I sat down at the computer and transcribed the copious notes I took while at the National Archives. A week of research took about a week to transcribe. Then I began to work what I had learned into the manuscript.

Then my computer crashed.

All I got was a black screen with a bunch of gobbledygook. I called the computer company. It must be your hard drive. You need a new hard drive.

I had backed up my files before my trip but not since I transcribed my notes from my week at the National Archives, a whole week of work lost, and my computer doesn't work. The phone rang. It was Wey Symmes.

Wey wrote *War on the Rivers* about his experience in the navy in Vietnam. Mutual friends gave a copy of his book to Mom and Dad. Mom read it and lo and behold, Wey mentioned my cousin Kenny who was killed in Vietnam. Mom wrote to Wey. He called her. It turned out, we were all going to be in Tucson the next month. While in Tucson, we met Wey and his wife, Terry. Wey asked about my book and said he'd recommend it to his publisher. He was now calling to say he had talked to his publisher, Stan Cohen, and he would publish my book. "Call him right now," he said. All I could think was my hard drive crashed, I lost a week of work, I need a new computer.

"Thanks," I said and hung up.

After I spoke with Stan, I called the family computer wiz, Dad. He said, "Don't you have some kind of disk?" I looked through everything that came with the computer. I found a CD and put it in, and *voila*, the computer booted up. I backed up everything and ordered a new computer.

CHAPTER FORTY-TWO

MOM HAD BEEN GREAT about copy editing my manuscript as I wrote. Dad and my brother, Jeff, read it and made helpful comments. Jeff advised working in more foreboding. Several friends read chapters. Now I wanted someone outside the family, someone who hadn't heard anything about the story, to edit the manuscript. Stan arranged to have Bob Jones, a retired newspaper publisher, do this. He made helpful comments, such as when Sarah was in jail and wrote to her son Bill and told him to burn the letter, Bob asked: "If she told him to burn it, how did you get it? The reader might like to know." I added an explanation, that the sheriff and county attorney got the letter and put it in the court file. I wonder if Bill ever saw it.

At the part where the couple demanded money from Grandma right after Grandpa Peter died, I didn't want to use their real names, so I called the wife "the wife" and referred to the husband as "the wife's husband." Bob said this was awkward. I needed to give her a name. That was something I had struggled with, so I wasn't surprised by his comment. I needed to come up with a pseudonym, which I would identify as such, but I didn't want to use just any name. I wanted it to be symbolic. I wanted it be a character revealing name, like Alfred P. Doolittle in *My Fair Lady*, he did just that—little.

My mind drifted again to Shakespeare, perhaps I could use something from Shakespeare, a character from Shakespeare like the person I was trying to name. I pulled *The Works of William Shakespeare*, which Uncle Ray had given me, off my bookshelf and started to thumb through it, reading the *dramatis personae* for each play. The most obvious choice, I couldn't use. How about Lady Macbeth? That didn't quite fit. Perhaps something that sounded like Shakespeare, I thought Ophelia, Portia, that sort of sound. What the woman in my story did was horrible, pilfering a grieving widow. It was appalling, it was awful, it was horrible, her behavior was atrocious. Atrocia. That's it! I'll call her Atrocia! Then I thought, maybe it's too extreme. I called Mom and asked if she thought it was too harsh. "I think it's perfect," she said.

INITIALLY I CONTEMPLATED including a dozen or so family pictures in the book. Now that I was publishing with Pictorial Histories, I thought, I'll use *a lot* of pictures, and I'll get historic pictures of the places and events in the book. It would be great to include a picture of everyone in the book. You'd read about a person, and then his or her picture would appear. Great idea, but I didn't want to deal with the pictures. I wanted it to happen by itself—as if some picture fairy godmother would swoop in and say, here you are, dear, here are the pictures you need. For some reason, I dreaded doing it, but once I forced myself into picture collection, I enjoyed doing it. I also discovered that adding pictures adds another whole level of complication to a book.

I thought I had looked at all of Grandma T's pictures at Mom and Dad's, but on my next visit, I opened a drawer and discovered loose photo album pages that must have been Grandma's. Where did these come from? I had never seen them before.

Aunt Aila and Auntie Mary also had some of Grandma's pictures. I had a vast collection from which to choose. So many good pictures, such photogenic relatives, which to use? I didn't think the book should morph into a family photo album, and I didn't want it to be too long. I had to pick.

As I organized the pictures chronologically, I couldn't help but notice how Grandma grew prettier and prettier as the years went by, *The Picture of Dorian Gray* in reverse.

One of the pictures of Sarah and Arthur in the boarding house had a large calendar hanging on the wall. The month and year were clearly visible. That gave me a reference point as to how long Arthur stayed in Butte.

It wasn't until a journalist interviewing me about the book asked, who took the pictures, that I got to wondering, who did take them? These pictures at the boarding house were taken between 1916 and 1920, at a time when owning a camera was not common as it is today. I wonder if one of the boarders was a photographer.

I remember when I was a little girl walking into Grandma's bedroom with Mom and Grandma one day and seeing a picture of a beautiful lady.

I asked Mom, "Who is that?" "Grandma," she said. For some reason the picture made a strong impression. That's the only place I ever saw it, and the only time I remember seeing it. When I decided to write *One Night in a Bad Inn*, immediately I knew the title and I knew that picture would be on the cover. It's her high school graduation portrait.

Auntie Mary and Uncle Ed have a large folding screen of family pictures in the living room of their new house. Grandma's high school graduation portrait and Peter's picture from the war are together in the same frame, with Grandma on the left and Peter on the right, looking over her shoulder. As soon as I saw it, I thought—that's the book cover.

There were still family members for whom I didn't have pictures at the right age. I wanted to use pictures of them close to the age they were in the story. It didn't make sense to include a picture of Aunt B in her eighties when I'm talking about her just having a baby. None of my relatives in this country had a picture of Uncle John Gribben as a young man. Cousin Rosaleen in Belfast found one for me. She said she asked our cousin Dennis O'Hara for pictures, and I didn't even know I had O'Hara cousins.

The pictures I had of Roy Walsh and Sheriff Mountjoy were microfilm copies from the newspaper articles and quite grainy. I began hunting for the negatives. I called the *Boulder Monitor*. They didn't have them. There had been a fire and lots of those old glass plate negatives were destroyed. Someone suggested I call Ellen Rae Thiel. I had called her about something else awhile back. I called her and explained about my book, and that part of it was about Roy Walsh and the murder, and that we had spoken by phone a year or so ago. She said, "I don't remember that, but I want to talk to you now!" Roberta Barrows had called her a few days earlier. She was looking for information about her great-granduncle Albert Johnson who was murdered at Renova.

Through Ellen Rae, I got in touch with Roberta. I hoped that she might have a picture of Albert toward the end of his life. I felt awkward calling her, explaining who I was, that my great-uncle Archie was the accomplice of the man convicted of murdering her great-granduncle Albert. We had a nice friendly chat, but unfortunately, no picture.

The first place I went to collect historic pictures of places in the story was the World Museum of Mining in Butte. The trouble with public photo archives is they have enormous collections, it's overwhelming, it's mind boggling. How do I pick? As I stood in the back room at the museum perusing photo album after photo album, selecting far too many pictures, a terrific hailstorm blew in. The hailstones slammed against the roof, making such a racket that I could not hear myself talk. For some reason, it seemed hilarious, it was so loud. I walked over to the entrance to Hell Roarin' Gulch and watched the ice pebbles ricochet off the road, staying clear so as not to be pelted.

Once it quieted down, I went back to work getting terribly carried away selecting far too many photographs.

Many pictures were not dated. I studied cars, eyeglass shapes, clothes, anything to at least establish a decade. It occurred to me that cultural anthropology would be an interesting field.

I still wanted to include pictures from the war. I didn't want random First World War pictures. I wanted pictures of the men in Peter's division, preferably his regiment. Though I didn't find any at the National Archives, I was not giving up on the idea. Then one day, another epiphany. I called the Military History Institute in Carlisle. Yes, they have photo archives. I sent the regiment and brigade and division numbers and the names of the towns, and before long, I had pictures. My favorite is the one of Peter's regiment marching down a tree-lined road through the French countryside. A little French girl and boy are watching them from a fenced pasture. It is a sunny, dry day. You can see the dust kicked up by the marching soldiers, you can feel the warmth of the day, you can sense the calm of the pastoral setting; yet they are marching off to war, to kill or be killed. So surreal.

Perhaps I wasn't looking in the right places at the National Archives. I queried them for pictures. Then I remembered that General Moffett had given me photographs when I met him in Belgium. I dug those out. I called the museum at Fort Lewis. The curator sent me some terrific pictures, including that one of the soldier leaping over the sandbags. Where I thought I had none, now I was awash in pictures and had to choose.

While reading the history of the times, and looking at pictures of those who peopled those times, I was struck by how some people seemed to fly off the page and make a strong impression. Their faces brimmed with character. I wondered why. General Pershing and Marshal Foch look like storybook figures of great generals. Central casting could not have done better. Where Eisenhower looks like the quintessential Everyman, Pershing looks larger than life, like a man who successfully led troops in a world war, tailor made for statues, as one writer called him. Sheriff Mountjoy, with those sculpted features, looks like the sheriff who always got his man.

Along with the pictures, I decided to include maps in the war narrative. I wanted to add the German lines of defense to the map showing the 91st Division's movements in the Argonne. This would support the dramatic climax when the 91st reached the Kriemhilde Line, the first American troops to do so, to stand firmly at the American Army's objective. I was very pleased with the way I had written it, swelling as it did with a mighty crescendo. And then came the dreadful order to withdraw—after losing all those lives to take all that land—a triumph followed quickly by a bitter pill. As I studied the two maps, I started to come to the disturbing realization that they may not have reached the Kriemhilde Line, as the regimental history said they did. I went back and studied the rest of my source material. I reread the operations summary written by General Johnston. He didn't say anything about the 91st reaching the Kriemhilde Line the day they took Gesnes. This would have been a stunning achievement. Why wouldn't he say if it happened? Again I studied the map showing the German lines of defense. I saw a communication trench. I plotted the troop positions on the map. It appears they reached the communication trench. Perhaps they thought it was part of the Kriemhilde Line. I cannot say for certain, but I don't think they did reach the Kriemhilde Line before they were ordered to withdraw. When in doubt, I couldn't say it happened, especially something that significant. I had to delete my wonderful passage. That hurt.

As I collected war pictures and worked with the book designer, Kitty Herrin, on deciding where to place them in the manuscript, I got to thinking more about the massacre at Gesnes which took a horrible toll on Grandpa Peter's regiment. I remembered reading that General Pershing replaced the corps commander right in the middle of the Meuse Argonne Offensive. I checked the dates on my time line. It was after the disaster at Gesnes that Pershing replaced him. I wondered if there was a connection. I checked indices for several books, looking for his name. I found him, but no explanation for why Pershing replaced him, and he wasn't just replaced, he was demoted. I emailed Mitch at the National Archives. He suggested I consult a friend of his, which I did. He and Mitch recommended *The War to End all Wars* by Edward M. Coffman. In Coffman's book, I found no explanation for the corps commander being replaced, though I found something else.

Coffman wrote that 46,992 American soldiers died of influenza and pneumonia in the First World War. This was more than twice the number cited by Clodfelter in *Warfare and Armed Conflicts*. Why the disparity? I figured there must be an official number in some official army document saying how many soldiers died of the 1918 Spanish Flu. I googled the subject and found an article which footnoted *America's Forgotten Pandemic* by Alfred W. Crosby. I got that book. It said 43,600 soldiers and sailors died from flu and pneumonia complications in 1918. Of that number, 5000 sailors died; 23,000 soldiers died of flu; and 15,600 soldiers died of pneumonia. Crosby footnoted the *War Department Annual Report for 1919*. Clodfelter's number matched Crosby's number for death from flu for soldiers. Apparently Clodfelter included only deaths directly from flu, whereas many more died of pneumonia which the soldiers contracted because they had the flu. They were all flu-related deaths. Coffman's number of 46,992 was a little higher than Crosby's number of 43,600 deaths. Crosby's number was for 1918. Perhaps Coffman's number included both 1918 and 1919. Rather than chase that down, I used a round number in my book, more than forty thousand servicemen, which worked better in the narrative anyway. This proved to be yet another case of what appeared to be conflicting information simply being several pieces of the same story, and once again I spent an insane amount of time finding out.

Chapter Forty-three

After eight years of research trips, reading books for research, taking notes, transcribing notes, visiting with family, hearing their stories, transcribing taped interviews, writing, rewriting, fact checking, double fact checking, discovering more story, doing more research, writing, rewriting, polishing, I finished the manuscript. It was ready to become a book.

The research was great fun. Every time I discovered the answer to a question on my to-do list, I felt a great sense of accomplishment. Even when my search culminated in a dead end as far as what I set out to find, inevitably I would stumble across something I didn't know I was looking for. I received tremendous help from my family and am profoundly grateful. As for paper sources, I requested many items from the able staffs of libraries and archives and courthouses and am profoundly thankful for their help, but by and large, I did my own research. I wouldn't have it any other way. I'd miss too much if I didn't do it myself. I'd miss the context, especially with newspaper research, which can be tedious, especially when reading microfilm. But as I perused those newspapers, becoming bleary-eyed and bleary-brained as the pages passed before me, I was gleaning a flavor of the times, of what else was happening, what people were reading about current events, what they were doing, what they were interested in. It helped put me there.

As for the writing, at the beginning I felt as if I were slogging through mud, glue-like gumbo, mud so thick you could build a house out of it. No matter how fast I wanted to go, I could go only so fast, and there was nothing I could do about it. How to say this, where to put that—not here, there, or maybe there. Such a wonderful sentence, but it doesn't work. It has to go. So painful.

The slogging part lasted for years, but as the story took shape, and I was down to just polishing the writing, I felt I had left the mud behind and was walking swiftly on nice, smooth pavement.

Toward the end, as I realized I was about to let go of my little one, I'd wake up with a start—did I spell Gaelic correctly? Did I spell it Gallic? I searched on the computer. Gallic. Oops. Fixed it. Did I hyphenate or not hyphenate Alsace-Lorraine consistently? I checked. Missed one hyphen. Fixed it.

While trying to come up with a title for this book, I pulled Grandma's book of poems off the shelf, the one Mom had given her, and looked again at the pages where she left markers. She had placed a metal marker with an image of the Blessed Mother at "Up-Hill" by Christina Georgina Rossetti:

> Does the road wind up-hill all the way?
> *Yes, to the very end.*
> Will the day's journey take the whole long day?
> *From morn to night, my friend.*
>
> But is there for the night a resting-place?
> *A roof for when the slow dark hours begin.*
> May not the darkness hide it from my face?
> *You cannot miss that inn.*

I've no doubt she did not miss that inn—the good inn.

I wouldn't have missed the good inn that was writing my book. The whole experience was a treasure.

You might say, that's all well and good, but why do this, why leave a perfectly good career and go traipsing across the globe, snooping around to discover what skeletons may be tucked away in the recesses of a vast family closet? Why not leave them lie? As Aunt Betsy said to her nephew David Copperfield, "It's in vain, . . . , to recall the past, unless it works some influence upon the present." If *One Night in a Bad Inn* had only been about people behaving badly, about self-inflicted pointless misery, I wouldn't have written it. It is the example of my grandmother Aila, Grandma T, that made it a worthy endeavor. Had I watered down the bad acts of her parents and her brothers and the footloose nature of her husband, I would have undercut her strength of character, and that wouldn't have been fair. It would not have been a service to the truth. "I was not going to live like that," she said. "I was going to be a lady." And that she was. And in telling her story, my hope is that her example will work some positive influence on the present.

NOTES

The following lists sources for quotes where the person or source is not cited in the text. Sources for historical content are listed in the bibliography for *One Night in a Bad Inn*, with a few additions below.

CHAPTER 2
Biographical information about Edith Stein: Edith Stein, *Life in a Jewish Family 1891–1916* (Washington, D.C.: ICS Publications, 1986).

CHAPTER 6
"The wind blows where it will": John 3:8, *New American Bible* (Nashville, Camden, New York: Thomas Nelson, Publishers, 1971).

"The ones that did good in this country didn't spend . . ." and "When things get really tough": Quoted by Jonathan Raban, *Bad Land: An American Romance* (New York: Pantheon Books, 1996), p. 209–210.

CHAPTER 7
"She was a bold unashamed rootin', tootin' . . .": Montana state highway marker shown in Don James, *Butte's Memory Book* (Caldwell, Idaho: The Caxton Printers Ltd., 1975), p. 77.

Biographical information about Teddy Traparish: Tracy Thornton, "King of fine dining," *Montana Standard*, December 12, 2004.

CHAPTER 10
William Alexander quoted by Daniel N. Vichorek, *Montana's Homestead Era* (Helena: Montana Magazine, 1987), p. 56.

CHAPTER 12
1870 article about the Welsh quoted by William D. Jones, *Wales in America, Scranton and the Welsh, 1860–1920* (University of Wales Press, University of Scranton Press, 1993), p. 204.

Paul J. Zbiek, *Luzerne County: History of the People and Culture* (Charlestown, MA: Strategic Publications, 1994), p. 42-43.

Chapter 13
"For him, the war had retained its romantic glow to the very end . . .": Stein, *Life in a Jewish Family 1891-1916*, p. 229.

Chapter 15
"there is no well or river or mountain peak . . .": Quoted by Trefor M. Owen, *The Customs and Traditions of Wales* (Cardiff: University of Wales Press, 1991), p. 120.

Chapter 16
Tuchman's observations about atrocities in the First World War: Barbara Tuchman, *Practicing History: Selected Essays* (New York: Ballantine Books, 1981), p. 43.
Quotes by J. E. Rendinell: Harold Elk Straubing, ed. *The Last Magnificent War: Rare Journalistic and Eyewitness Accounts of World War I* (New York: Paragon House, 1989), p. 199-206.

Chapter 17
"History is a hill . . .": Gilbert Keith Chesterton, *All I Survey*, 1933, G. K. Chesterton's Works on the Web, http://www.cse.dmu.ac.uk/~mward/gkc/books/All_I_Survey.txt
"To have 'an opinion about Ireland' . . .": William Makepeace Thackeray, *The Irish Sketch Book of 1842*, found in *The Works of William Makepeace Thackeray, Kensington Edition, Volume XX* (New York: Charles Scribner's Sons, 1904), p. 476.
Casement quoted by Jonathan Bardon, *A History of Ulster* (Belfast: Blackstaff Press, 1992), p. 452.
Count von Bernhardi quoted by Barbara Tuchman, *The Guns of August* (New York: Bantam, 1962), p. 11.
"were confident that industrial progress . . .": John Dos Passos, introduction to *First Encounter* (New York: Philosophical Library, 1945).

Chapter 27
"Helena June10—Governor Stewart today received a telegram from Forsyth . . .": *Anaconda Standard*, June 11, 1917.

Chapter 33

Background on the depression of 1919-1921:

Milton Friedman and Anna Jacobson Schwartz, *A Monetary History of the United States, 1867-1960* (Princeton University Press, 1963).

Thomas E. Woods, Jr., "The Forgotten Depression of 1920," article posted on the Ludwig von Mises Institute web site, November 27, 2009, http://mises.org/articles.aspx?AuthorId=424

"the convent was not founded . . .": Kieran Kavanaugh and Otilio Rodriguez, trans, *The Collected Works of St. Teresa of Avila, Volume One* (Washington, D.C.: ICS Publications, 1976), p. 70.

"one night in a bad inn" and "The bad inn lasts only a night": Kieran Kavanaugh, text prepared, *St. Teresa of Avila: The Way of Perfection* (Washington, D.C.: ICS Publications, 2000), p. 442.

"didn't think Moses was in his right mind . . .": *Forsyth Times Journal,* May 28, 1914, p. 4.

Chapter 40

"To speak little . . .": John P. McClernon, selected and arranged, *Sermon in a Sentence, Volume 2: St. Francis De Sales* (San Francisco: Ignatius Press, 2003), p. 54.

"What is the meaning of goodness . . . ": *National Velvet*, directed by Clarence Brown, screenplay by Theodore Reeves and Helen Deutsch (1944; Culver City, CA: Metro-Goldwyn-Mayer).

"Certainly the squalid and worthless . . .": Tuchman, *Practicing History: Selected Essays*, p. 54.

"For Michelangelo . . .": Will and Ariel Durant, *The Story of Civilization: The Reformation* (New York: Simon and Schuster, 1935), p. 831.

ALSO BY CHRISTY LESKOVAR

One Night in a Bad Inn tells the lively true story of two colorful families, one Welsh, one Irish, who overcome scandal, war, murder, and mayhem on a desolate Montana homestead, in the raucous mining town of Butte, and on the bloody battlefields of the First World War. It was a 2007 High Plains Book Award finalist.